SOCIAL WORK IN HIGHER EDUCATION

Already published in this series, in association with CEDR
(Series Editor *Robin Lovelock*)

Changing Patterns of Mental Health Care A case study in the development of local services *Jackie Powell and Robin Lovelock*

Partnership in Practice The Children Act 1989 *ed. Ann Buchanan*

Disability: Britain in Europe An evaluation of UK participation in the HELIOS programme (1988-1991)
Robin Lovelock and Jackie Powell

The Probation Service and Information Technology *David Colombi*

Visual Impairment; Social Support Recent research in context
Robin Lovelock

Workloads: Measurement and Management *Joan Orme*

Living with Disfigurement Psychosocial implications of being born with a cleft lip and palate *Poppy Nash*

Educating for Social Work: Arguments for Optimism
eds Peter Ford and Patrick Hayes

Dementia Care: Keeping Intact and in Touch A search for occupational therapy interventions *M. Catherine Conroy*

Suicidal Behaviour in Adolescents and Adults Research, taxonomy and prevention *Christopher Bagley and Richard Ramsay*

Narrative Identity and Dementia A study of autobiographical memories and emotions *Marie A. Mills*

Child Sexual Abuse and Adult Offenders: New Theory and Research
eds Christopher Bagley and Kanka Mallick

Community Approaches to Child Welfare International perspectives *ed. Lena Dominelli*

In preparation

Valuing the Field Child welfare in an international context
ed. Marilyn Callahan

Parents in Need Reflecting on social work assessment where both child care and parental mental ill-health are involved
Sue Beresford

Social Work in Higher Education
Demise or development?

Jaure West

KAREN LYONS
University of East London, UK

Ashgate

Aldershot • Brookfield USA • Singapore • Sydney

Published by
Ashgate Publishing Ltd
Gower House
Croft Road
Aldershot
Hants GU11 3HR
England

Ashgate Publishing Company
Old Post Road
Brookfield
Vermont 05036
USA

Ashgate website: http://www.ashgate.com

British Library Cataloguing in Publication Data
Lyons, K. H. (Karen Hamilton), 1944-
    Social work in higher education: demise or development?
    1. Social work education - Great Britain
    I. Title II. University of Southampton. Centre for Evaluative
    & Developmental Research
    361.3'0711'41

Library of Congress Catalog Card Number: 99-76358

ISBN 0 7546 1007 1

Printed in Great Britain by
Antony Rowe Ltd, Chippenham, Wiltshire

Contents

Foreword

Sonia Jackson

How do we account for the precarious foothold of social work in British universities? Apart from a brief period in the 1970s when the workforce requirements of the newly established social services departments seemed to guarantee the future of social work education, the subject has faced a constant struggle to survive as an academic discipline. Yet Schools of Social Work are springing up all over Eastern Europe, while in the United States, where over three thousand social work educators regularly gather for their annual conference, social work academics occupy grand buildings and have access to the levers of power.

One of the main characteristics of social work education in the United Kingdom is its inward-looking quality, and probably the majority of social work teachers are barely aware of the contrast between their position and that of the continental and North American colleagues. They are too enmeshed in the endless negotiations and meetings which take up so much of their energy and have severely limited their capacity to compete with colleagues in less applied subjects when it comes to research ratings and lists of publications. This is the first book, based on thorough research and empirical evidence, to look at the current state of social work in higher education both from an historical and an international perspective.

Even twenty years ago, British social work was in a position to provide a model for the world. In most countries social work students were still taught by academics from other disciplines, with an add-on of social work theory and methods, and fieldwork placements having little relation to the theoretical component. In this country, the idea of an integrated course explicitly designed for the learning needs of future social workers was well advanced. In addition, the social work profession had developed ideas about combating racism and discrimination through training long before it became fashionable, and the idea that practice should be informed by research rather than intuition was making a real headway.

So what happened to create the present situation, where statutory social work is increasingly downgraded to a bureaucratic exercise involving minimal engagement with people, there is a chronic shortage of high quality research directly concerned with social work theory and methods, and the very existence of social work as a university discipline is under threat?

Karen Lyons has done a most valuable service by unravelling the strands that contribute to this sorry state of affairs and tracing their antecedents. She sets the problems of academic social work within the wider context of higher education generally, as well as noting that other professions too have been under attack in recent years. Social work, however, suffered uniquely from a hostile climate in the media as well as in Westminster. The most significant blow was Margaret Thatcher's highly predictable refusal to fund a three-year programme, followed by CCETSW's attempt to save face by fudging the non-graduate/postgraduate issue. If the qualification for social work is set at sub-degree why should the taxpayer subsidise expensive degree courses, still less postgraduate study? Postqualifying education too has been blighted by the confusing and illogical structure imposed on it.

In all this, the Central Council, with its increasingly symbiotic relationship with central government, emerges as the villain of the piece. The social work teachers surveyed by Karen Lyons are in agreement that the onerous requirements laid down by CCETSW for formal partnership structures in place of pre-existing collaborations based on different though complementary functions, have been immensely time-consuming and produced little benefit to students or the profession. They are also costly, making social work an unpopular subject with university administrations.

However, one of the author's most striking findings is the invisibility of social work within higher education. In two out of three institutions social work is subsumed within departments whose title does not even indicate its existence. Moreover, social work academics rarely occupy influential positions in the governance of universities and this makes the subject a highly vulnerable target in times of financial stringency.

At present, social work in higher education does indeed seem headed for demise. Current trends would see social work downgraded to sub-degree level, taught mainly in further education colleges with no research traditions and based on the discredited 'competency' approach, which is wholly inappropriate to a complex occupation like social work.

But there is hope in the new demand for evidence-based practice. Where is the evidence to come from? It requires a new alliance between service providers and academics which clearly defends the independent position of social work in higher education. Universities have lasted so long because their function as transmitters and generators of knowledge has value for society. New perspectives, in social work as much as any other subject, are only likely to emerge from institutions that are free to ask fundamental questions, not bound by the day-to-day requirements of service provision.

Obviously, this is a view that the author holds strongly, but her book is no mere polemic. Its argument is based on careful, historically based analysis and empirical research which carries conviction. All social work educators have reason to be grateful to Karen Lyons for throwing such a clear light on the problems of the discipline within higher education and for suggesting some ways in which they might be overcome.

Professor Sonia Jackson
University of Wales, Swansea

Preface

A prolonged period of Conservative government in Britain (1979-1997) resulted in profound changes in the nature of social welfare, including education. One of the characteristics of this period has been a decrease in the status and autonomy accorded to professions, and a change in the relationship between 'the providers' and 'the consumers' of services. More specifically, the years from 1989 to the mid-1990s were marked by rapid legislative and organisational change in the personal social services. The period has also seen significant change in the institutional policies and culture of higher education, now continuing under the New Labour administration.

Changes in both these sectors have impacted on the arrangements for the education of social workers, responsibility for which is shared between the professional accrediting body, employing agencies and higher education institutions. The starting point for the research on which this book is based was a recognition that, in line with other moves promoting deprofessionalisation and instrumentalism, qualifying training might be relocated outside the higher education system.

An initial question, 'can social work survive in higher education?', prompted an exploration of the external influences and internal characteristics which have resulted in this sense of vulnerability. The research utilised interdisciplinary perspectives, grounded in a policy framework, and an inductive approach to collection of empirical data, to examine the view that social work education is open to conflicting policies and values from higher education and the professional field. The possibility that the subject would share similarities with other forms of professional education was also examined.

The book therefore presents a case study of the epistemology and relationships of a particular form of professional education. Consideration of the literature pertaining to the three contextual factors, social work, higher education and professional education, and of the empirical data derived from social work educators support the concluding argument. This posits that biography, culture and structure interact to produce a discipline with inherent tensions, partly due to its position on a boundary between two systems and partly reflecting the nature of the subject. While its location within higher education is deemed appropriate by social work educators, decisions about its location and form are largely exercised by other interest groups: its survival and development therefore require constant negotiation.

Acknowledgements

I would like to express my thanks to the many people who have contributed to this book, particularly those social work educators who gave their time, experience and views through completion of questionnaires and participation in interviews during the data gathering stage of the research.

But a wider number of people have also given encouragement to this enterprise, directly and indirectly, including those associated with JUC SWEC and the Department of Government at Brunel University. In this connection, I would especially like to express my appreciation to Mary Henkel, whose steady support, critical eye and stimulus derived from her own research and writing also provided me with a model of PhD supervision.

My thanks also go to Robin Lovelock (CEDR) for encouragement to publish; to Avalon Associates of Chelmsford for final checking, formatting and preparation of camera ready copy, and to Claire Lyons for assistance with preparation of the bibliography and indexes.

I am, of course, responsible for the conclusions drawn and any errors of fact or judgement which readers might ascribe to this final product.

PART 1

BRITISH SOCIAL WORK EDUCATION IN CONTEXT: POLICY CHANGE AND PROFESSIONAL EDUCATION

PART I

1   British Social Work Education

Introduction

Radical policy change has affected expectations of higher education, the personal social services and the professions. These changes date mainly from the accession to power of a Conservative government in 1979, marking a sea change in ideology and policy paradigms, not least those affecting the welfare sector. The changes gathered force and momentum with ensuing electoral victories, until 1997, when 'New' Labour came to power in an indelibly altered environment.

The pace of change has been at least as significant as its direction, in its impact on the users and providers of a range of services. Established assumptions about the nature of the welfare state, the remit of higher education and the power of professionals have all been challenged: organisation and practice in both social work and higher education have been changed by political, legislative and fiscal means, within a broader reshaping of the economic and social structure of the country (Pollitt, 1990; Burrage and Torstendahl, 1990; Becher and Kogan, 1992; Clarke *et al.*, 1994; Barnett, 1994).

In the area of education for social work, a sense of strain, and even a questioning of the viability of the subject, became evident in the early 1990s (Cooper, 1992; Pinker, 1993). Concerns about the survival of social work in higher education prompted a series of research questions:- 'why is social work education so vulnerable?'; 'is social work different from other forms of professional education and, if so, how?'; 'how far is the sense of crisis shaped by external forces or by innate internal characteristics?'; 'what role do social work educators play in defining or developing or even in problematising the subject?'; 'how have recent changes been experienced by social work educators and how do they view the subject and its future?'

These questions reflected wider and long-standing debates about the nature and status of professional subjects in higher education. In the USA, Schon (1983) had written about the crisis in professional education, and in the British context, Becher (1989) had suggested a lack of research into the

3

nature of professional subjects as opposed to academic disciplines. Becher's focus on the epistemology and culture of disciplines provided a useful starting point for the research detailed in this book, and the study has been paralleled by a growing body of literature about professional education in Britain (Bines and Watson, 1992; Yelloley and Henkel, 1995; Eraut, 1994).

The research took place also in a broader climate of perceived threat to higher education values, methods and assumptions about purpose and autonomy and in the context of ongoing dispute and uncertainty about the role of social work in society. These factors informed the research design as an exploratory case study, using an inductive and interpretive approach to draw out the characteristics of social work as a discipline, relative to its location in higher education, its professional field and professional education as a generic concept. These three aspects of the framework are discussed in Part 1 of this book after an analysis of the origins and recent development of social work education.

The substantial middle part of this book is based on data from questionnaires, interviews and secondary sources relating to social work as a subject area in England and Wales in the 1990s (see Appendix 1: Research Methodology). The discipline is not regarded as synonymous with the qualifying training course (the Diploma in Social Work), though in some institutions this would be the main focus of work. The data primarily reflect the perspectives of social work educators themselves. The main characteristics of the subject and the factors which contribute to the particular culture of social work as a discipline are identified, and the findings identify strengths and weaknesses of social work education, particularly in the context of changed environments.

The implications of the findings for current and future prospects of the subject are discussed in Part 3. The study is broadly informed by a social policy orientation, but interdisciplinary perspectives are also drawn on.

Setting the Scene

This first chapter gives an overview of policy developments and change in British social work education, providing the background to the research and a theoretical basis for its focus. Origins as a subject area in higher education are dealt with only briefly, but early and periodic concern about the nature and status of the subject area and its place in the academy was apparent. The chapter then looks at events and debates in the 1970s and 1980s which formed a more immediate background to developments in the 1990s. These are discussed in some detail since they informed the research question and have an immediate bearing on the prospects for social work in higher education beyond the millennium. The chapter concludes with a summary of some of the main issues identified.

There was a relative lack of material about British social work education (as opposed to texts about the nature or aspects of the wider field of social work) when this research commenced. Notable exceptions (Jones, 1978; Harris *et al.*, 1985) were augmented by a relative flood of edited collections during the mid-1990s (Yelloly and Henkel, 1995; Doel and Shardlow, 1996; Ford and Hayes, 1996; Gould and Taylor, 1996; Jackson and Preston-Shoot, 1996; Vass, 1996). The appearance of these texts might suggest a growing concern about, or interests in, the discipline.

Less detailed discussions of British social work education can also be found in books about comparative social work (Jones, 1992; Lorenz, 1994), in edited texts about the state of (British) social work (Parsloe, 1990; Timms, 1991; Jones, 1996a; Webb, 1996), in texts about other or wider subjects (Clark, 1991; Henkel, 1994), and occasionally in journal articles in related fields (Cannan, 1995). An analysis of the two British journals ostensibly concerned with social work education (*Issues in Social Work Education, Social Work Education*) revealed relatively few articles dealing holistically with the nature of social work as a discipline, with some notable exceptions (Brewster, 1992; Cooper, 1992; Clark, 1996; Sheppard, 1997). However, this exercise gave useful insights into the importance attached by educators themselves to particular aspects of the social work education process.

Finally, the leading journal in the professional field, *British Journal of Social Work*, has a much wider focus and has therefore carried very few articles in the 1990s about social work education specifically, with occasional important exceptions (Clark, 1995; Sheppard, 1998) and an annual presentation of (three or four) abstracts relating to the subject. In the wider field, recent editions of *Research in Higher Education Abstracts* reveal virtually no references to social work education except Henkel's contribution (1994) to a text about professional education, and occasional case studies, for example, on teaching about gender in the subject (Reynolds, 1994). The implication - that there is either very little research being undertaken about social work education, and that publication of material relating to the subject area is largely confined to social work journals (not covered by the abstracting service) is one of the issues explored further.

Origins of Social Work Education

The identification of a variety of social problems in 19th century Britain led to a range of policy measures and practical responses incorporated into organisational frameworks (Walton, 1975; Parry and Parry, 1979; Jones, 1983). The establishment of social work education in the early 20th century can be seen as evidence of a growing sense of vocational identity among philanthropists and social reformers and a concern to provide 'professional' standards of intervention - the initiation of the 'professional project' (Macdonald, 1995).

As early as 1896, a scheme of lectures on social work had been established for its volunteers by the Charity Organisation Society (COS). This organisation participated in the foundation of a School of Sociology and Social Economics in London (1903) and a School of Social Science at Liverpool University, both offering opportunities for practical work as well as courses. Smith (1965, p.54) describes how these schools provided a general training for social workers, 'not to be confused with special vocational training for a particular job' (Smith, 1965, p.54). Despite satisfactory operation over a ten year period, the School of Sociology experienced financial problems. It was taken over in 1912 by the London School of Economics and Political Science (LSE) and became part of a new Department of Social Science and Administration. Other courses were also established at around this time, for example, at Barnett House, Oxford, and Bedford College, London, the latter continuing a more sociological tradition than the LSE course (an interdisciplinary rivalry which has continued throughout this century).

Courses at this time offered teaching in college on a range of 'academic' and 'professional' subjects (origins of status differences between social science academics and social work educators) and students spent an equivalent length of time in practical work (Smith, 1965). Thus, issues concerned with funding; the relationships between college-based learning and practice; and academic as opposed to professional knowledge, were already on the agenda of social work education. More broadly, the subject area was already a site of conflict over the role of the state in welfare provision (under discussion by the Royal Commission on the Poor

Law), with implications for the role of welfare professionals (Jones, 1979, p.77).

Jones contends that early social work development laid a basis for a form of social work concerned to 'socialise its clients into appropriate social habits...[and to reach]...the common goal of maintaining and reproducing a reliable working class' (Jones, 1979, p.75). It was also significantly based on the medical model, and notwithstanding the Settlement movement (Parry and Parry, 1979), social work education promoted a highly individualised form of social work which has persisted with only occasional challenges in the UK, and is widespread elsewhere (Suin de Boutemard, 1990).

Lorenz has identified the different ideological positions which informed the development of social work education in a number of European countries (Lorenz, 1994). Christian, philanthropic and feminist ideals all played a part in shaping the early course aims and content, though socialist influences were perhaps less in evidence, with the exception of the course established at Ruskin College, Oxford. However, socialist ideals have periodically motivated some social work educators and had particular relevance to a more recent stage of development, discussed later.

Three of the texts discussing historical beginnings (Smith, 1965; Jones, 1979; Lorenz, 1994) have illustrated the need for social work education to 'grapple with the dialectic tension between, on the one hand, preparing (students) for very specific tasks and duties within given organisational parameters, and, on the other hand, relativising and questioning these organisational constraints from the transcending positions of ethics and fundamental views on the nature of society and human behaviour' (Lorenz, 1994, p.40). The education/training dichotomy, which played an important part in the earliest stages of social work education, has continued to be a major concern to a range of interest groups and is central to the crisis concerning the future shape and location of social work education.

The inter-war years were noted by Jones (1979, p.72) as 'a period of relative quiescence' in social work education, notwithstanding the social changes and economic problems of the time. This raises the issue of relevance to the social concerns of the day. However, just as wider welfare policies were characterised by 'administrative responses', the organisation of social work continued through establishment of professional organisations. These approved a slowly growing number of training opportunities, that is, the professional project proceeded.

Social work education continued to be fragmented (reflecting organisational and professional divisions): the Institute of Almoners approved training for social work in hospitals, while the Home Office approved courses initially in the Probation and subsequently Child Care fields. From the outset, it was mainly women who took advantage of training opportunities and who predominated in the 'care' roles (in hospitals, schools and a few clinical settings), while significant numbers of (largely untrained) men worked in the 'control' areas (Probation, Mental Welfare, NSPCC), mirroring domestic roles and Victorian norms (Walton, 1975). The implications of gender are also further explored in this study.

The inter-war years saw the beginning of a form of social work research distinct from the important and well known social surveys which had informed earlier developments (Pinker, 1971). A ten-year study of social casework (1924-34) was summarised in an unpublished paper 'Social Casework in Action' by an LSE lecturer, Clement Brown (Walton, 1975). Its non-publication at the time raises questions about social work academics' credibility and confidence - another area for exploration in this study.

The Late 1940s to 1969

Jones identified a period of 'gradual but increasing ascendancy [in social work] in the post 1945 period' (Jones, 1979, p.72), related to significant changes in philosophy and policy regarding state welfare provision (Glennerster, 1995), and reflected in social work education. In fact, Jones' publication in 1979 marked the point at which this development could be said to have been reversed. The path of social work education, even in these expansionist days of welfare and professional enterprises, was not smooth. Jones mentions cryptically that during the 1950s 'social work successfully fought to keep its courses in the university sector, *despite the opposition from many social studies departments*' (Jones, 1979, p.78, author's italics), presaging one aspect of the insecurity subsequently experienced.

Social work education at that time did have an influential advocate in Eileen Younghusband, who noted that 'the removal of social work education from the university sector would lower the standards and status of courses' (Younghusband, 1951, p.172). She contributed significantly to the further development of social work education through a report, commonly named after her (1959). This laid the basis for a generic approach to training (pioneered at the LSE in 1954) and also to the growth of social work education, including at non-graduate level in the 1960s. This latter development coincided with the establishment of the polytechnic sector and a general expansion in higher education as well as growth in the personal social services. However, with hindsight, it can be seen as the precursor of a shift from post-graduate to non-graduate courses which subsequently became the norm. It also marked the first paradigm shift from specialisation to generalism, in education as well as practice, another issue of periodic concern to educators.

Notwithstanding the impact of developments in social sciences and the growth in academic social research in the 1950s and 1960s (Payne, 1991, p.3), there was academic disfavour towards social work education in the 1950s, arguably related to its general adoption of perspectives from psychiatry, psychology and psychoanalysis, in tune with the emphasis on family stability after the upheavals of war (Bowlby, 1951). This resulted in the prevalence of individual case studies as a means of analysing and communicating ideas about social work, and reflected a form of practice which ignored wider societal factors and strategies. This approach, continued into the 1960s, provided a relatively secure form of professionalism but countered the positivistic approach of social sciences and their own efforts to establish academic credibility.

During the 1960s the psychodynamic approach became 'naturalised' (Payne, 1991), and structural analysis and the teaching of theory or skills relevant to intervention in community development or at policy level received little attention. While the 'rediscovery of poverty' was spearheaded by social scientists in the mid-1960s (notably by Abel Smith and Townsend (1965) at the LSE), it was not until the 1970s that social work courses became more influenced by sociological and policy perspectives and began to develop radical critiques of social work. From 1970 to 1977, a collective produced 25 editions of the differently informed and 'irreverent' *Case Con* (Langan, 1993, p.59), which challenged the prevailing orthodoxy; and during this decade social work education became more heterogeneous.

This delayed response to changing circumstances contributes to a criticism made of social workers more recently - in a period of anxieties about child abuse - that they fail to use research findings and to adapt their organisation and practice. Thus, social work education has periodically demonstrated a lack of timely attention to wider research and analysis, and been criticised for failure to produce social workers equipped to deal with emerging problems. The belated adoption of 'new' knowledge and perspectives then puts the discipline out of step with the demands and opportunities of the field, public and government attitudes, and the possible contributions of related subjects. The dangers of an introverted and 'precious' approach to social work education or, conversely, of an over-confident assumption by the profession of the role of critics and conscience of society, are examined later.

The 1970s

1970-1971 marked an important point in the unification of British social work and an apparent strengthening of its role and identity. Along with the establishment of local authority Social Service Departments (SSDs) following the *Seebohm Report* (1968), the main professional associations (with the exception of the National Association of Probation Officers, NAPO), formed the British Association of Social Workers (BASW). Additionally, the government strengthened the regulation of social work education through the establishment of the Central Council for Education and Training in Social Work (CCETSW). This body was a QUANGO charged with promoting the growth, rationalisation and standardisation of social work education. It replaced a smaller body, the Council for Training in Social Work established by legislation in 1962. The legislation was amended in 1971 to give the new council extended powers, and again in 1983 when the size of the council was significantly reduced and became less representative of the profession and more subject to government influence, a trend continued into the 1990s.

A new professional qualification, the Certificate of Qualification in Social Work (CQSW) was established replacing earlier awards and providing generic training, related to the changed external context of social work practice. SSDs had quickly become the major employers of social workers and had developed generic teams rather than perpetuating old divisions related to client groups. Social work education was unique in offering a professional qualification at any one of four academic levels - non-graduate (two years); undergraduate (usually as part of a four year degree in social science or sociology); postgraduate diploma (1 year) or masters level (two years). This ensured the possibility of entry to the profession by a wide range of applicants. It could also be interpreted as the avoidance of conflict with established educational interests (since most postgraduate courses were offered in the university sector) by a body whose powers were yet to be tested, in a period which generally demonstrated a consensus rather than a conflict approach to policy change.

The four academic levels may also suggest a degree of uncertainty about the academic status of the subject. The shift which occurred then to a preponderance of non-graduate courses (about 50 per cent) might also be seen as evidence of a degree of anti-intellectualism within the social work profession (Jones, 1996a), as well as scepticism about its academic credentials. However, Jones had previously noted that a relative increase in the number of social work courses at masters level in the 1970s (partly through upgrading of postgraduate diploma courses) could be seen as 'another example of the image creating manoeuvres of social work' (Jones, 1979, p.79). The issue of the appropriate level of professional qualification, combined with course length and content, became a major preoccupation for CCETSW in the 1980s and continued into the 1990s, when it was apparently resolved - at least in CCETSW's view - but ambiguity, uncertainty or conflict about the qualifying stage of professional education for social work has continued.

The 1970s were an important period during which tensions in the field around establishment and maintenance of professional values and authority were mirrored by similar conflicts in social work education Professional values might be said to have 'lost out' to bureaucratic and technocratic pressures. Social work education was marked by a new wave of American theories and models apparently suited to the new conditions in British social services - crisis intervention theory; task centred work; and the systems model (Payne, 1991). It was also strengthened by larger scale and more credible forms of research, notably into organisational forms (e.g. Rowbottom *et al.*, 1974); modes of delivery (Goldberg and Fruin, 1976); and the social work role (DHSS, 1978).

However, radical critiques were also being developed by British academics rooted in the wider social movements of the 1960s and informed by Marxist perspectives. Although not a uniform feature, they played a significant role in the shaping of some social work thought and action (Bailey and Brake, 1975; Corrigan and Leonard, 1978). Growth of unionisation and industrial unrest occurred in a few social service departments in the late 1970s, related to increased bureaucratic and financial stringency, resulting in polarisation between practitioners and managers (Langan, 1993). This could be seen as evidence of social work training failing to prepare students for the reality of life in a welfare bureaucracy. The earlier characterisation of social workers as 'lady bountifuls' was replaced by that of 'trendy lefties' at a time when a shift to the right was occurring in public attitudes.

In the early 1970s, CCETSW had been more preoccupied with the *quantity* of educational provision than its form, but from the outset it was heavily influenced by the 'needs' of local authority departments. The first CCETSW Annual Report (1971) recorded that, from 1961-1970, output of qualified social workers had increased from 325 to 1,521. By 1975, 130 social work courses recommended 2,650 students for qualifying awards (Jones, 1979, p.72). However, only about 40 per cent of local authority social workers were qualified, predominantly in 'field work' rather than in residential and day care services; and growing demand, assisted perhaps by growing dissatisfaction with CQSW courses, led to the establishment in 1975 of the Certificate in Social Services (CSS). This two year non-graduate award was offered jointly by employers and colleges outside the university sector and was sometimes referred to as an employment-based route. It set an important precedent for the development of social work education and training.

The two qualifications, although intended for people in different roles, became synonymous with training for field workers (CQSW) and for staff in residential and day-care settings (CSS). This exacerbated tensions and status differences between the two groups of workers, reflected in the different institutional levels of awards as well as course content and ethos. The CSS addressed far more directly the training needs of employing agencies, and brought into sharp contrast issues about professional loyalty and accountability, as well as critical thinking, emphasised on CQSW courses.

The fight for power between employers, educators and CCETSW was illustrated in microcosm by CCETSW's closure in 1977 of a course in the polytechnic sector which had resisted admission of an education welfare officer, employed by one of the institutions' funding authorities. This event brought social work educators into conflict with their own institution and resulted in a high court case against the institution which CCETSW won (Parsloe, 1980). All the social work educators involved in the case at its inception (1975) had been replaced by the time a new course was approved (in 1980), and most had returned to the field.

Around this time, CCETSW proposed CQSW reform to ensure its relevance to employer needs. This provoked a spirited response from a group of academics at Warwick University who suggested that the consultative document showed a preference for 'the pragmatic, the technical, the uncritically active...[and] an indifference to social policy and macro-perspectives [with] an underlying contempt for theory' (Barker *et al.*, 1978, p.18). They further criticised the document as 'educationally unsound, ...politically naive and set on getting social work education to commit suicide' (p.22). This robust defence of social work education (and outspoken attack on CCETSW) did not halt a process which saw CCETSW and employers gain increasing influence over the scope and nature of social work education during the 1980s and into the 1990s.

Thus, the end of the 1970s could be viewed as a watershed in the development of social work education. Internally, the balance of power between CCETSW and academia was shifting and some of the theoretical perspectives being espoused by educators were increasingly viewed with suspicion. External factors included the election in 1979 of a Conservative government, with its new agenda for the public sector and welfare services, though as Glennerster noted 'it was the economic circumstances of 1976 that finally broke the continuity in social policies in the post war era' (Glennerster, 1995, p.167).

The 1980s

Social work education entered the 1980s with its confidence shaken and resources depleted (Brewer and Lait, 1980). The immediate result of the conflicts of the late 1970s and concerns about relevance was more emphasis on skills training in social work education (Richards, 1985) and the decade was not characterised by significant theoretical developments. Two writers produced useful overviews of the theories, methods and approaches taught on social work courses throughout the 1980s (Coulshead, 1988; Payne, 1991), both of which illustrated an eclectic approach to theory compared to the dominance of the psycho-dynamic paradigm of an earlier generation.

There was little development of research about social work education, with the exception of work by Gardiner (1988). Social work educators were slow to appreciate the potential relevance of new thinking about reflective practice advocated by Schon (1983, 1987), although related ideas about the adult learner took hold (Harris *et al.*, 1985). The shift away from radical critiques was replaced by research and teaching about developments in the field, for instance community social work (Brown *et al.*, 1982; Hadley and McGrath, 1984) and a growing preoccupation with child abuse and protection (Howe, 1986; Stevenson, 1989). The latter, in turn, led to an increasing emphasis on law teaching on courses (Bray and Preston-Shoot, 1992), a significant theme in the recasting of qualifying training for the 1990s.

However, sociological thinking was not entirely quelled and found expression in increasing attention on courses to the power differentials between different groups in society, notably, at that stage, ethnic minorities and women (Dominelli, 1988; Hanmer and Statham, 1988). These replaced an earlier preoccupation in the social sciences with class inequalities. Social work education developed anti-racist and black perspectives, and subsequently anti-discriminatory or anti-oppressive policy and practice.

Government cuts in higher education spending in the early 1980s and reorganisation within and between institutions had some unplanned consequences, including the loss of three social work courses in London, at Bedford College, Brunel University and Chelsea College (all at masters level), but 'CCETSW was not consulted, nor did the DHSS...participate in the process; perhaps they were not invited to comment' (Kogan and Kogan, 1983, p.106).

CCETSW's earlier preoccupation with quantity of training had by now shifted very substantially to concerns about quality (adopting a later definition of 'fitness for purpose') which CCETSW sought to address through structural changes. A major, though poorly prepared, proposal by CCETSW in 1984 (Paper 20.1), dubbed the X/Y debate, reflected an accepted division between two forms (levels) of training, and gave rise to acrimonious debate (Bamford, 1984). CCETSW subsequently produced a new proposal for a three year training programme leading to a qualifying diploma in social work (QDSW), citing in support, European norms and the Commission's Directive on level and length of professional training. An internal paper by Barr was published in 1990.

However, the British government was unmoved and declined to fund a third year of training. One explanation of this refusal was offered by Henke (1988) who saw the decision as a backlash against increased public expenditure (of £1.5 bn) from the Treasury Contingency Fund (for various unrelated purposes) rather than a rational response to a proposal costed at £140 million and which had received some support from six government departments, including the (then) Department of Health and Social Security. However, others might have interpreted the decision as part of a wider move to weaken a professional group which found little favour with either the government or the wider public.

Whatever the motives or reasons behind the refusal, this defeat, described by a leading academic in the context of EC recognition, as 'a blow to the standing of British social work and social work education'

(Parsloe, 1990, p.20), had considerable impact on the morale of social work educators, who were generally in favour of a longer training period. It resulted in a hastily revised set of proposals being put forward by CCETSW for a Diploma in Social Work (DipSW). This retained some of the features of QDSW, but required it to be taught within two years, as a replacement for both the CQSW and CSS awards.

Developments in the 1990s

The Diploma in Social Work

The DipSW proposals, laid out in Paper 30, issued in 1989 (with minor revisions in 1991), signified the successful shift to a training paradigm in preparation for social work practice, relative to an educational one. With the exception of its adherence to anti-racist and subsequently anti-discriminatory perspectives, it demonstrated the dominance of political and employer influence over professional interests (including those of social work academics). Paper 30 specified the knowledge, values and skills needed to achieve competence in social work practice (CCETSW, 1989, p.13) and required proposals for new courses (renamed programmes) to be submitted jointly be colleges and agencies; to offer an area of particular practice (APP), to implement and monitor anti-racist policies, and to be assessed by CCETSW approved External Assessors.

The establishment of formal partnerships drew heavily on the CSS model and formalised many existing informal relationships between CQSW courses and local agencies. Social work educators had expressed support for partnerships in 1986 in one of 28 recommendations made in a joint report issued by the Association of Teachers in Social Work Education (ATSWE), the Joint University Council Social Work Education Committee (JUC SWEC), and the Standing Conference of Heads of CQSW Courses (SCHOC) (Hooper and Robb, 1986). However, in reality it introduced further bureaucratisation to qualifying training and a decade later Jackson and Preston-Shoot (1996, p.5) referred to DipSW partnerships as 'time-consuming and largely pointless formal structures'. This move could also be seen as an attempt to ensure relevance to practice without necessarily achieving a particular goal, namely ensuring quantity and quality of placements.

Despite CCETSW's avoidance of the term, the second requirement firmly reinstated 'specialisation' within the curriculum, usually related to client (or now user or consumer) groups and reflecting the reorganisation taking place in social service departments in the early 1990s. The third requirement reflected the patchy development of anti-racist training on CQSW courses in the 1980s, and repaid the efforts of the Mickleton Group, formed in the mid-1980s by social work students and educators to lobby CCETSW. As a result, a Black Perspectives Committee had been formed (1987) to augment the representation by the solitary black member on CCETSW Council (Pierce, 1994). This undoubtedly affected 'the emphasis placed on anti-racist values in the formation of professionals who would be operating in a multi-racial society.

However, this area in particular was to be subject to a backlash against politically correct social workers in the early 1990s (Webb, 1990; Pinker, 1993) which triggered a review even before all revised courses were established. The changes from CQSW and CSS to DipSW were originally to be phased in over the period up to 1995. It is perhaps not surprising that among the early validations, ex-CSS programmes predominated, with later changes taking place to CQSW courses in the old university sector. By 1993, 46 new DipSW programmes were in place with only six CSS courses but 29 CQSW courses remaining (CCETSW, 1993, Annual Report and see Part II).

CCETSW did not specify a curriculum for social work education, but the requirement to produce a practice curriculum, which addressed the competencies to be assessed, proved a challenge and provided the stimulus for recent literature discussing the appropriateness or otherwise of a 'competency-led' approach to professional education (Timms, 1991; Jones and Joss, 1995; Yelloly, 1995; Clark, 1996; Ford, 1996; Parton, 1996; Vass, 1996; Froggett, 1997).

Two other developments were instigated by CCETSW in the early 1990s. The first concerned *practice teacher training and funding* arrangements. The requirement that all practice teachers should receive training for this role, and some additional resourcing from government, was partly a response to the lack of a third year at the qualifying stage, but also sought to address issues of quality. It undoubtedly had some impact in this respect, but also tended to exacerbate the problems of supply of placements; to place further demands on college and agency staff, and probably to shift further the balance of power from academics to the field. A minimum of two placements, accounting for 50 per cent of the overall programme, has remained the norm from the inception of social work education. By the mid-1970s the old-boy (or more appropriately old-girl) mechanism for securing placements from a network of former students and colleagues was creaking under the strain of the rapid expansion of training opportunities and the impact of changes in the field.

By the 1980s the placement situation had reached crisis proportions, prompting surveys by social work educators (Collins *et al.*, 1987) and the Association of Directors of Social Services (ADSS) (Parker, 1987). Meanwhile, in London, social work educators and agency training officers initiated regular meetings and developed the 'Cluster System' aimed at increasing the supply of placements and rationalising their allocation. An evaluation of this system in a report on the costs of social work education suggested that the system had achieved its first goal, if not the second (Rustin and Edwards, 1989) and it is likely that this activity also fed into the CCETSW thinking about the DipSW model of partnership.

More recently, under pressure from the Department of Health (DoH), and following an explosion of placements in the voluntary sector relative to a decrease in statutory placements, CCETSW radically restructured the funding of placements in line with purchaser/provider principles, pushing social work educators into a competitive market place with potentially serious implications for the viability of some courses. This move is not critically analysed in recent literature about social work education, but the 'placements issue' is a recurring item in the documentary material analysed, and is further discussed in Part II.

The Continuum of Training

The second development concerned CCETSW's promotion of a *continuum of training* since 1991 and reflected an extension of its brief from qualifying training to an increased concern with the pre- and post-qualifying stages. The concern with pre-qualifying training acknowledged that social workers constitute only 10-15 per cent of social service staff and reflected the governments' agenda to increase training opportunities for unqualified staff. CCETSW was active in the Care Sector Consortium, with its remit to develop National Vocational Qualifications (NVQs) for a range of pre-professional workers in the social and health care fields (Yelloly, 1995). Such training is generally offered within employing agencies in conjunction with the further education sector and was not explored in this study. It accelerated a trend towards shifting agency resources from funding professional and post qualifying training outside the agency, to meeting the training needs of a larger number of workers within the agency.

The proposals in relation to the post qualifying stage (PQ) were built on the recognition that a two year training programme can only lay a basic foundation for practice, which needs to be consolidated (through post qualifying awards, PQSW) and extended (through advanced awards, AASW). A small number of universities had previously offered courses and academic qualifications beyond CQSW, without distinquishing between the post-qualifying and advanced stages. Courses had been approved by CCETSW, but despite various lengths and models of courses (including part-time opportunities) and some CCETSW bursaries to cover fees of students, take-up had been low. There were regional variations in availability, and there was no necessary correlation between the needs of the field, the courses offered and participation rates.

Social workers usually needed agency permission to attend such courses, but applications were generally made on the basis of individual interest, and often bore no relation to either staff development profiles or workforce planning strategies of organisations. There is impressionistic evidence to suggest that individuals attending part-time MA courses used them to progress their careers, often out of the organisations which had allowed, for example, half-day release for two years. (There are early indications in a recent Dept. of Health/Welsh Office Consultation Document (1998) that these tendencies have continued even with the development of a more systematic approach to post-qualifying awards.)

The only qualification previously offered in-house by agencies was a 60 day additional training course for staff involved in mental health work leading to the CCETSW award of Approved Social Worker (ASW). This had been introduced in the early 1980s amid concern that one or two year generic courses were failing to provide sufficient training for this specialist role. Its introduction was resisted by many unionised social workers, as against the principles of genericism and creating an elite group within the workforce. However, within a decade this was well established (usually offered without formal HE involvement), and, given the increasing disquiet about practice in the child care field, some were surprised that a similar requirement had not been introduced in that area of practice also.

The new proposals developed further the requirements for agency/higher education institution (HEI) partnerships in devising and providing PQ and advanced awards, already a requirement of practice teaching programmes. It also required the formation of regional consortia aimed at rationalisation - relating the supply and nature of such programmes to local needs - and standardisation - ensuring some uniformity of standards within a region and nationally. Both the timing and the form of this new initiative were unfortunate. Agencies were preoccupied with the needs of large numbers of unqualified workers and developing NVQ provisions, and social work educators were still involved in devising or implementing new DipSW programmes.

However, both parties recognised a vested interest in involvement in the scheme, and initially, large amounts of staff time and CCETSW funding were committed to developing regional consortia (whose activities and business plans had to be approved by CCETSW) and in establishing criteria for approval of programmes by validation panels. In the event, very few programmes had been approved and awards made by the mid-1990s, provoking government pressure on CCETSW to achieve targets. With the Research Assessment Exercise approaching in 1996, some social work educators reduced involvement, and the impact of policies in this area has continued to be relatively patchy: in less than a decade this was one of a number of areas of social work education and CCETSW operation under review (DoH/Welsh Office, 1998).

A further implication of the establishment of the continuum of training was the assumption that qualifying training would normally take place at the *non-graduate diploma level*, emphasising CCETSW's acceptance of the down-grading of the British social work qualification relative to social work education abroad (Cannan *et al.*, 1992; Hokenstad *et al.*, 1992), and indeed relative to other forms of professional education in the UK.

Further Change

By 1992 (the starting date of this research), it seemed as if the new form and structures of social work education had been established, albeit they placed increased bureaucratic pressures on social work educators, further prescribed their academic freedom, and posed fundamental questions about the nature of the educational process, content and assessment for professional practice. In 1992, Jones described the new DipSW qualification as employment-led with 'regulations that are...detailed, directive and technical...[leaving] little opportunity for developing analytic skills' (Jones, 1992, p.55). Thus, the technocratisation of social work, increasingly evident in the 1970s and 1980s, would apparently be completed through the medium of the social work education process in the 1990s. This was paralleled by its increasing bureaucratisation, also detailed in practice (Howe, 1986) and now evident in regulations concerning partnership arrangements for both DipSW and the post qualification awards.

But the opportunity to consolidate new developments was not yet available. The early 1990s was a period of significant changes in the scrutiny of the quality of research, institutional arrangements, and teaching and learning opportunities in higher education. Thus, social work educators were involved to varying degrees in the Research Assessment Exercises (RAEs, 1992 and 1996), institutional visits by the Higher Education Quality Council (HEQC), and subject area review by the Higher Education Funding Councils for England, Wales and Scotland (HEFCE, HEFCW, and SHEFC) (1994), discussed further later.

Nor were changes in the social work discipline itself complete. Notwithstanding the funding by the DoH of a research project into 'readiness to practice' of students qualifying in 1992 and 1993 (Marsh and Trisselliotis, 1996), 1993 saw further changes, prior to any results from the funded research. The Secretary of State for Health announced the governments' intention to 'reform' social work. This included a restructuring of CCETSW itself, including abolition of the Black Perspective Committee, a reduction in the size of the Council (further reducing professional participation and excluding representation of the Association of Metropolitan Authorities (AMA)) and a review of training under a new chairman, Sir Jeffrey Greenwood (Francis, 1994). The previous chairman, an academic, had resigned in February 1994 following a clash with Tim Yeo, then Junior Health Minister (Cervi, 1993).

The restructuring was apparently on the grounds of the need to adapt to changes triggered by the new legislation (in the areas of child care, community care [vulnerable adults] and criminal justice), introduced in the period 1989-1991 with significant implications for social work organisation and practice. However, it was also intended that CCETSW should require courses to adopt a 'more common sense approach' to social work with less use of jargon, and it came in the wake of the previously mentioned accusations of political correctness and bigotry in social work practice, for which the education and training programmes were blamed. The immediate impact was the production by CCETSW of a revised Paper 30 heralded in 1994, but in fact not issued until February 1995, with a requirement that all programmes should be revised, submitted for re-approval and implemented by Autumn 1995.

This was an impossibly short timescale for many institutions and programmes. The latter included nine remaining CQSW courses which were planning to convert to DipSW (under the previous regulations) in

Autumn 1995. It may have been the last straw in the case of the LSE course, which had its last intake (to its new Diploma) in 1995, though doubtless there were other factors in this case. It was also apparently a factor in the near demise of the Barnett House course, which was 'saved' by the intervention of Baroness Lucy Faithfull (an ex-Children's Officer from Oxfordshire and continuing supporter of the social work enterprise, including three year qualifying education, until her death in March, 1996). Jones (1996b) saw the review as evidence of the governments' inner direction of CCETSW and of the influence of managerialism on CCETSW and social work education. However, yet one more review into the DipSW was to be undertaken before the end of the decade (JM Consulting, 1998) and the consequences of this latest policy development, alongside other changes, have not yet been fully realised.

Nor was the review of DipSW the only change in the mid-1990s. In 1994 the government set up a review of education and training of probation officers which recommended that DipSW should no longer be the qualification for entry to this field of practice (Dews and Watts, 1995). Ward (1996) identified a long-standing antipathy between the Home Office and CCETSW, as well as disputes among the educators responsible for probation training as behind this development.

Despite separately identified competencies for probation officers, additional requirements prescribing the content of probation APPs, the significant investment of probation agencies in partnership programmes, and important evidence that the 'fit' between education and training of students and the requirements of employers was most evident in the probation field (whose students also proclaimed the highest levels of satisfaction with their education (Marsh and Trisseliotis, 1996)), efforts to argue against this action were ignored and 1995 was the last year for admission to DipSW programmes of students (with Home Office sponsorship) wishing to enter the probation service. The debates surrounding probation training in social work education are usefully discussed in Nellis (1996), Ward (1996) and Williams (1995). More recent developments have resulted in a new award for probation officers, incorporating a vocational qualification but awarded at degree level.

Concluding Comments

This review of social work education has described events leading to a sense of crisis in the subject area in the early 1990s and continuing uncertainties at the close of the decade. It has identified some recurring issues and the increasingly turbulent environment in which social work educators operate. The 'associational effects' of social work with people in crisis, excluded or in conflict with society must play some part in this scenario. Added to this is a sense of the marginal position of social work education. It is neither fully acknowledged as a specialist form of professional practice, nor apparently conforms to the 'mainstream' of academic norms and expectations. This raises questions about the identity and careers of social work educators themselves, discussed in Part II.

Other themes identified in this overview, which are further explored, are the academic location of the social work subject area, and its relation to practice (in both epistemological and bureaucratic terms), its resourcing, the 'ownership' and direction of social work education, the implications of gender, the place of research in developing its knowledge base, the effect of professional values as represented in tensions around education for anti-racist and anti-oppressive practice, and the possible influence of comparative European or international perspectives.

The foregoing discussion demonstrates that social work has a long established position in British higher education, but not a secure one. From a comparative perspective, with the exception of qualifying courses at masters level, the UK has the shortest length and lowest academic level of education and training for social work anywhere, but probably the highest proportion of time spent in practice placements. Further, the UK is unusual in the extent of prescription exercised by a body which is not a professional association, nor an academic institution, nor a government ministry (although CCETSW is clearly an agent of the state). Additionally, it is probably the only country in which such concerted efforts are made to ensure that supply of places is matched by demand for trained workers (Cannan *et al.*, 1992; Hokenstad *et al.*, 1992).

From this analysis, social work education developments have clearly been increasingly influenced by CCETSW over a 25 year period, although its own status has not always been secure. While CCETSW was viewed by social work educators as a relatively benign agency in the 1970s, it was perceived as incompetent and lacking intellectual and political capacity in the 1980s, and has since been seen as operating as a conduit for government policies. A debate at a conference run by the Association of Teachers in Social Work Education (ATSWE) in 1996 explored whether CCETSW had defended social work education against government attacks or had 'sold out' to government policies.

It could be said that CCETSW became increasingly powerful vis-à-vis social work education, but increasingly weak in relation to a government which (up to 30/4/97) had seemed determined to curb the scope and powers of public service professionals and the welfare sector. But a change of government did not mean a halt to (or reversal of) changes in the welfare sector and shortly after this research had been completed the demise of CCETSW itself was announced, alongside significant changes in the structures regulating social work and its allied field of education and training.

As demonstrated in many other areas, central government has the power to change the 'rules of the game' and the structures which operationalise policies, and social work education has been no exception to increased state intervention in the pursuit of the goals of deregulation, accountability, quality and consumer choice (Pollitt, 1990; Henkel, 1994). There are additional factors related to the nature and role of social work which compound its vulnerability. What has also become clear is that early conflicts between the field of practice (agencies) and academic institutions, were originally, though not exclusively, mediated by professional associations which, since 1971, have been replaced by CCETSW, a body in which the participation of social work educators, whether as council members or officers, has significantly declined.

Despite the major part played by CCETSW in the developments outlined above, this research did not set out to chart specifically its role, nor that of any other particular bodies, but rather to explore the views of social work educators on the nature of the subject and responses to the recent changes. The wider context of developments in the field of social work, changes in higher education values and policy, and the nature of knowledge and professional education, are discussed next.

2 Social Work: New Paradigms and the Professional Debate

Introduction

There is an inevitable inter-relationship between a specific area of professional education and its field of practice. In any field, practice predates the establishment of education and training programmes, but thereafter, the balance of power between the two varies. While education becomes a specialism relative to the profession, it also regulates entry to it and may constitute the 'cutting edge' of professional practice through research. In other cases, it may be out of step with the field, a criticism periodically levelled against social work education and one of the reasons given for change.

However, educational arrangements and processes also sometimes *reflect* the uncertainties and turbulence of a profession. One of the writer's contentions is that recent trends in social work education mirror a weakening of the profession as a whole, thus increasing a distrust and competition between people who share similar values and goals. This chapter examines developments in social work since 1970. Chapter 1 sketched the origins and early history of social work: the more recent history illustrates paradigm changes in the role and organisation of social workers, with consequences for the education and training process.

Payne (1991, p.1) observed that social work is 'widely enough spread for international associations ... and a shared language and literature to exist ... but there is no agreed definition ... [decisions about boundaries, objectives and roles] ... vary according to the time, social conditions and cultures within which [they operate]'. The extent to which social work is organised as part of state welfare or provided on a more *ad hoc* basis by the voluntary or private sectors is variable, although some aspects often have a state mandate.

In England and Wales, social work has been closely associated with local authority social service departments (SSDs) since 1970 and a lack of differentiation in the use of the term 'social worker' has been significant in public perceptions of the role. In its statutory form, social work has experienced variable fortunes, according to the political will and economic circumstances of local and central governments. Increased levels of central government intervention through the 1980s and 1990s have been noted in the literature, related to a wider redefining of local authority roles.

Unification and Genericism

The Seebohm Report (DHSS, 1968), with its proposals for unified community-based, family-orientated social service departments, was written during growth in provision of welfare and in professional confidence. The rediscovery of poverty in the mid-1960s gave rise to government initiatives to combat social disadvantage (Education Priority Area Projects, 1969-1972; Community Development Projects, 1971-1976) which enhanced the power of some occupational groups but also contained notions of prevention and participation. The new departments were established in accordance with the Local Authority Social Services Act (1970) and espoused universalist and redistributive ideals alongside encouragement of individual effort.

These departments reflected social work values concerning the uniqueness and worth of individuals and their right to acceptance and self-determination (Kogan, 1971), while creating hierarchical and bureaucratic structures which some saw as being at variance with professional values. Hall (1976) suggested that the Seebohm changes had been influenced less by strong public or political feeling about social work, than by social workers themselves (the Seebohm Implementation Group), unhindered by strong opposition from other interest groups. The medical profession, for instance, was preoccupied with reorganisation of the health service. However, underlying the initiative was a concern for better co-ordination of services, which 'one door' access aimed to provide.

The formation of new departments brought together social workers previously employed separately to respond to the needs of different client groups, with the important exceptions of workers employed in secondary settings, education, criminal justice and health (although responsibility for the last group transferred to SSDs in 1974). The voluntary sector was apparently marginalised and social work in the private sector seemed to be a contradiction in terms. The move was paralleled by the incorporation of most existing associations into a unified professional body (BASW). About a year later, CCETSW was established to address the varied training needs of existing and potential staff in the new conditions. This signalled the start of an increasingly close association between the goals of education and training and the needs of SSDs as the main employers.

In line with the expansionist mood of the times, SSDs grew apace. Bamford (1982) suggested that the number of social workers employed increased by 50 per cent between 1971 and 1974; the number of people seeking help nearly doubled to 15 per cent of the population by 1975 (Glampson and Goldberg, 1976); and social service expenditure in 1975 showed a 400 per cent increase over 1948 (Judge, 1978). Analysis of organisational form, and of emerging levels and other divisions of work, was a feature of academic inquiry into social work in the 1970s (Rowbottom *et al.*, 1976; DHSS, 1979).

However, social workers, managers, politicians and the public still struggled to agree on the nature and scope of the social work task. The pace of growth, the variable levels of staff and management training and the raised public expectations produced strain in the system at an early stage. Optimism was shaken by the first in a series of child abuse scandals (the Colwell Report, 1974) which led to significant changes in the management of social work and inter-professional relationships, and heralded an erosion of public confidence in the profession (Stevenson, 1989).

Increasing bureaucratic controls, combined with resource constraints, led to growing social worker dissatisfaction, including strikes, in the late 1970s. This industrial unrest coincided with the election of a Conservative government with radical views on the state and professional roles, relative to individual responsibility; distribution of wealth; and the powers of the local state *vis-à-vis* central government or the market. Personal social services were not the main initial target of policy change by the new regime but there were shifts in focus from the 'monopolistic' position of local authorities as the primary source of social work and social care, and towards control of professionals.

Continuity and Change: The Return to Specialisms

Ten years after the establishment of SSDs, a new 'enquiry into the roles and tasks of social workers' was initiated by government. The resulting preface to the Barclay Report (1982) stated: 'There is confusion about the direction in which [social workers] are going and unease about what they should be doing and the way they should be organised and deployed'. It also suggested that 'Too much is generally expected of [them]' and described social work as a 'relatively young profession' (p.vii), excuses which failed to convince an increasingly sceptical public as the decade progressed.

The Barclay Report (1982) concerned itself with social work in all its forms (including outside SSDs) and settings, and supported a move towards community social work, which 'requires of the social worker an attitude of partnership' with clients, relations, neighbours and volunteers (p.209). It presaged the philosophy underpinning legislation nearly a decade later. Some departments actively promoted community social work in the early 1980s (Hadley and McGrath, 1984), informed by practitioner concerns about client and community empowerment and management hopes of containing costs. But even given the 'generic' basis of the Seebohm departments, many maintained or developed some specialist teams (Lyons, 1984).

Continuing anxieties about child abuse resulted in increasingly reactive local authority policies and social work practice, constrained by procedures and economic stringency, but rising demand was also occasioned by growing numbers of frail elderly people. Reviewing 1984, the ADSS warned of the effect of cuts in government expenditure upon this client group, and drew attention to rapid growth in private care. They also noted large variations in local authority spending per head of population (still evident in later research (Bebbington and Kelly, 1995)); and an absence of data about the workforce (since a survey in 1976) on which to base planning (ADSS, 1985). A ministerial speech in 1984 heralded government intervention to promote the development of a mixed economy of care, although the full impact of a split in purchasing and providing arrangements was not felt until the early 1990s (Langan, 1993).

Meanwhile, SSDs were being more tightly managed within the bureaucratic framework, as evidenced in the growth of guidelines and procedural documents (particularly in relation to child abuse) and in the use of performance indicators, target setting and other mechanisms of the new managerialism (Pollitt, 1990). SSD priorities and social work practice became increasingly dominated by the claims and anxieties of child protection work, and the effects of failures in this area (Howe, 1986; Stevenson, 1989). It was also a significant factor in the juridification of social work (Stanford, 1992) and a new phase of legislation around 1990, which resulted in reorganisation of services into specialisms by client group (now 'users' or 'consumers', in line with the commodification of welfare).

Further features of the late 1980s were a more public acknowledgement of the particular needs of minority ethnic groups, and failure of SSDs to organise appropriate responses (ADSS, 1989); and some development of open records (though departments lagged behind their counterparts in the education sector in both these areas). Despite public perceptions of social workers as preoccupied with racism and discrimination, anti-oppressive values were not dominant in the policies and practice of many departments and workers, affecting the quality of care received by some client groups (Bebbington and Miles, 1989). Such concerns had a direct effect on the framing of DipSW requirements.

Growth in the voluntary sector, usually assisted by funding from SSDs, and the beginnings of the contract culture, were in evidence. Specialist services were provided by established voluntary organisations, such as the NSPCC, and by new organisations addressing unmet needs, including those of minority ethnic groups. Some initiatives gave greater emphasis to user involvement and sought to implement ideas about normalisation and empowerment (Lyons, 1992) to a greater extent than the statutory sector. New responses, such as telephone helplines, and new roles, for example 'advocates', were also established, largely outside SSDs.

By the end of the 1980s, social workers were required to operate within a supply-led welfare system, 'determined by budgetary resources rather than by the needs of clients' (Jones, 1992, p.51). New legislation reflected some public concerns, but also signalled the clear intention of government to limit the powers of professionals and the scope of public services in welfare, as in other sectors. The 1989 Children Act, 1990 National Health Service and Community Care Act, and the 1991 Criminal Justice Act had considerable implications for both social work practice and the organisation of services, and marked the most important change since the Seebohm reorganisation.

The Children Act maintained social work in child care as predominantly still the responsibility of SSDs, although with increased emphasis on partnership, with other agencies and professionals in planning and delivery of services, and with parents and other family members in devising and implementing care plans. The emphasis remained on protection of children at risk (see later). But the narrow interpretation given to 'children in need' resulted in a lack of resources for family support work (despite a growth in family centres, but see Cannan (1992)), and limited responses to children with disabilities or mental health problems or at risk of offending, and young carers. Intentions to 'hive off' adoption and fostering tasks to the voluntary or private sector were averted by the change in government, but there is considerably more use (than a decade ago) of services provided by voluntary organisations under contract (Hill and Aldgate, 1996).

The NHS and Community Care Act, concerned with services to vulnerable adults in the community, has arguably had the most impact on social work practice and the position of SSDs. It represents most clearly the marketisation and commodification of welfare, and the limitation of (professional) discretion. It formalised the purchaser-provider split, with SSDs as the purchasers of services which should be provided by agencies in the voluntary and private sector, or informal care. The implications in terms of expectations placed on women, as family members or low paid carers, has been remarked upon (Langan and Day, 1992). While social workers and other staff (renamed care managers) retain responsibility for some assessment work and care planning, direct work with users is carefully prescribed and limited by budgets. There has been growing public concern about the quality of services available, particularly in relation to people with mental health problems.

The third Act clearly incorporated the Probation Service into a criminal justice system possibly more concerned with retribution than rehabilitation, in the face of rising crime levels. The role of probation officers was redefined as 'policing' offenders in the community, and social work skills and approaches were no longer thought appropriate. This was reflected in the removal of probation training from DipSW programmes, and also in the changes in probation (Harris, 1996) resulting in 'exit' (Hirschman, 1970) noted in research (La Valle and Lyons, 1996a).

As the 1990s progressed, social work became a more fragmented occupation, with an increased range of work carried out by people not called social workers (for instance, care managers), who are thought not to need social work qualifications (probation officers) or who operate outside the statutory sector and have other, or no, qualifications. Increasing numbers of staff now work on temporary contracts and their commitment to particular employers or users is short term: their training, supervision and affiliation needs are also different. Characteristics of the workforce and their perceptions of these changes have been explored (NISW, 1995; La Valle and Lyons, 1996a, 1996b; Balloch *et al.,* 1999). The range of job titles listed by respondents to CCETSW's 'first destination' surveys (1993-1997) gave evidence of the increased range of posts and settings which newly qualified social workers were entering (Wallis Jones and Lyons, 1997).

By the end of the 1990s social work might be described as being at a cross roads in terms of its future development. Pessimists see evidence of deprofessionalisation and even 'erasure' (Pietroni, 1995) while others have more confidence in the ability of social work to adapt to changed conditions. Recurring themes in this account concern the nature of the task, in particular the social work role in protecting children and other vulnerable people, and the professional status of social work. These are now examined further.

Task and Mandate: Care, Protection and Control

One explanation for the problematic position of social work is in the apparent growth of violence within families, and the failure of social workers to prevent abuse of various kinds. Child deaths are not a new phenomenon (the 1948 Children Act in part had its origins in the death of a boy who was fostered (Heywood, 1978)), nor did the British discover 'baby battering' (Kemp *et al.*, 1962), but child protection work assumed an increasing profile following the death of Maria Colwell in 1973 and some thirty subsequent public enquiries into child deaths (Stevenson, 1989). Concerns since the late 1980s about child sexual and ritual abuse brought into public question social work judgements and intervention, as well as training and inter-professional co-operation.

Public criticism had largely focused on the practice (and training) of fieldworkers, but from the early 1990s events in the residential care sector (Kincora, Staffordshire) prompted investigation and calls for improved scrutiny and training of residential workers (Warner, 1992). While these events in the community and residential sector have had a significant impact in relation to training (qualifying and in-service), the other response has been organisational and administrative, reflected in central and local government guidelines and procedures, including the establishment of area review committees and child protection registers. Anxieties about child protection work were also an important spur to the establishment of specialist teams, even before the changes resulting from the 1990 legislation (Ottway, 1996).

It has become clear that violence is not restricted to children, although initiatives in relation to 'wife battering' from the late 1970s have occurred in the voluntary rather than the statutory sector, and links between domestic violence and child abuse have only been made more recently. Since the mid-1980s there have also been concerns about 'elder abuse', in neglect of isolated old people or maltreatment by their carers (Eastman, 1994). Such concerns have extended to other vulnerable adults in the community or residential care. In the 1990s, the experience of violence took a new turn with the murder by a person discharged from psychiatric hospital and supposedly in receipt of 'community care' (The Clunis Enquiry, 1994), resulting in the requirement for health authorities to keep registers of discharged patients who are mentally ill, and for all such people to be allocated a key worker who should be either an approved social worker or a psychiatric nurse.

The rise of violence in society can be linked to a variety of factors; increased attention and assessment; greater poverty; a reduction in community-based resources and preventive strategies; and increased responsibilities placed on individuals in a society described as having 'minimalist and authoritarian social policies' (Jones, 1992, p.48). Community care legislation and other measures (including those aimed at unemployed 17 and 18 year olds) have placed families (particularly women) under increasing pressure. Recent initiatives by 'New' Labour, for example in relation to lone parent families, unemployed people and pensioners, indicate a continuing concern to contain welfare expenditure and to break the 'dependency culture'.

The cumulative effects of policies on people who were traditionally clients of social workers were documented (Becker, 1997) and links have been drawn between the increasing desperation of users of social services and the violence and stress experienced by social workers (Payne, 1991; Jones, 1992; Lyons *et al.*, 1995). While previous connections were made between the poor standing of social work in the public esteem and the stigmatisation of people who use social services, Jones (1992) went further in suggesting that working with the 'new poor' had produced 'a harder face of social work as it moves increasingly towards becoming an agent of a restrictive and punitive state' (p.52). This has chilling echoes (noted also in Payne, 1991) of the subversion of social work in pre-war Nazi Germany (Lorenz, 1994) and is a far cry from the earlier aspirations of social work. It may also explain a disowning of the title 'social worker' and the growth of differently titled posts.

There are additional levels of explanation on why social work experienced such a loss of public confidence and became a target of hostile intervention by government. Government agenda are assumed to reflect the will of the people (through the ballot box), and one criterion on which they are periodically judged is their effectiveness in dealing with the perceived social problems of the day. They thus have a considerable interest in how policy is implemented. The political will is marked by legislation and funding decisions, and social workers since the 1970s have been responsible for implementation of an increasing range of Acts, marking significant changes in policy direction.

Reasons for the implementation gap between policy intent and execution offered by policy analysts include insufficient resources or knowledge and skills (Rein, 1983) and conflict of values (Kogan, 1975). Each might have underpinned actions by social workers which were subsequently perceived as inadequate or at variance with government intent.

From a different perspective, Parton (1996) saw the growth of social work as occupying the space which can be called 'social' between those already occupied by health, education and the justice systems, but the boundaries are unclear and subject to contest and renegotiation. In addition, effective care often requires the collaboration of professionals across disciplinary and organisational boundaries, and the apparent inability of social workers to secure this, in particular cases, has caused criticism and loss of public trust. There has also been an apparent inability by social workers to 'explain' their role, not only to other professionals, but to the media, and thus to the public, creating a vacuum to be filled by misunderstanding and distrust.

The third perspective in analysis of the role of social work and its difficulties is loosely based in psycho-analytic theory. It concerns how social work reflects back to society the worst aspects of itself. Recent decades have seen social workers apparently 'discovering' (and then failing to deal adequately with) aberrant behaviour - child abuse, sexual abuse, ritual abuse and, most recently, paedophilia. These can be seen as things the public would rather not acknowledge or which, if believed, they want someone to 'deal with' (Campbell, 1993). In similar vein, social workers have failed to stem the increase in homelessness, addictions, marital breakdown, single-parenthood, and juvenile and adult crime, and have become an easy target for blame. Do they not, after all, sympathise with feminists, homosexuals and ethnic minorities - seen by some as the root causes of society's current problems?

Social work is difficult because the subject matter is problematic, and the form and quality of the response is determined not just by the values, knowledge and skills of workers and managers, but also by the demands of government and the perceptions of other professionals, the press and the public. Societal attitudes are ambivalent. Social workers may be regarded as necessary, but too closely associated with the poor and deviant to be respectable; or too concerned to operate as a counter-profession and conscience to be comfortable colleagues and citizens. In any case, their actions are seen to require careful scrutiny and control, hardly appropriate to an occupational group which might aspire to professional status.

Professional Status, Accountability and Regulation

The establishment of social work within unified departments in 1970 apparently marked a strengthening of the social work professional project (Macdonald, 1995), but in fact paved the way for increased governmental intervention and the potential deprofessionalisation of social work. Henkel (1994) has pointed out the inevitable relationship between social work and the social policies of states, and its mandate to carry out functions which reflect the differing agenda of governments. The professional status of social work can be debated in relation to the theory of professions, as well as to policy directions affecting all professionals. In 1991, the outgoing chief of the Social Services Inspectorate (Department of Health) said:

> Profession is perhaps a courtesy title, since social work possesses few of the distinctive characteristics of the established professions. Employment is unregulated, without minimum requirements for education and training. Satisfactory means do not exist for debarring incompetent, criminal or otherwise unsatisfactory practitioners. Social work possesses a core of knowledge derived in part from the intellectual product of other disciplines, and a developing methodology, as yet largely untested by research (Utting, 1991).

This statement reflects a sociological view of what constitutes a profession from the 1960s. Professions possess key attributes, notably, a body of knowledge, a code of ethics and control of training (Volmer and Mills, 1966). Social work, along with teaching and nursing, was deemed a semi-profession by Etzioni (1969), an epithet which has persisted.

Subsequent writers have challenged earlier conceptions of 'profession', and Johnson (1972) suggested that the functionalist account of professions distorts reality 'because it neglects historical evaluation' which indicates that a given reward structure is 'the result of the arrogation by groups with power to secure claims and create their own system of legitimation' (p.37). Thus, some saw the establishment of SSDs as an opportunity for social workers to increase power at the expense of other occupational groups (Hall, *op. cit.*).

Howe (1986) saw problems around the professionalisation of social work as being for technological and ideological reasons. Industrial unrest in the late 1970s reflected a general mood of egalitarianism, or even radicalism in SSDs, which resulted in large scale unionisation and only a relatively small number of the increasing workforce joining the professional association. BASW's efforts to keep in step or regain ground resulted in the publication of a pamphlet (*Clients are Fellow Citizens*, 1980) and the opening of its membership to unqualified social workers soon after.

But scepticism remained about the desirability of social work seeing itself as a 'profession' (thus self-seeking and remote from the needs of clients), and some social workers were hostile to any suggestions of elitism in their ranks. This was illustrated in the problems surrounding the introduction of the Approved Social Worker qualification in the early 1980s, and in previous debates about the establishment of a General Social Work Council.

Schon (1987) saw a relationship between the mandate (and status) given by society to certain occupational groups to exercise social control and operate autonomously in specialised fields, in exchange for their specialised knowledge and skills. In one sense, this applied to social work in the early Seebohm departments and, in part, it was social work's failure to demonstrate sufficient knowledge and skill and to exercise control in relation to abuse, which led to withdrawal of public support, quite apart from the values and divided views of social workers themselves on the matter. However, Schon also noted the difficulties of professionals meeting expectations in periods of increasing turbulence and regulation, factors salient to the wider social conditions within which social workers operated and the bureaucratisation of SSDs in the 1970s and 1980s.

Friedson (1986) noted the extent to which bureaucratisation of professional groups results in increased rules and sanctions with a concomitant decrease in professional authority and power. The other side of this coin had been noted by Mishra (1981, p.129) 'Where the professional element is weak, services may have a greater tendency towards bureaucratisation'. Variations in professional autonomy between different branches of social work were explored by Roach Anleu (1992) in the Australian context, and her findings about varying levels of autonomy between social workers in different settings (hospital, child care department, and probation) had parallels with the British scene, at least until the early 1990s, when managerialism was impacting universally on professional autonomy.

Regarding the sociology of the professions, Witz (1991) asserted that 'the generic notion of profession is also a gendered notion as it takes what is, in fact, the successful professional projects of class privileged male actors at a particular point in history and in particular societies to be the paradigmatic case of professions'. She suggested that 'the creation and control of occupational boundaries and inter-occupational relations may be crucially mediated by patriarchal power relations' (p.675), undoubtedly significant for the semi-professions characterised by their predominance of women. This position is reinforced when linked with different training patterns and paradigms, as discussed later.

The position of social work has also to be seen against the backdrop of policy change affecting all professional groups, summarised thus by Henkel (1994): 'the combined forces of managerialism, market philosophies, consumerism, technological and concomitant societal change seem likely to force a reappraisal of occupational categories and power' (p.101). The fragmentation of social work can also be seen as increasing specialisation which gives rise to sub-groups with differential status, including some who experience deskilling and deprofessionalisation (Shaw, 1987). Debates about current and future developments in social work education thus contain questions about the survival of some forms of social work (and concomitant training) relative to the demise of others.

The principle that professionals have to be accountable has gained increasing recognition. An argument in favour of social work within local authority structures was that this ensured accountability, and a measure of representation and participation. Social workers are accountable to the public via departmental directors, answerable to locally elected representatives on social service committees. A concern about growth of services in the voluntary and private sectors is loss of democratic accountability (underpinning the growth of inspectorial systems), as well as possible territorial injustice, due to uneven spread of services.

But even in the statutory sector, 'straight line' accountability (electorate-politicians-employees-consumers) may be disrupted in various ways (Bolderson and Henkel, 1980). Social workers may have divided loyalties, where professional practice in relation to a particular user conflicts with departmental policy or resourcing. If welfare policies and practices fail to protect the interests of individual consumers, they can then seek redress via commissioners, tribunals, professional regulatory bodies, or agency complaints procedures.

In the case of social work, although CCETSW has regulated education and training, and BASW has produced a Code of Ethics and has a well used Advice and Representation Service for its members (separate from any services which might be available through union membership), there has been no universal regulatory body, despite periodic and partial recognition that this would be in the interests of both the public and profession. Efforts in the early 1990s to secure such a body were signalled by the publication of a report (Parker, 1991). This advocated for a Social Services rather than a Social Work Council, in recognition of the wide range of workers whose activities impact on people needing care, protection or control. Despite a high level of support from the occupational field and associated interest groups, (costed) proposals, submitted in 1993, were not acted on.

However, a GSSC Development Project continued to press for implementation, for instance in its response to a White Paper, 'The Obligations of Care' (1996). The White Paper stated the (then) government's preferred reliance on employers to define and enforce expected standards of conduct and practice, but where an increasing range of agencies offer social work and care, and where workers are less likely to have secure, long-term employment with one employer, it was argued that a Council was necessary (Brand, 1997).

Proposals were reactivated following the change of government and in 1998 a new White Paper, 'Regulating Services' signalled the intent to establish a General Social Care Council. An earlier recommendation, that consumers should be represented on any such Council, has been more than met by the intention that the Chair of the Council will be a lay person and that membership will be largely drawn from the users of services. The role of the Council is to strengthen public protection and ensure that staff are equipped to provide social care. It is charged with setting enforceable standards; with registration, re-registration and de-registration of individuals; with the reservation of specific jobs (for example, ASWs); and with the regulation of social work training. The (English) Council will cover about one million employees in the care sector, including about 40,000 social workers. It will operate alongside other regulatory mechanisms, including the independent regional Commissions for Care Standards and a new body concerned with training strategies (TOPPS) which will take over many of the functions undertaken by CCETSW.

Concluding Summary

This chapter has reviewed changes in social work over a thirty year period, noting particularly the paradigmatic changes in 1970 and around 1990. The development of social work during this time has been intimately bound up with the fortunes of SSDs although, even in the mid-1990s, social workers formed only 15 per cent of the departmental workforce (SSI, 1995/1996). The shift in professional and public values between 1970 and the late 1990s has played a significant role in the extent to which social workers have been seen as being in or out of step with public and governmental expectations.

However, while social work may be expected to support the dominant values of society (reflected in its control role), it also should mediate tensions within society, often experienced as value conflicts between the majority and marginalised or excluded minorities. It has a mandate to protect vulnerable members of society: it was its apparent inability to do this from the mid-1970s which led to its increased regulation and loss of public trust. Bringing to light sexual abuse, and revelations of (sexual) abuse of those in the care of SSDs by workers, have further alienated the public and demoralised the profession.

Demoralisation was exacerbated by the nature and pace of policy and practice changes in the early 1990s, coupled with resource constraints and increased violence and blame from service users. This was linked to the worsening of social conditions for a minority of the population as well as the encouragement of a competitive and individualistic society. Social workers were seen as having borne the brunt of policies formulated by a government unsympathetic to the goals of a welfare state (Jones, 1992; Langan, 1993), although other services and professionals also felt the impact of different political values. Most recently, the White Papers, 'Modernising Social Services' and 'Regulating Services', suggest further change and increased regulation.

While concerns about the 'break-up' of SSDs and the deprofessionalisation of social work may be exaggerated, the monopoly position of local authority departments as the providers of social work and care services diminished within a more pluralist system, and the role of British social workers seems more proscribed than their counterparts elsewhere. Some recent developments also suggest new opportunities for social work practice, with concomitant challenges for the education and training system. There are also indications of effectiveness studies which suggest that not all practice has been bad (Cheetham, 1996). Thus, the key question, about the 'survival' of social work education, in part reflects uncertainties about the future of the wider occupational group from which it derives. The other significant determinant is the system within which the discipline is located, which is examined next.

3 Higher Education: Changing Policies and Expectations

Introduction

Changes in higher education over two decades provide a backdrop against which to explore developments in professional education and social work education in particular. These changes are here examined from a policy perspective, with a focus on events which signify value shifts in expectations about higher education. The chapter concludes with a review of the debate about academic freedom and accountability, provoked by recent changes, and then of the 'Enterprise' and related schemes which are indicative of change in the functions of higher education.

Discussion follows on the changing relationships between the individual academic, the basic unit, the institution, and the central authority: and on the dominant values which these elements in the system may represent. Broadly speaking, these can be identified as professional (individual academic and basic unit), managerial (institutional), and market values (government). Phases in the development of UK higher education policy range from autonomous institutions, then the domination of central management, to a preoccupation with external markets (Becher and Kogan, 1992).

Post-War Development of the Higher Education System

Higher education up to the 1940s was described as having 'evolved by drift and policy accretion...the result of centuries of disjointed incrementalism' (Stephens and Roderick, 1978, p.167). Universities offered discipline-based degrees and postgraduate research opportunities to an elite minority. The value shift promoted by the Second World War, and the passing of the 1944 Education Act, laid the basis for a more egalitarian system and for a wider range of opportunities at further and higher education levels.

The 1963 Robbins Report recommended rationalisation and extension of the higher education system, primarily through the establishment of polytechnics. The report maintained the objectives of higher education as to promote general powers of the mind, transmit a common culture, and ensure the advancement of learning, but also included 'instruction in skills'. It adopted the social demand principle; that is, courses of higher education for all qualified by ability, attainment and inclination to follow them; and it saw the new polytechnics (based on existing colleges, firmly rooted in their localities) as affording a major expansion in access to a wider range of courses.

This binary system with (initially 29) polytechnics as 'equal to but different from' the (45) universities signified both a concern 'to meet the growing demand for vocational, professional and industry based courses which could not be met by the universities' (Kogan and Kogan, 1983, p.21), and an early attempt to bring part of higher education under public control. Establishment in 1964 of the Council for National Academic Awards (CNAA) to validate courses offering awards in the new public sector HEIs also indicated a concern with standards (and status). The establishment of the polytechnic sector (and also of the Open University) exemplified innovation (Hall *et al.*, 1975) in a period of incremental policy change in the educational field during the 1960s and 1970s (Kogan, 1975).

There was consensus between both major political parties as to the need for higher education expansion, and the liberal educational values underpinning it: 'higher education was thought to be good both for individuals and for the country' (Kogan and Kogan, 1983, p.19), and even in 1972 this 'benevolent orthodoxy' prevailed as shown in a government White Paper, 'Education: a Framework for Expansion'. Such values underpinned a considerable expansion in student numbers in the higher education sector (a four-fold increase from 1945-1970), although numbers did not quite reach the recommendation of the Robbins Report for a doubling of the progression rates (that is of 18 year olds to HEIs) from 8 per cent (1963) to 17 per cent (by 1973), reaching only approximately 13 per cent by 1982 (Kogan and Kogan, 1983, pp.15-18).

There was a considerable increase in part-time student numbers (mainly in the polytechnics and Open University), the beginning of a more diverse and flexible sector, with access for a wider range of the population. While the 1970s generally lacked a clear policy direction for higher education, the system continued 'edging towards a mass rather than an elite system, and one more responsive to social need' (Becher and Kogan, 1992, p.37), despite downward revisions of higher education student targets and cash limits on university funding from 1975 onwards. The mid-1970s saw the beginning of a move away from consensus in the policy process and increased conflict in policy formulation (Hall *et al.*, 1975) in the field of higher education as elsewhere.

Professional academic values continued largely unchallenged in to the 1970s, despite the relationship between local authorities and the polytechnics, and Crosland's introduction of the audit of universities (in 1967): they underpinned the widespread autonomy of HEIs and their structure as self-governing communities of scholars. Becher and Kogan (1992, p.23) noted that academic values were 'assumed to be invariant and unassailable', but that they were beginning to be challenged from within by professionals espousing vocational and multi-disciplinary values. Differences existed in attitudes to the growth of more varied courses and open access, and in the emphasis given to research (creation of knowledge) and teaching (transmission of knowledge), related to status differences between pure and applied theory.

It has been suggested that vocationalism, now so prevalent, took root in the 1970s, amidst growing unemployment and technological and industrial change (Stephens and Roderick, 1978). This division in the academic community was later to be exploited by a government committed to decreasing the power of the professionals and changing the culture of all public services.

Policy Change Since 1979

Barrett and Fudge (1981) identified the time when political power changes hands as a paradigm change (rather than incremental shifts) in the policy-making process, as a different value system informs government intent. The period since 1979 has been marked by increasing intervention by governments determined to reduce public spending. Despite the economic boom years of the 1980s, economic considerations and instrumental values have prevailed in the formulation of social policy. The government 'think tank' (Central Policy Review Staff) in the early 1980s suggested public spending cuts in four areas - health, defence, social security and higher education, and withdrawal of government funding from HEIs at this time was only averted by ministerial resistance (Deakin, 1994).

Effects of policy change involving a value shift at governmental level were soon felt in the higher education sector, with 13 per cent cuts in funding (less fee income for home students, compensated in part by increased fees for overseas students) over the period 1979-1982. Kogan and Kogan (1983, p.12) described the government of the early 1980s as having 'little notion of the consequences and costs of its actions [but] its policy, begun in ignorance and confusion, gathered particular biases as it developed...it led to changes in the purpose and running of higher education...and shifted the line between universities and polytechnics'. Decreased funding impacted on HEIs across the binary divide, affecting humanities and social sciences in particular, and resulted in cuts in staffing (mainly through retirement and voluntary severance) and widespread reorganisation or 'rationalisation'.

The cuts had unanticipated consequences in that there was not an overall reduction in student numbers. While the University sector generally chose to reduce its intake to protect staff student ratios (SSRs) and research activities, the polytechnic sector cut the unit of resource and continued to increase its intake. In 1981/1982, 13.2 per cent of 18-21 year olds were in full-time higher education, of which 7.5 per cent were in the university sector and 5.2 per cent in the polytechnics. By 1982/1983 the proportion had shifted to 7.2 per cent in the universities and 6 per cent in the polytechnics (Kogan and Kogan, 1983). Additionally, between 1979 and 1987, apart from an increase in full-time students (19.3 per cent), graduates (20.9 per cent) and post-graduates (27.1 per cent), there was also a considerable increase in the numbers and proportion of part-time students (34.2 per cent), predominantly in the public sector HEIs (DES, 1989).

One consequence of the continuing rise in student numbers was the creation in 1982 of the National Advisory Board (NAB) as a national planning body for local authority controlled higher education, charged with approving student numbers in subject areas. A further consequence was the strengthening of the managerial role within institutions. Growth had taken place on a relatively *ad hoc* basis, subject mainly to the criterion of academic viability, but reductions and restructuring had to be 'managed'. Policies aimed at promoting government priorities were also introduced; for example, assistance with redundancy schemes, funding for 'new blood' appointments, and money to purchase information technology. Income generation began to play an increasing part in higher education resourcing. Money from research grants, consultancy contracts and services generated 16 per cent of university income in 1981, but 27 per cent by 1987 (Walford, 1991).

In the polytechnics, subject to local authority control and structured hierarchically, the managerial roles of senior staff increased during the 1980s (and has been further emphasised in the 1990s). In 1985, the Jarratt

Report recommended that university vice-chancellors should become chief executives and adopt a strong corporate planning approach. It proposed managerial rather than collegiate ways of working, with devolution of financial responsibilities to cost centres and monitoring and evaluation, through performance indicators.

A study by Boys *et al.* in 1985/1986 stated that the most strongly established HEIs 'continued to work on the autonomous model of academic government' but that there was increased emphasis on managerial ways elsewhere. Noting the limited manageability of academic institutions, the authors nevertheless recognised the need for leadership in managing change in a turbulent environment, and identified leader performance as a key factor in how well an institution maintained its position in the mid-1980s (Boys *et al.*, 1988, pp.162-63).

External auditing and monitoring exercises have led to increased managerial control and accountability within institutions, and the managerial role was given further emphasis in the 1987 White Paper, 'Higher Education: Meeting the Challenge', which preceded the 1988 Education Reform Act (ERA). The transfer of managerial thinking into HEIs resulted, by the early 1990s, into mission statements, new logos and other manifestations of corporate image previously associated with the business world (Boys *et al.*, 1988).

Another indication of management values was performance related pay, agreed between the CVCP and Association of University Teachers (AUT) in 1987, and finally agreed in the polytechnic sector in the early 1990s. This followed a threat by the DES to withhold funding from dissenting institutions, but exacerbated difficult relations between staff and management in many institutions. The introduction of managerialism (defined by Becher and Kogan (1992, p.179) as 'a pathological obtrusion of management values as promoted by a particular government ideology') has been as much about effecting a culture change within institutions as about extending the regulation and rationing functions which are fundamental to the policy-making process (Hall *et al.*, 1975).

The 1988 ERA heralded the independence of polytechnics from local authority control (from April, 1989), and CNAA accreditation, and the replacement of NAB by the Polytechnic and Colleges Funding Council (PCFC). The Act disbanded the UGC (established 1919) and removed university funding from the hands of academics, giving its successor body, the University Funding Council (UFC), and the PCFC, stronger powers to implement government policy through funding mechanisms, thus 'effecting a nationalisation of higher education funding' (Letwin, 1992, p.274). However, both these bodies were relatively short-lived, being combined into national Higher Education Funding Councils (HEFCE, HEFCW and SHEFC) in 1992.

Policy Developments in the 1990s

The early 1990s, and a change in leadership of the Conservative government, did not see the advent of new policy trajectories in higher education, but rather a continued vigour in implementing policies initiated under 'Thatcherism' (Sullivan, 1994). Competition was an important theme, emphasised as a concern for consumer choice and rights. The 1980s had seen a steady increase in the age participation rates of traditional entrants and an increasing number of entrants from non-traditional backgrounds (Schuller, 1991). Becher and Kogan (1992), commenting on the move to a mass education system, identified a shift from a strong centralist approach in higher education policy to one based on market values, with three key players, the government (via the funding bodies), the employers and the consumers (students).

In relation to *government* influence, the funding councils require institutions to bid for allocations, these being dependent on certain criteria. In the case of subject area reviews, varying proportions of funding are allocated depending on judgements about quality. These are based partly on 'value for money' and 'fitness for purpose' criteria, relating back to earlier concerns about the relevance of what courses offer, gauged by responsiveness to the market (that is, employers). Research Assessment Exercises (RAEs, 1992, 1996) have been another important device for assessing quality and distributing funding, and have resulted in increased research output (McNay, 1996) but also increased institutional competition. Both these mechanisms have promoted market forces within higher education, and shifted the balance of power between higher education and government (Barnett, 1994).

Various policies were introduced from the mid-1980s to promote increased contact between HEIs and *employers*, and responsiveness of the former to the latters' requirements (Boys *et al.*, 1988) including in 1987 the Enterprise Initiative by the Department of Employment. The 1988 ERA pushed the public sector institutions to become 'entrepreneurial, flexible and responsive' after vesting day, for example, through the appointment of members of industry and commerce to newly constituted governing bodies, the break up of national negotiating machinery on academic pay, and competitive development of courses and services (Walford, 1991).

This process culminated in a White Paper (DES 1991) which laid the basis for the 1992 Further and Higher Education Act which abolished the binary divide. Thus, polytechnics which satisfied certain criteria were designated universities and the framework for a mass higher education system was established, though without increased resources. Sullivan (1994, p.41) has suggested that 'one of the reasons behind [the abolition of the binary line]...was that the new universities had developed as successful polytechnics by adopting market values. ...The insertion of these institutions into an enlarged university sector would, it was hoped, encourage the old universities to compete for contracts in the real world of markets'. The expansion of higher education, catering for a more diverse student population through more varied and flexible programmes (with modularisation, credit accumulation and transfer, and approval of prior (experiential) learning), has been accompanied by increasing emphasis on technological change and modernisation of industry to promote British competitiveness and economic growth (Sullivan, 1994).

In relation to the *consumer* element, privatisation has not yet been a significant feature of the higher education sector (Hill and Bramley, 1990). However, the burden of funding has been substantially shifted from the state to the consumer (or students' families) through the reduction (and subsequently the abolition) of student grants, the introduction of a loans scheme and the debate about fee levels and payment, contrary to the egalitarian ideals underpinning higher education for most of the post-war period. The full cost basis for overseas student fees has established a broad minimum and some (prestigious) institutions charge more.

This approach is also evident in intended 'top-up fees' and in variable fee levels of post-graduate courses. Undoubtedly, one consequence, if not a motive, of the government's encouragement of increased part-time and open learning educational developments will be a direct shift of costs from LEAs to consumers - or perhaps to their employers. While there were concerns that increased costs might deter some students, initially there was little indication of a decrease in demand. A 43 per cent increase in student numbers between 1989 and 1994, continued more slowly in the mid-1990s with a 2 per cent increase in enrolments (to over 1.6 million) from 1995 to 1996, of whom 32 per cent were part-time (HESA Reports, 1995-97). However, UCAS figures at the end of 1998 showed a 1.8 per cent drop in applications overall, with particular decline in the numbers applying for science places and a 10 per cent fall in applications from mature students (*The Times Higher*, 5/2/99), and the latter trend is a source of concern to social work courses.

Apart from the 'marketisation' and 'massification' of the system, another contentious area of higher education policy in the 1990s is the monitoring of processes and outputs and their relationship to funding. The issue of accountability is inescapable in publicly financed services but the establishment and operation of separate bodies, the Higher Education Quality Council (HEQC), concerned with institutional processes and since replaced by the Quality Assurance Agency (QAA), together with the operation of the quality assessment divisions of HEFCs (concerned with teaching and learning in subject areas and research), have resulted in a significant increase in external scrutiny. This is compounded in subject areas which are also subject to professional review, and in many quarters has been linked to concerns about academic freedom.

Accountability and Academic Freedom

Accountability has been defined as '...the obligation of professionals, individually and collectively, to justify their actions and decisions to legitimate audiences' (Becher, 1994, p.161). Policy change in the 1980s and early 1990s prompted considerable debate, both about accountability and about the nature of academic freedom. Kogan suggested (1988, p.18) that the problem with accountability in education is that, while education is financed and sponsored as a public activity, it is carried out in institutions which are largely closed to public scrutiny and difficult to supervise from outside. Additionally, in the face of multiple interest groups to whom the teacher or lecturer should be accountable, (s)he may claim 'the right to self accountability on the basis of expertise and the moral authority of a profession'.

Ferguson (1994, p.93) stated that changes in education were central to the public policy reform project - the education system was seen as 'expensive, not self-evidently adequately productive, insufficiently accountable, monopolistic, producer dominated, resistant to consumer demand and, at worst, self-generating and self-serving'. However, he noted that in higher education 'more academic autonomies' had been retained, relative to school teachers, notwithstanding the ubiquitous penetration of managerialism.

It is debatable how far policy change has penetrated higher education at the level of individual academics and basic units (Departments or

Schools). Becher suggested that there have been some signs of 'collective resistance against the coercive demands from central policy makers...many centrally announced reforms leave no lasting deposit because internal constituencies are not effectively summoned to support them. When a system is bottom-heavy, groups at the grass roots are key participants in implementing policies and reforms' (Becher, 1994, p.178). However, one effect of ERA was to change the conditions of academic tenure. This, and fiscal pressures, have altered the composition of the workforce to a core of permanent staff and a periphery of temporary (and usually poorly paid) employees, for whom the notion of academic freedom may seem remote. Additionally, more recent moves to institutional, as opposed to national, setting of pay and conditions of service are resulting in a more differentiated workforce with significant variations in pay within and between institutions, as well as a decrease in the amount of time over which academics have control, and which traditionally was designated for research and scholarly activity (reports in *The Times Higher*, 29/1/99 and 5/2/99).

Concerns about academic freedom were signalled in 1988, when the Society for Research in Higher Education (SRHE) took this theme as its conference focus. The concept was defined by one speaker as 'the right of academics and other scholars who need to exercise the same functions, to pursue research, to teach and to publish, without control, restraint and the threat of sanctions from the institutions that employ them': he linked the threat to academic freedom to a wider government agenda to suppress freedoms of all kinds (Turner, 1988).

Another speaker, Barnett (1988), described academic freedom as 'the self-serving rhetoric of an interest group' and apparently challenged the relevance of the concept: in fact, he was questioning the extent to which academics are expected, or accept the responsibility, to perform a critical function in society, ideas he developed further in two subsequent publications (Barnett, 1992; Barnett, 1994). Concern was expressed that academics have moved from a professional to a technocratic role, an idea paralleled in debates about other professional roles and professional education, and linked to the development of utilitarian values in higher education. In a review of the edited collection of the conference proceedings (Tight, 1988), Flood Page observed that there was too little mention of responsibility, and if not coupled with this, 'academic freedom degenerates into selfish privilege' (Flood Page, 1989, p.631), echoing the views of critics that academic freedom is a discredited and outmoded concept.

Observing the changes experienced by British academics (as reported in Eggins, 1988), an American reviewer commented, 'These papers [illustrate] the degree to which the government has been successful in dictating the agenda for debate and the terms of the discourse. Change, even turbulence, has become the order of the day in British higher education' (Foster, 1989, p.624). He characterised British higher education as 'an academy in retreat' but also noted 'a fine mist of resistance, reserve and reservation [floating] through the essays' and some evidence of 'ingenious adaptations and coping strategies' (pp.625-26). Such commentary accords with policy writers' views on the role of professionals at the policy implementation stage (Barrett and Fudge, 1981; Rein, 1983). It illustrates the way in which academic freedom is a variant of professional autonomy, to be used responsibly, in this case for the purpose of developing knowledge, understanding and critical perspectives in the interests of society (Barnett, 1994).

Writing in defence of the first publication of League Tables of HEIs, Cannon (1993) proclaimed 'accountability is at the heart of publication', and suggested that previous strands of accountability (through open collegiate structures in the universities, and local democratic controls in the case of polytechnics) had been undermined by managerialism and severing links with local government. He further stated that the increasing complexity and diversity of the sector, and consumer needs for accurate data on which to base judgements (choices), justified publication (in *The Times Higher*) and that this should be seen as being of potential benefit to all participants. This new openness about higher education's achievements and failings can be seen as a response to criticism and the declining reputation of the sector in the preceding decades, chronicled for instance by Silver (1990), as well as a plank in the marketisation strategy, and a corollary of the 'painful transformation' from an elite to a popular system (Ball and Eggins, 1989, p.1).

Some of the literature, and recent debates about the restructured quality assurance system, suggest a shift to a more proactive stance by academics in the face of government pressures on higher education, and the perceived threat to academic freedom. However, traditional conceptions of higher education, including ideas about research, the learning process, the role of students and relations with employers and communities, have been substantially challenged, and some of these changes are now explored through examination of a particular policy, the Enterprise Initiative.

Enterprise in Higher Education

The Enterprise Initiative, launched by the government via the Manpower Services Commission (MSC), continued a broader strategy (including the technical and vocational educational initiative (TVEI) in schools and funding of technical equipment) to upgrade the skills of the British workforce, and to ensure that higher education courses provided education and training relevant to the country's economic needs. A decisive shift from liberal educational values to the imposition of instrumental values was evident in a government White Paper of 1987, which stated 'the Government and its central funding agencies will do all they can to encourage and reward approaches to higher education which bring [institutions] closer to the world of business' (Boys *et al.*, 1988, p.12).

The government had already established the National Council for Vocational Qualifications (NCVQ, and a parallel body in Scotland) in 1986. The Enterprise programme and related initiatives (for instance, the PICKUP scheme providing pump-priming funds for higher education courses for managers) have had a significant bearing on funds available to HEIs and, *inter alia*, the nature of changes promoted in teaching, learning and assessment. Some HEIs, particularly in the public sector, were already promoting an 'entrepreneurial strategy' in the early 1980s (Lockwood and Davies, 1985), and universities were increasing their income from research contracts, though in 1987, only 3 per cent of this funding came from industry (Walford, 1991, p.175). The Enterprise scheme injected a substantial sum into selected HEIs over the first five years of operation (£100m in 1987-92) for projects which would 'inbed (*sic*) initiative into the curriculum' (Becher and Kogan, 1992, p.48).

The broad objective of the Enterprise Initiative was to promote teaching, learning and assessment strategies which would produce self-reliant students with specific skills (competencies), readily transferable to the world of work. As part of this exercise, initial funding criteria required proposals to be jointly submitted by HEIs and industrial or other external agency partners. Tasker and Packard (1993) suggested that this resulted in mutually profitable relationships between industry and higher education, but that continuing differences in the value systems and interests of each remained and should be respected.

Wright described the Enterprise Initiative as 'the most important instance of planned curriculum development in higher education' (Wright, 1992) and saw this as a means of promoting a more active student role in the learning process. He related it to the development of modularisation and credit accumulation and transfer schemes (CATS), though these were also responses, in part, to the declining resource base of HEIs, and recognition of the increasing difficulty for some students of sustaining full-time attendance. The emphasis on skills, divorced from historic associations with specific trades and occupational cultures, has also been seen as promoting abstract qualities in an individualised and mobile workforce (Cohen, 1990).

While advocates of the scheme appreciated its practicality, its capacity for income generation, and the employability of its graduates, it was also found to require planning to harness and focus its effects. If initiatives were not built into the strategic developments of units and institutions, results were likely to be random and short-lived. It was not surprising, therefore, that a subsequent development, promoted by the HEFCE (1993/1994), made available £0.7m to support effective teaching, learning and assessment by projects which spanned more than one HEI. The focus of the five projects approved in the later scheme (out of 118 proposals received) was also indicative of government priorities: maths learning and assessment; supplemental instruction; effective teaching and learning in fieldwork (archaeology, geography, geology); course design for resource-based learning; and effective engineering education (HEFCE, 1993).

Meanwhile, the disbanding of the Department of Employment and the aggregation of its former training functions with the Department for Education (into a combined Department of Education and Employment, 1995) regularised the increasingly close relationship between education and training in the service of the economy, and reconceptualised a higher education objective as the development of transferable skills. Thus, some of the issues which have long confronted educators of students for the professions have become more general questions for all academics, and a shift from educational values favouring theoretical knowledge to those valuing applied knowledge seems to have been achieved, though not without the continuing reservations of some academics (Barnett, 1994).

The question initially asked by Halsey and Trow in the 1960s, in response to the Robbins Report, 'How would academic men (*sic*) in Britain adapt themselves and their institutions to a period of expansion and redefinition of higher education' (Halsey and Trow, 1971) has been posed even more acutely in the past decade. The Enterprise Initiative played an important part in attempting to reconstruct HEIs on lines suggested by commercial and industrial undertakings. Although in the early 1990s Halsey was confident that the essential idea of the university (as a place for pursuit of truth and intellectual development) would remain (Halsey, 1992), the challenges to the academic role and the nature of universities have been sharpened by the increased power of consumers in the market place.

Concluding Comments

This chapter has traced policy changes affecting higher education over the post war period, and particularly in the 1980s and 1990s, emphasising the values informing these changes. Ferguson (1994, p.96) summarised the objectives of educational reform (since 1979) as follows: 'the creation of competitive markets in service provision; establishing the powers and rights of consumers; the subordination and curtailment of producer power and interests; the pursuit of efficiency and economy (in the interests of reduced public expenditure); the promotion of excellence over equity; and the encouragement of diversity in the interests of consumer choice', all to be achieved by empowering the consumer, controlling the producer and promoting the role of the (industry inspired) manager.

As Kogan noted in 1988, the extent of changes taking place in the education system could not have been readily envisaged. Following a change in government and a major inquiry into higher education (the 'Dearing Report', 1997), policy change and new initiatives are likely to be a continuing feature of the higher education scene. The relationship between HEIs and society is still in the throes of redefinition. A mass higher education system with limited resourcing is now an established fact. Increased student responsibility and new thinking about teaching, learning and assessment methods require system-wide adaptations, not least at the level of the basic unit.

The effects of significant and continuing change on academics and other staff in the system have been considerable, and the strategies for resisting and adapting are varied. There is evidence of individual 'exit' rather than the raising of a concerted academic 'voice' (Hirschman, 1970) in the face of new conditions, but the changes have produced important debates on accountability and academic freedom, on the values, knowledge and skills to be promoted, and how these may be transmitted. These debates - about higher education purpose, content, form, resourcing and academic role - are considered next in relation to professional education and regarding social work.

4　Professional Education and Knowledge

Introduction

The changing ethos of higher education has coincided with a growth in interest in the place and form of professional education in HEIs. Becher (1989, p.32) noted the 'near total neglect' of professional subjects as a focus of academic inquiry, and attributed this to the difficulty of distinguishing them from their 'surrounding domains of professional practice'. But there has been a burgeoning of literature about professional education since the 1980s, and this material, together with wider literature about conceptions of knowledge, is the theme of this chapter.

The professions themselves are examined first, pre-figured, by the earlier discussion about the field of social work. In the 1960s Parsons described academics as 'the keystone in the arch of a professionally oriented society' (cited in Curry *et al.*, 1993, p.82) and their changing fortunes illustrate a general weakening of professional power in recent decades.

Professional educators have been subject to shifting expectations (related to their field of practice) and closer scrutiny of employer interests, through professional accreditation bodies, for considerably longer than their disciplinary colleagues. Tensions exist between professional education and the professions.

Distinctions between subject disciplines and professional education are based on the epistemology of particular subjects, and the notion of a hierarchy of knowledge, both in higher education and wider society. Traditional conceptions of knowledge are being challenged, and the changing role of HEIs has led to a reappraisal of teaching, learning and assessment methods. This chapter explores some of the issues common to all forms of professional education which have a bearing on the particular challenges and changes which social work is experiencing.

Some Characteristics and Issues of the Professions

Siegrist (1994, p.3) summarised the history of the professions as intimately linked with 'the social processes of modernisation and rationalisation; with professionalisation and bureaucratisation, with the development of school cultures and the meritocratic system and with juridification, medicalisation and technical and economic progress'. He comments that there is no single theory of the professions, nor an adequate definition. Although used as a generic term, it is a changing historic concept with particularistic roots (Freidson, 1986). Earlier writers advanced a trait model to define professions, related to expertise, ethics, education, and entry, in which knowledge was seen as a core trait (Macdonald, 1995).

The process by which some occupational groups have become professions has been summarised thus: random entry to an occupation has given rise to voluntary formation of associations or guilds, which subsequently organise training. There follows the imposition of entry and training requirements, with accreditation of courses and licensing of practitioners (Matarazzo, 1977). Johnson (1972) described this professionalising process as a device for asserting occupational control, and others have also commented on the notion of occupational closure (for example, Torstendahl, 1994).

The question of which occupations are designated 'professions' is a source of continuing debate - not least within aspiring occupational groups, as illustrated earlier in the case of social work. Any list produced is likely to be longer than those professions originally recognised - law, medicine, the clergy and the military - but additions are likely to be contentious, or may be acceptable in one country but not elsewhere. Thus, American writers recently suggested a list classified into three clusters - helping, entrepreneurial, and technical professions (Curry *et al.*, 1993, p.xiii) - which would be arguable or incomplete in a British context. Pragmatically viewed, 'contemporary eclectic academic approaches to professionalism mirror everyday usage', which extends the term to groups of employees that lack many of the attributes functionally associated with professional status. So whether teaching qualifies, 'depends on what criteria of professionalism one adopts' (Taylor, 1994, p.43).

While class, with its variations in education, has been a factor in entry to and status of professions, recent literature has also questioned the role of gender. Blackstone and Fulton (1975) examined the position of women in entry to and progression in academic posts, and there is now some monitoring of both gender and race in the statistics gathered by the

Higher Education Statistics Agency (HESA). Theoretical work by Witz (1991) on professions and gender was alluded to earlier. Her arguments have particular significance concerning occupations where women predominate, sometimes referred to as the 'caring professions', and their associated educational fields. Thus, Becher writes that 'women are significantly under-represented in the physical and social sciences but they appear in sizeable numbers in female oriented subject areas such as...home economics and in relatively low status fields such as library science and education' (Becher, 1989, p.125). However, concerns about how professions are defined have been less important in the UK recently than the changes affecting most professional groups (Henkel, 1994).

Education for the Professions

The relationship between professions and the professional schools has always been complex. Professional schools regulate initial entry to, and standards achieved by, those aspiring to a particular profession, but are themselves regulated by representatives of the relevant profession, as well as by academic peers. Since the universities act as a certifying agency for professions, it is appropriate that professional education should be closely aligned to the external professional requirements. However, the relationship between professional practitioners and managers, and professional educators and researchers, may well be a site for conflict.

Concerns about the nature and standards of professional education are by no means new, nor limited to the UK, nor to one profession. In 1910 the Carnegie Foundation for the Advancement of Training sponsored the Flexner Report into the state of medical education and, subsequently, the Reed Report on legal education in 1921, both in the USA (Boyer, 1990). More recently, an American national project was established in response to widespread dissatisfaction with the prevailing model of scholarship (based on European traditions). This recommended a broader conception of scholarship more congruent with the diversity of HEIs and 'more appropriate, authentic and adaptive' (Boyer, 1990).

Also writing of the American scene, Hixon Cavanagh (1993, p.107) states that 'evidence suggests a discontinuity between the education to which aspiring professionals are exposed and the nature of work demands encountered in professional practice'. She cites the work of Winguard and Williams (1973) as evidence of the mismatch between professional education and practice. This research found no relation between academic grades and subsequent professional performance in the fields of medicine, business and teaching. A more recent British study (Lyons *et al.*, 1995) found no correlation between the career patterns of social workers and the academic level of their professional qualification, although this did not suggest irrelevant or inadequate education.

Hartman (1989, p.500), looking at six professional schools in an Australian university, found that 'control from outside [the HEI] is seen by academics to retard change...and [to create] too little flexibility in syllabus operations...[conversely, university courses are]...typically seen by outside professionals to be removed from the world of practice, too theoretical and quite radical in orientation'. He also noted the tension between commitment to traditional academic norms and scholarship 'relative to the transmission of distinctly vocational skills and attitudes' required of professional educators. A Swedish writer notes 'there has been a growing tension between the interests of the practitioners and the interests of teachers and researchers, who are seeking more control over a distinct discipline' (Svenson, 1994, p.133).

Similar concerns are apparent in British professional education, and public criticism has provided legitimacy for increased levels of government intervention. 'The professions themselves are facing a difficult period, and one in which Government intervention seems in a number of countries to have become more active than at any other time in their long existence. That intervention has commonly taken the form of exercising direct control over the process or outcomes of initial training' (Becher, 1994, p.ix).

This is clearly seen in Britain in the case of teaching and social work (Graham, 1996; Jackson and Preston-Shoot, 1996), but has also been experienced by educators in more established professional fields. Vang (1994), writing of changes in health care in the 1980s, noted consequent challenges to medical education. Graham (1996) suggested that government sponsorship of research in the teacher training field (through the Teacher Training Agency) could result in government control and redefinition of the knowledge base, a salutary warning for all forms of professional education, related to concerns about the whole enterprise of higher education (Barnett, 1994).

Concerns and criticisms of professional education can be explained partly by its position on the boundaries between academic institutions and the competing claims of professional fields. Conflict because of differing value systems and overt power struggles are not unusual and may be compounded by societal dissatisfaction with particular professions, or 'experts' in general. Some of the issues are related to conceptions of knowledge and the status given to research and pedagogy, both within institutions and by wider society, and these are considered in the next section. However, an aspect which merits discussion first is the form which accountability to the field might take.

Partnerships and Accountability

Reference has already been made to the necessary relationship between professionals and professional education, and to issues of accountability facing all professionals, including academics. What range and nature of external relationships do professional educators experience? Burrage (1994) suggested that professional education is the product of the interaction of four sets of interests - the profession/practitioners; the state; the educators; and the users. Whether by 'users' Burrage means students, or users of the 'products' of higher education (employers) or consumers of the services which professionals provide, is unclear.

At one level, the users of education are clearly students, and educational resourcing (including student funding), methodology, notions of reflective practice, and student self-responsibility, suggest an increasing role for them. The extent of representation of students in the various systems for planning and monitoring educational programmes seems likely to be variable. The previous government's promotion of citizen charters of various kinds suggests that professional education should be more susceptible to feedback and input from users of professional services, and there is some evidence that this is of wider concern in higher education (Haselgrove, 1994).

Government influence is a relatively recent innovation, in contrast to continental Europe where professional education has long been more formally prescribed by the state (Heidenheimer, 1989; Burrage, 1994). In the main, formalised relationships have traditionally existed primarily between representatives of practising professionals and the educators. Bodies to restrict entry to particular professions have existed since the 19th century (the General Medical Council was established in 1858); and most of them also regulate the training which their aspiring members should undertake; for example, engineering institutions have supervised 'schools' since the 1920s (Torstendhal, 1994). There is thus a very direct link in accreditation of courses in Britain and elsewhere. In the USA, for instance, Burrage (1994) notes that systems for external scrutiny and accountability, including professional bodies, have been in place 'for decades'.

More locally, recent government and professional initiatives in the UK have also encouraged or required the active participation of representatives of the professions, particularly employing bodies, in planning and delivery of educational programmes. This has been particularly evident in the areas of teaching and social work (Taylor, 1994; Henkel, 1994). The British requirements for partnerships in both social work and teacher education has put into practice a proposal by an American writer for 'deliberative curriculum enquiry as a strategy for curriculum design that more closely mirrors reflective practice,' including deliberation among the stake holders (Harris, 1993, p.18).

The trend towards closer collaboration is also observable in response to the Enterprise Initiative and similar policy (funding) devices. Thus, work placements have become an increasingly important aspect of many courses (whether concurrent, or offered on a 'sandwich' basis as a year or shorter periods outside the institution); and cessation of student grants and emphasis on 'employability' may enhance this trend. But placements exert their own demands on practitioners and educators if students are to derive maximum benefit, and in the early 1990s Bines and Watson cautioned against expecting too much: 'Neither funding nor training is necessarily available to develop...the role of the practice teacher/professional mentor...or the contribution of practising professionals to the course as a whole' (1992, p.22). In general, it is unclear whether partnerships secure enhanced development of professional knowledge or increased tension between professionals and educators, but some findings about the resourcing implications of them in relation to social work are reported in Part II.

On the Nature of Knowledge

It was mentioned earlier that knowledge is a 'core trait' of professions but it can be argued that the particular forms of knowledge created and utilised in professional education differ from traditional conceptions of knowledge, based on the Cartesian paradigm (Henkel, 1995). Some of the literature about the nature of knowledge and about epistemological issues raised by education for the professions is now considered.

Over thirty years ago, Polanyi proposed that knowledge is a function of the whole personal experience. He used 'the idea of "personal knowledge" as the basis of an attack on the scientist notion that real knowledge is public and objective in character' (Barnett, 1994, p.106).

Polanyi elaborated the notion of *tacit knowledge*: this suggests that all new learning takes place in the context of existing knowledge derived from the totality of individual experience, some of it beyond the conscious recollection of the learner (Polanyi, 1962). This concept has proved important in developing ideas about curriculum and pedagogy in the area of professional education, and builds on ideas originally propounded by Dewey, in support of liberal education. Dewey's view that 'knowledge is humanistic in quality, not because it is about human products...but because of what it does in liberating human intelligence and human sympathy' (Dewey, 1916, p.23) has echoes in some of the subsequent literature presented here.

Ideas about knowledge in relation to the individual learner can be placed alongside more structural approaches to an exploration of its nature and place in society, developing in Britain in the 1970s. Thus, Bernstein wrote, 'How a society selects, classifies, distributes, transmits and evaluates the educational knowledge it considers to be public, reflects both the distribution of power and the principles of social control', and suggested that formal educational knowledge is realised through the 'message systems' of curriculum, pedagogy and evaluation, the last being the 'valid realisation of this knowledge on the part of the taught' (Bernstein, 1971, pp.202-203). Barnett expressed this slightly differently: 'knowledge is not so much transmitted as painfully authenticated by each student'(1994, p.26). Both these points have considerable relevance to current debates about professional education encapsulated in the questions, 'how far should curricula be prescribed?' and, 'do methods of pedagogy enable and appropriately assess the individual learning of students relative to practice?'

Habermas, writing during the 1970s and 1980s about different forms of knowledge, suggested that scientific knowledge (concerned with predicting the workings of the natural world and controlling it) has been valued in society at the expense of hermeneutic knowledge and emancipatory knowledge (concerned with comprehending and communicating with each other, and developing views of the world which lead to changed self-understanding, respectively (Habermas, 1978)). This public prioritising of different forms of knowledge has been reflected in the higher education system where scientistic knowledge, representative of instrumental interests and strategic rationality, has often predominated over communicative and critical interests.

These ideas are central to any consideration of societal values and culture, and underpin Habermas' espousal of a revaluing of the place of communicative action and critical reflection, in the interests of developing a healthy 'life world': both necessitate the development of a more open society, where knowledge and actions are not distorted by power relations. Such ideas also illuminate the relationship between, and relative status attributed to, different forms of knowledge, as represented by disciplines.

Toulmin suggested that knowledge is developed by 'communities of knowers' and that each discipline is characterised by its own body of knowledge (concepts), methods and fundamental aims (its epistemology). Academics are concerned with issues of stability and transformation, in terms of transmission to the next generation and modification by research (Toulmin, 1972, p.139). He further identified disciplines as constituting both 'a communal tradition of procedures and techniques for dealing with theoretical and practical problems' and 'a profession comprising an organised set of institutions, roles and men (*sic*) whose business it is to apply or improve these procedure and techniques', that is, disciplines have both an internal and an external 'life story' (p.142). Toulmin also advanced the notion of the 'enculturation' of students into the collective concepts of the discipline through a form of apprenticeship, successful completion of which is marked by the student's ability, not only to internalise the knowledge, but also to critique and develop it (p.159).

The relationships between epistemology and knowledge communities were further explored in Becher's research (1989) about the culture of disciplines, and in the distinctions he drew between hard, soft, pure and applied knowledge forms, which he also related to the likely learning styles of students (see Appendix II). These dimensions (knowledge and the knowers) are as relevant to a discussion of professional education as they are to thinking about traditional academic disciplines, and are explored in this research.

More recently, Barnett's work, about the changing perceptions of the nature of higher education, (1990) and about the relationship between knowledge, higher education and society (1994) have underlined the shift which has taken place in conceptions of knowledge and the role of academics in transmitting and assessing it. He suggested that the predominance of instrumental values in society have resulted in knowledge itself being commodified, and increased emphasis being placed on the acquisition of skills and functional knowledge. In these circumstances, academic work increasingly resembles training rather than education, and the development of critical thought, once the aim of higher education, is discouraged.

In place of terms such as 'understanding' and 'wisdom', Barnett (1994) identified a new vocabulary which superficially suggests some convergence between disciplines and professional subjects, in terms of goals and methods. However, there is a danger that this is at the expense of critical reflection in *all* subject areas. Additionally, Scott (1984) had noted a shift from 'knowledge as a process' to 'knowledge as a product'; and Barnett saw modularisation as a device for the fragmentation of knowledge and weakening of disciplines, both matters of concern to professional educators.

Finally, the concept of inter-disciplinarity is relevant to professional education. Barnett suggested that this was 'more a feature of the higher education discourse than its practice' (1994, p.127), and concluded that new forms of organisation and thinking, including the weakening of disciplinary frameworks, diminish the possibility of inter-disciplinarity developing at other than a superficial level. If the potential for inter-disciplinarity has been minimised, this may also in part explain the vulnerability of some forms of professional education which require interdisciplinary approaches. However, it can be suggested that individual forms of professional education, while drawing on knowledge from other areas, make it their own in the particular way that concepts are combined and used.

It would be appropriate now to review some of the literature about knowledge *vis-à-vis* professional education more particularly and about the specific aspect of its assessment in this context.

Knowledge and the Reflective Practitioner

Jones and Joss described 'The nature and application of knowledge...[as]) a key dimension of professional work' (Jones and Joss, 1995, p.21), and noted the inadequacy of single conceptions of knowledge. They cite Walker (1992) in referring to three forms of knowledge considered appropriate to professional performance, namely, content knowledge (public bodies of theories, procedures and information); knowledge as a cognitive process; and practical knowledge of the practising professional (Jones and Joss, 1995, p.21). They further suggest that while a knowledge base is essential for all professionals, the degree of theoretical orientation, the values attached to the knowledge, how knowledge is applied and the existence or not of explicit practice theory vary between professions.

In the same volume, Henkel examined 'some of the profound shifts in theories of knowledge that have been made in the course of the 20th century', exploring particularly pragmatism and hermeneutics (Henkel, 1995, p.68). She suggested that both these paradigms (the first emanating from a scientific tradition, the second humanistic) reject the Cartesian view of knowledge and replace it with one which has 'action embedded in it'. Within these paradigms both (social) scientists and professionals are reflective participants in, rather than privileged observers of, particular phenomena or situations. Further, knowledge has moral, intellectual and personal dimensions and its development requires continuing dialogue between and within communities. Within these frames, professional education can be seen as 'a process of moving between grounded understanding of one's own practices, strengthening...[them]...and confronting theories, paradigms and practices which challenge them' (Henkel, 1995, p.78).

These ideas relate to the emphasis in much professional education given to recognising and even starting from the 'situation and experience' of students (McNamara, 1990) and the value placed on learning by doing or experiential learning (Gibb, 1988); and have a clear association with the works of Schon, concerning the nature of, and conditions for, producing reflective practice (Schon, 1983, 1987). Schon, drawing on the work of Dewey (1933), Polanyi (1967) and others, advocated the redevelopment of professional education to combine the teaching of applied science with coaching in the activity of 'reflection in action'. He described artistry as 'the exercise of intelligence', 'a kind of knowing', and suggested that while applied science and research-based techniques are important, they are 'bounded by the art of problem framing, implementation and improvisation' (Schon, 1987, p.13).

Schon further stated that learning all forms of professional artistry requires the use of practicums - specially designed settings and scenarios where students individually and collectively 'practice' under supervision. 'These "virtual worlds" with their own culture, language, norms and rituals must have legitimacy in the academic world and not be isolated from their professional world...rather they should provide a "bridge" between the two worlds' (Schon, 1987, p.347). Schon's work has been widely used recently on both sides of the Atlantic to advance debates about the conditions necessary for professional learning and the appropriate forms of knowledge in their education. Harris, in the USA, has written that:

> This [new] epistemology suggests the importance of systematically eliciting the general principles and strategies embedded in the knowing-in-action of expert practitioners...[and] extends the sources of knowledge for practice

from university based basic and applied...research to knowledge-of-practice emanating from the analysis of masterful practice (1993, p.50).

Rice and Richlin (1993, citing Boyer, *op cit.*) summarised four dimensions of scholarly work - discovery of knowledge; integration of knowledge; transmission of knowledge (requiring synoptic capacity and knowledge of pedagogical theory); and the scholarship of practice - suggesting that giving recognition to the third and fourth areas in higher education would have a significant effect in halting a drift by professional educators away from promotion of knowledge relevant to professional practice. They quoted Brown and Gelertner (1989) in support of their concern about and reasons for the mismatch between professional education and the needs of practice: 'academics [wish] to make the discipline more academically respectable and theoretically credible and less like practical training' (Rice and Richlin, 1993, p.64).

Rice and Richlin further suggested that fields in which educators retain a role in professional practice (for example, accountancy, architecture, business) have adopted a more pragmatic view of research, and they follow Schon in advocating that the wisdom embedded in practice (phronesis), and theory derived from practice, should be given equal weight with more traditional forms of academic research and scholarship (Rice and Richlin, 1993, p.313). In summarising the various themes in this American text about professional education, Curry and Wergin suggested that 'Faculty need to reflect on...how their teaching, research and service activities take place not in an academic sanctuary but in an environment that models the kind of professional expertise increasingly demanded by the larger society' (Curry *et al.*, 1993, p.322).

Assessment and Competencies

The relevance for professional education of traditional assessment methods has recently come into question, with, at least in some fields, an increased emphasis on the need for assessment to reflect not just what the student has learned in relation to content knowledge, but also whether this learning can be demonstrated in practice. A shift towards outcome-based assessment, including the use of 'competencies', is evident in a number of fields of professional education.

The origins of the competency movement in British higher education lie in government attempts to create a national framework of vocational certification across a range of occupations. The Training Agency in 1988 defined competencies as follows, 'the ability to perform the activities within an occupation or function to the Standards expected in employment'. Competence includes the ability to transfer skills and knowledge to new situations; to organise and plan work; to innovate and cope with non-routine activities; and to deal effectively with co-workers, managers and customers (Yelloly, 1995, p.53).

Writing of social work, Henkel (1994) described competencies at NVQ level as 'reductionist and atomistic' and suggested that the challenge to professional education is to devise competencies which reflect the holistic and reflective conceptions of professional practice. However, the assessment of competencies involves complex judgements and Jones and Joss (1995, p.20) have suggested that, in some situations, competence can only be inferred rather than directly observed. In fact, it is precisely in assessing key attributes of professionals such as artistry and judgement that assessment using a competency-based approach may fall short. This would seem to throw assessors back on their own professional or intuitive judgements about standards of performance - a subjective position which the use of competencies seeks to avoid. Jones and Joss summarise that professional competencies must include elements of knowledge, values, understanding and behaviour and must be combined in ways appropriate to a given situation.

Assessment of work-based competencies are also seen as appropriate to post-qualifying or continuing professional education which is often part-time, learner directed and/or making use of credit accumulation schemes and 'assessment of prior [experiential] learning' (APL/APEL) (Bines and Watson, 1992; Curry et al., 1993; Yelloly, 1995). While the competency approach is not yet well established in higher education assessment, it obviously has relevance to the future development of professional education, and some efforts have been made to develop competencies which address the cognitive, reflective and affective processes involved in the area of post-qualifying education for social workers (Winter and Maisch, 1992).

From the foregoing it is clear that, while the location of professional education in the university sector may add legitimacy to the status of professional knowledge and promote extension of knowledge through research, it also poses questions about discipline-based assumptions on the value of particular forms of knowledge, scholarship and research, as well as about the practical aspects of how learning is structured and assessed, which extend beyond the particular subject which is the focus of this research.

Conclusions: Professional Education and Higher Education

Professional education is of necessity closely related to its occupational field of practice and some of the tensions experienced can be attributed to turbulence in the field, or to conflict on the boundaries between two systems. However, the position of professional education in higher education may also be questioned as carrying with it dangers of either too close an association with academic norms and values (and thus remoteness from the field) or insufficient attention to research and theory development (and thus lacking academic credibility). There are deeper questions related to how knowledge is conceived and to the value placed on particular forms of scholarship and pedagogy, and to the expectations society has of higher education.

In 1989 Becher wrote of the low status of professional education in the universities, attributing this to its role in transmitting knowledge rather than creating it (Becher, 1989, p.3). However, professional schools are beginning to challenge the hierarchical conception of knowledge that makes application of knowledge derivative and consequently second best, and it has been suggested that scholarship must be put in a broader context, including application and relevance (Rice and Richlin, 1993, p.310).

In summary, an American writer suggested the following reasons for the mismatch between academic environments and professional education:

(i)   academics are influenced by a culture that rewards scientific knowledge and research (more than practice);
(ii) the disciplinary specific organisation of academic institutions creates barriers to curriculum integration (necessary in most forms of professional education);
(iii) the effects of poor curriculum integration are made worse by inappropriate evaluation methods (Hixon Cavanagh, 1993 p.109).

These are all issues identified in recent British literature and discussed above. Further, as Schon suggested in 1987, greater confidence in the value of practice knowledge (and research in this area), as well as an expanded definition of what constitutes scholarly work would undoubtedly benefit professional education and enable it to develop in ways more appropriate to professional needs, without jeopardising its place in higher education (Boyer, 1990; Rice and Richlin, 1993). At the moment, professional educators may feel they are between a rock and a hard place, either pursuing research calculated to establish academic credibility (and with perhaps little immediate value to the field) or undertaking applied research (for which they gain little academic credit).

Both Toulmin (1972) and Becher have made connections between the culture of disciplines and the people who create and transmit their codes and values. Becher has also suggested that many academics in the soft pure and applied areas could be regarded as 'late bloomers' (Becher, 1989, p.120) in research terms - a notion of particular relevance to professional educators who may have spent time in professional practice prior to changing career.

However, as has been pointed out, 'the research culture, the essence of the university stamp, demands a considerable theoretical input which ultimately differentiates professional training from trades' (Hartman, 1989, p.507). Other writers mentioned here have written of the vulnerability of professional education in particular, associated with changes to the professions externally, in addition to the changes taking place in higher education, including the declining resource base (Bines and Watson, 1992; Henkel, 1994). It is possible that the shift to more utilitarian values prompted by government policy in the UK, and also evident in higher education in other parts of the world, and some of the changes in relation to expectations of students and outcomes, will promote re-evaluation of the role and status of professional education, as part of a wider renegotiation of the relationship between higher education and society.

Certainly, some professional schools have long been concerned with promoting educational approaches in teaching, learning and assessment which are now gaining greater currency in higher education, and ideas of partnership - not withstanding the value conflicts and tensions inherent in them - are not new to many professional educators. Bines and Watson (1992), while recognising the impact on professional education of recent policy and societal changes, also gave examples of a range of innovations and developments which have taken place in professional education in one British university, despite the threats and restrictions commonly being experienced.

In conclusion, it seems as if some of the trends and practices evident in professional education are being given greater legitimacy, both by recent research and literature and by more general concerns about the role and nature of higher education outlined in the previous chapter. However, the question arises about whether this is at the expense of some necessary autonomy in the relationship between academics and society and in the scope for critical thinking (Barnett, 1994), not least in relation to education for the professions. This literature review suggests that some of the issues raised in the research about social work are general to the wider field of professional education, and this supposition will be returned to in the light of the empirical data in Part 3.

PART 2

CHARACTERISTICS OF CONTEMPORARY SOCIAL WORK EDUCATION

5 Social Work in Higher Education: Rationale, Location and Scope

Introduction

This chapter opens the discussion about the nature of social work as a discipline by considering some of the structural characteristics of the subject area. These include its organisational location and scope, and some aspects of its epistemological characteristics and its relation to other disciplines. Material is also presented about its relation to the professional field, in the form of collaborative arrangements with agencies. Evidence is drawn from a survey (1994), interviews (1996), and an analysis of JUC SWEC documents, as well as wider literature (See Appendix 1 *re* Research Methodology and Appendix 3 *re* JUC SWEC).

The chapter commences with a discussion of the rationale for social work's location in higher education, based on the views of leading UK social work academics. They voiced strong support for the subject's continued existence and development as a discipline in higher education. However, the survey data suggest that, within higher education, there is no consensus about the location, scope, boundaries and alliances of the area, and this results in a fluid and vulnerable position, particularly when combined with rapid internal and external changes. Changes affecting social work education are occurring in the organisation and practice of social work as well as in higher education. Questions about the mission, resourcing and mode of operation of HEIs have also impacted on social work, and the subject area finds itself in an institutional context subject to critical review.

Although social work originated in the 'old' universities, it more recently became predominantly (two thirds) located in HEIs outside the university sector. However, with university status for most polytechnics by the time of the survey, 43 out of 64 of the survey respondents were in universities and a diminishing number in colleges or institutes of higher education (increasingly becoming colleges of established universities). Continuing differences between 'old' and 'new' universities (ex-polytechnics) in academic ethos, expectations and resourcing, are referred to in the analysis. Unlike teacher education, social work education has been consistently located in HEIs concerned with various forms of professional education, which occupy a minority position relative to discipline-based studies and where the emphasis given to research activities has varied considerably.

The Rationale for Social Work in Higher Education

At the interview stage a direct question was asked of the interviewees on whether social work should be in or out of higher education. All respondents said that social work education *should* remain in higher education, although three respondents qualified their answers. These qualified responses included digressions about the level at which qualifying training should be offered, or suggestions about the need for clarity regarding the roles and tasks for which students are being prepared and the particular challenge which offering qualifying training in higher education poses. All respondents were asked the reasons for their views.

The knowledge base was identified by most respondents as requiring a close association between those who create knowledge and those who transmit it. Respondents saw a necessary connection between the social sciences and preparation for professional practice, as well as holding expectations that social work academics would themselves be involved in the creation of knowledge through research. Social work 'needs research and dissemination of new ideas through academic publications...students should be exposed to new ideas'. 'The skills involved [need to be placed] within a much wider context, [students] need to have a good basic education in relation to the social science knowledge base, and to be able to use this professionally'.

The nature of the social work task was also thought by all respondents to require exposure to higher education, in preference to role-related training programmes. One respondent described social work as 'a very complex activity which requires [the exercise of] intellect, not just a bureaucratic or routine response'. Another saw it as 'emotionally, intellectually and theoretically demanding'. One cited sound academic training as enabling students to 'think, write and analyse' and to use these abilities to inform their judgements about interventions, while another referred to the 'high levels of conceptualisation, flexibility and articulation' needed for practice. Although only one respondent used the term 'reflective practice', it was clear that respondents recognised the need for an informed and thoughtful approach to actions undertaken in complex situations; and one respondent suggested that the term 'education and training' should represent 'a properly sophisticated relationship between theory and practice'. Another spoke of the 'essence' of social work being the exercise of 'discretion and judgement...a professional activity which requires creativity and a developed intellect...[this is] what [higher] education is about delivering'.

Comparability was suggested by two respondents as a rationale for social work's continued existence in higher education (not as the only or main reason), citing the need for social work education in the UK to have a comparable status with educational programmes outside the UK: the British 'weakness' in this area has already been mentioned. More importantly, in a domestic context, both respondents were concerned about the need for comparability (in terms of educational status) with occupational groups with whom social workers frequently interact, or may be compared in public and academic exercises. One respondent observed, 'Social work would have an anomalous position relative to other professions and occupations if it came out of higher education'.

Public accountability was another reason given. One respondent cited the expectations of the public and the risk to individual users, if social workers were not educated at an appropriate level. Responsibility for *continuing professional development* was mentioned: social workers were seen as having to take continuing responsibility for evaluating their work and for maintaining and developing their knowledge and skills.

In summary, respondents saw 'the essence [of social work] as being about people...making decisions over matters which are not replicatable', and thought that preparation for such work is necessarily located in higher education with its goal of developing the intellect and analytical skills. In contemplating its possible removal from higher education, one respondent voiced concern about the 'potential erosion [of social work] as a professional and political activity', if it were not subject to 'critical debate' as part of the educational process.

Turning to another data source, the support of JUC SWEC for maintenance of social work in higher education might be assumed, consisting, as it does, of social work educators. Such support is often implicit, but sometimes also explicit, in its documents. In the 1991 Annual Report, the chairperson expressed the Committee's concern to work with related interest groups 'to avoid wasteful duplication and fragmentation of effort' in promoting social work. However, her comments also justified the Committee's separate identity, noting 'the broad social science and policy perspective for which [JUC SWEC] stands, its concern with scholarly as well as practice standards, and its regard for the research base of social work' as a rationale. The 1995 Annual Report commented on the Committee's active role in preparation for the Research Assessment Exercise with the intention of 'helping to improve the performance of social work as an academic discipline'.

JUC SWEC's position is also clear in its concern about actual or potential loss of courses or areas of practice from social work education. For instance, after some course closures in the 1980s, the chairperson noted in the 1989 Annual Report that there had been 'no further erosion of social work places' in higher education that year. In the 1995 Report, the intended closure of the LSE course was remarked upon - 'it is to be hoped that the decision...does not mark the beginning of a trend'. This statement was made in the context of considerable preoccupation with the proposed withdrawal of training for the Probation Service from higher education, which would affect nearly one third of the subject area.

The same Annual Report noted that a number of bodies, including the Committee of Vice Chancellors and Principals (CVCP) had 'clearly perceived...the [DEWS Report] proposals as constituting a threat to higher education, as well as to social work and the quality of Probation practice and research, and that they have opposed them in the fiercest possible terms'. The fact that this opposition was over-ruled perhaps says more about the level of political determination and intervention in the welfare sector (including higher education) than the motivation or effectiveness of particular interest groups, as represented here by JUC SWEC.

 This study demonstrates reasoned support from social work educators for the maintenance of social work in higher education, but it is clearly not a secure position. The apparent inability of the educators to defend (let alone develop) the position of social work as a legitimate academic enterprise with a theoretical core (compared to the increased vocationalism and prescription in CCETSW requirements for courses leading to professional awards) has been noted in the literature (Timms, 1991; Jones, 1996a). The tensions inherent in any form of professional education include the 'dual mandate' or potentially conflicting expectations of the university and the field, and Hartman's Australian study (1989, *op cit.*) of the consequences of an 'academic location', in terms of the tensions experienced by teaching staff, has relevance to the UK.

The location of professional education (including social work) 'at the intersection of two social institutions' was noted by Halpern (1985) in America and this undoubtedly contributes to feelings of low status, marginalisation, and having to manage tensions at external as well as internal boundaries. Harris (1990) suggested that the fundamental task for British social work education in the 1990s would be the management of its relationships with *three* distinct worlds - academic institutions, the agencies and CCETSW. The evidence confirms this view. Even in the 1980s, JUC SWEC records suggest that a considerable amount of academic time and energy had been taken up responding to various drafts of CCETSW proposals, as well as in trying to 'manage' more local aspects of the academy-field relationship.

Formalisation of this relationship in the early 1990s into DipSW (and Regional) Consortia may have diverted social work educators from their academic task (including theory development) and weakened their defence and development of a subject that was already marginal in higher education.

The Naming and Organisational Location of Social Work

Assuming a continuing place for social work education in higher education, questions arise about organisational location and visibility of it as a named subject area. The evidence from the survey suggests that while it is frequently a basic unit in terms of organisation and delivery of teaching, ideology and peer system (Boys and Kogan, 1984, p.45), it is rarely this in financial and managerial terms and usually fails to attain the status of *Department (or School)*. In only 16 HEIs (evenly spread between old and new universities) were respondents heading distinct basic units. More often, social work constituted a subject area or section within a department, and in only five such cases was its existence directly signalled in a 'combination title', such as 'Department of Social Work and Nursing'.

In the remainder of cases (about two thirds) social work was subsumed within departments whose titles did not indicate its existence. The majority of these (16) included 'social science' or 'social studies', or 'community studies' (8) in titles; while eight other titles signalled the disciplinary basis of the department, for example, social policy (5) or sociology (2). A few titles suggested a possible interdisciplinary bias, but not necessarily the existence of social work, for example, 'Human Studies'; 'Education and Administration'; 'Management and Professional Education'. These more venturesome titles were a feature of the new universities. The extent to which social work does *not* constitute a basic unit, and its relative *invisibility* in terms of departmental titles further suggests that it is a weak subject area.

However, there is considerable variation in how academic institutes 'draw the map of knowledge' and how they accommodate newly emerging or interdisciplinary studies (Becher, 1989, p.19). Further, organisation of content into departments has been noted as highly arbitrary and a product of historical accident (Campbell, 1969), so perhaps the above findings are not conclusive in suggesting an identity problem. However, the study shows that social work does not have a clear profile as a subject area in higher education under departmental headings in a majority of cases. This is not an area explicitly addressed in JUC SWEC documents or in the wider literature.

Turning now to the *Faculty* base of departments of, or containing, social work (excluding a small number of institutions without this level of organisation), the majority of departments were within 'Social Science' faculties or in faculties bearing 'combination' or 'qualified' titles, for example 'Social and Political Science' or 'Applied Social Science' (16 in all). A further 14 departments were in faculties featuring Health in the title, such as Health and Human Sciences; while a third group (12) were in more broadly based faculties, for instance, Cultural and Community Studies. While the majority of respondents were in *Arts, Human or Social Science* Faculties of some kind, eight respondents were located in *Science* Faculties. There was little difference between old and new universities in this matter.

This question - 'is social work an art or a science?' - has been identified in the academic literature (England, 1986), although addressed to the internal context and style of the subject area rather than institutional framework. The science/art split may be an unreal or unhelpful dichotomy, but it can be seen as a further indication of disagreement about the nature of the subject, social work's identity problem, and its marginal position. It is also likely to have a bearing on the alliances of social work with other subjects.

Alliances

The relationship between social work and other disciplines further indicates its wide ranging or unclear nature. In the survey data, only seven respondents claimed to have *no* particular associations with other subjects. The wording of the questions made it difficult to gauge the rationale and quality of those associations and relationships described by the remainder. Alliances fell into two broad categories, those with *academic* subjects (62 mentions); and those with other *professional* subjects (57 mentions) and these were not necessarily exclusive. Thus, over a third of respondents, drawn fairly evenly from old and new universities, included subjects in both categories in their returns.

Proportionately, more respondents from the old university sector listed only alliances with academic subjects (12), whereas respondents from the new or non-university sector were more likely to list alliances only with other professional or occupational subjects (14). Of the academic subjects listed, social policy (including policy studies or social administration) was the most frequently cited (22) relative to sociology (16), psychology (11) and law[1] (10). Other subjects were listed by only two or three respondents (economics, anthropology, 'social science', criminology, European studies) or were single cases (geography, humanities, gender studies).

Regarding association with professional or occupational subjects, 'health' was noted by just over a quarter of respondents (17), followed by youth and community work (10) and education (6). Three respondents mentioned associations with other health-related professional subjects (psychiatry, medicine, dentistry) and two with occupational therapy. Other 'subjects' mentioned were counselling (4), professional studies (3), social care (2), housing (2), nutrition (1) and management (1). The relationship with 'subjects allied with medicine' reflects a category previously used by HEFC, and historical and current connections between social work and health, in practice and education.

The foregoing suggests some recognition that social work education has logical associations with both academic and other professional subjects, as evidenced by many respondents (24), and that there is some tendency to seek, or to maintain, 'academic' alliances in the old university

---

[1] Although categorised as a 'social profession' by Becher (1989), law is included here as an academic subject, on the grounds that it is studied initially at undergraduate level and not all degree holders proceed to professional studies.

sector, relative to the greater likelihood of the grouping of 'professional' subjects in the new and non-university sector. The continuing predominance of social policy as an associated subject is in contrast to lack of recognition of this subject in other European countries (Jones, 1985), and the stronger alliances of social work education elsewhere with either sociology or psychology (Cannan *et al.*, 1992). A more pronounced emphasis on a relationship with law might have been anticipated given concern expressed about the need for good preparation of students in this area (CCETSW, 1988), but it is likely that law teaching is carried out in-house by either social work educators or specialists from the field.

Epistemological Characteristics

A wider question concerning the epistemological character of social work education was put to interviewees in the form, 'how would you describe the area of social work education?' This sometimes gave rise to answers about the scope and level of social work qualification, but many respondents addressed the issues of location, boundaries and relationships with other fields of knowledge, as intended.

There was a general tendency to favour the development of social work as a rigorous *academic subject* with a close association with the *social sciences*, 'otherwise it's in danger of losing its critical edge'. However, this summary statement over-simplifies the levels of analysis offered by some respondents, about the 'core' of social work and its relationship with particular disciplines. One respondent spoke of the difficulty of social work 'securing a place within the intellectual territory' of the social sciences and of identifying 'its core intellectual or academic terrain'. Another spoke of social work's tendency to 'raid other disciplines for ideas, translate and adapt them...[it is] derivative and its intellectual content is five or ten years behind the mainstream'.

Similar ideas were expressed more positively by another respondent, that it is 'a multi-disciplinary subject...putting together knowledge and practice experience from a range of [other] areas...what makes it special is how disciplines are brought together for a purpose'. Yet another person also thought it appropriate for social work to draw from a wide range of other disciplines, 'including some areas we haven't thought about'. This would certainly support comparative literature about social work education, since the range of subjects included in curricula abroad is often wider than, or different from, that of British courses. Another respondent suggested that social work is 'no different from medicine which draws on a range of other subjects'. The *interdisciplinary nature* of the subject and the assumption that, while social work may be unique in some ways, it shares some characteristics with other forms of professional education, are further examined in Part 3.

Two other themes emerged from interviewees' responses to the question about subject area. One was a regular reference to *practice*: 'it is about inquiry and writing, reflecting what is happening in practice', or 'the mix of intellectual learning and practice is particularly well developed in social work education', or 'the theory-practice debate is fascinating ...[it's] not just an "application" relationship'. The last respondent also stressed the educator's role in 'managing the teaching-research-practice interplay'. The other theme concerned *values* and the likely value conflicts both within the subject area and between the subject and its various neighbours and associates (including practice).

Only one respondent placed social work education as 'one of a number of related occupational groups - health, education, social care [with] no clear boundaries between them [and] competing for territory'. He further suggested that the boundaries of each are shifting 'according to societal expectations and requirements'. Another person explicitly rejected a close association with health studies (on the grounds that this subject was not based on the critical use of the social sciences). A number of respondents indicated that the area is contested and/or that it lacks clear, identifiable boundaries, but one interviewee at least thought this should be a strength not a weakness. One interviewee also asserted that social work 'must develop a stronger identity as a distinct discipline with its own body of knowledge', suggesting that this is a challenging task for social work educators.

This raises two related questions concerning the epistemological nature of social work education on the one hand and its organisational form within the university on the other. Traditionally, social work education has been seen as drawing on disciplinary knowledge (specifically from the social sciences including social policy and law) rather than constituting a discipline in its own right. Referring briefly to the literature, social work can be categorised as both 'immature' (lacking the existence of clearly defined paradigms) (Kuhn, 1962) and 'unrestricted' (following problems into other areas) (Pantin, 1968). Its lack of status as a discipline and marginality in the higher education enterprise, perhaps partly explain its omission, along with all the other social professions (except law), from Becher's discussion of epistemological and cultural characteristics of selected disciplines, though it undoubtedly falls within the 'soft applied' domain delineated by him (Becher, 1989). That is, its content is concerned with a broad range of problems, with lack of clarity or agreement about its theoretical paradigms and methodology (soft); and it is open to external influence (applied).

However, this lack of clarity about its nature, content, methodology and boundaries is not peculiar to social work, and has even been experienced within a subject area formally categorised as a discipline, that is anthropology (Geertz, 1995). Geertz quoted a dictionary definition of 'discipline' which lists seven possibilities of this term, including, 'a branch of knowledge or teaching', and 'training expected to produce a specified character or pattern of behaviour'. He further stated that 'the idea of a discipline, in any of these senses...fits anthropology none too well. At once broad and general, wildly aspiring ["The Study of Man"] and particular and miscellaneous, strangely obsessive...it has always had...a blurry image. Neither method nor subject matter exactly defines it...' (Geertz, 1995, pp.96-97). The relevance of Geertz's comments to social work education is apparent, and indeed there is a possible relationship (in terms of relevance of knowledge, methods and values) between social work education and anthropology not normally acknowledged or explored, although social work educators and anthropologists co-existed in at least two departments at the time of the survey with individual staff teaching in both areas.

Another term, 'domain', was used by Trist (1972) in his discussion of social research and typologies of research organisations. He suggested use of this term as an attempt to integrate, rather than fragment the disciplines (under a broadly systemic approach) in relation to problem resolution, and this also has relevance to the nature of social work education. Becher (1989) used the term, domain, to describe a cluster of disciplines or subjects with similar characteristics. This variation in use, and lack of accepted and current usage and meaning of the term, coupled with the traditional connotation of 'disciplines' as theoretical rather than applied branches of knowledge, suggest the use of the term 'subject' or 'subject area' in this discussion as relatively neutral, notwithstanding the assertion in some of the data and literature that social work is a discipline.

It is relevant to note here some examples of similar concerns about location and epistemology in the social work education literature. For example, Sheppard (1995), in a discussion about social work, social sciences and practice wisdom, argued that good practice should be characterised by *critical awareness* and that this capacity, together with rigour and imagination, is best developed through an educational rather than a training process. Clark (1995, p.570), in a critique of competencies as the basis for professional training and drawing on a study of how practitioners use theory, stated that 'good practice must be based on a deep appreciation of the foundation principles and the fundamental logic and method of relevant fields of enquiry; ...in addition to drawing on relevant findings from diverse topics...[and that it] takes on the character of a discipline'.

The Scope and Scale of the Subject Area

The basis for identifying social work departments or subject areas in HEIs was the CCETSW list of social work qualifying courses (programmes). However, it was known that this did not include all institutions with an interest in social work education, for example, at post-qualifying or research degree level, and it was considered by the researcher that social work education as a whole was not solely concerned with the qualifying stage of training - at whatever academic level this may occur. Information about the range of activities carried out within the subject area, particularly as reflected in awards offered, was sought through the survey.

Some interviewees also spontaneously addressed this topic, although it was not the focus of a specific question. Thus, one respondent said, in answer to the question about the area of social work, 'it's not just DipSW. One of the problems with social work education and training is that it is couched in these terms - it should be broader'. Other responses, mainly about level of qualifications, are considered after a discussion of the findings from the survey.

The survey data demonstrate that, by the summer of 1994, provision of a qualifying *DipSW programme* as the sole award-bearing activity existed in only eleven out of 64 institutions: seven of these were in the new university/college sector (all at DipHE level), and four were in the old university sector (at undergraduate (1) and masters (3) levels). Many institutions offered a DipSW (at whatever level) and either a *practice teacher training programme* (9, all in the new university sector) or *courses at post-qualifying level* (8, primarily in the old university sector). About one third of the respondents (21), fairly evenly divided between the old and new sectors, offered qualifying education, practice teacher training *and* other post-qualifying courses.

A minority of institutions (13, mainly F/HEIs and sometimes franchised) offered the continuum of training including some awards at the pre-qualifying and post-qualifying stages (the latter usually being practice teacher awards); and a very small number (2) offered programmes leading to qualifying, post qualifying and advanced awards (as defined by CCETSW and described earlier). However, a number of other respondents signalled their intention to promote developments in the area of post-qualifying and advanced awards, having established the DipSW at non-graduate level. It should also be noted here that by the summer of 1994, 16 institutions were (still) in the final stages of CQSW provision (at various academic levels) although by the Autumn of 1995 all institutions surveyed planned to be offering DipSW.

These findings suggest that many institutions conformed with CCETSW's original intention regarding implementation of DipSW programmes well within the five year transitional period, originally proposed in 1989. Initially, it seemed as if conversion to DipSW would be completed in a shorter timescale, as indicated in the JUC SWEC Annual Report of 1990. This noted that 'the remainder [of courses] are expected to award DipSW by 1993'. However, an early flurry of activity on the part of some courses subsequently slowed. It was also the case that new programmes not approved for commencement in the Autumn of 1993 were then subject to 'planning blight' by the announcement of the review of DipSW in December 1993.

With regard to the *academic level* of qualifying professional awards (DipSW and CQSW), the survey indicated fairly equal numbers at DipHE and post-graduate level. The minority position of undergraduate degrees continued, with only five programmes at that level in this sample. However, the low number of undergraduate courses had, in fact, risen from 5 per cent of CQSW courses in 1980 to 8 per cent of qualifying programmes in this survey. The 1994 data also showed that a small number of institutions (four) had developed a 'two-plus-one model', that is, they were offering a professional qualification at DipHE level with the option to proceed or return to a third year for a 'top-up' degree. This can be seen as indicating a measure of dissatisfaction with only a two year professional programme and/or a broad support for academic awards which conformed to CCETSW's continuum of training.

The extent to which such degrees have been perceived and used by students as an immediate extension of their DipSW studies, or how far they have attracted previously qualified workers (back) into educational and/or approved post-qualifying programmes, was not explored by this study. With reference to the academic motivation for such a move, it was apparent from JUC SWEC minutes (1988/1989) that there had been strong support in principle for three year training (the QDSW proposals, assuming appropriate levels of resourcing and notwithstanding some reservations) and in 1995 a JUC SWEC representative spoke at a national conference promoting three year training as the basis for a professional award.

There was some support for the view that qualifying training should be (minimally) at degree level in the responses of the interviewees in 1996, with most interviewees mentioning this explicitly, for example, 'the ideal minimum academic level should be a degree. Three year training should be the norm'. In its comments on the CCETSW review of DipSW, the British Association of Social Workers also supported the idea of a qualifying award at degree level, although it carefully avoided suggesting that all awards should be in the form of three year undergraduate, college-based programmes (Colvin, 1995).

Further support is indicated in some of the social work literature. Sheppard concluded that social work 'should as a minimum be a degree level subject', not only because of the applied 'product' nature of its knowledge base, but because also of its 'process' nature' which he likens to the inductive social research paradigm (1995, p.289). On a different note, Jones saw the introduction of top-up degrees, 'outside of CCETSW's ambit of control', as evidence of the wishes of staff and students to extend and deepen their knowledge base, including in relation to social science and policy (1996b, p.16). It seems evident that social work educators have developed their own strategies for circumventing the government policy to limit social work qualifying training to two years. This accords with, for example, views on the role of professionals at the implementation stage of the policy process (Rein, 1983), and is further discussed in Part 3.

This trend towards degrees, with CCETSW's requirements being met within two years of a three year programme or spread across the three years (observable initially in the 1994 data) raises questions both for the place of *qualifying training at post-graduate level*, and for CCETSW's plans in relation to *post-qualifying and advanced awards*. With regard to the first, there was clear evidence that social work educators, in meeting CCETSW's requirements for a minimum period of two year training, took the opportunity to devise programmes carrying a masters degree, rather than a post-graduate diploma. There were 20 such examples in the 1994 sample, and by 1997 this number had increased to 30, although the overall proportion of routes at this level (relative to undergraduate programmes) has declined.

Turning to CCETSW's 'continuum of training', there was not universal acceptance of a distinction between post-qualifying and advanced awards, and this has posed some problems for programme designers and approvers alike in deciding the appropriate level for specific awards. Thus, if increasing numbers of students obtain a basic qualification at degree level, the rationale for locating awards associated with induction and consolidation or, more particularly, practice teaching at this level is obscured, and the position of social workers obtaining their first qualification at masters level is even more anomalous. Subsequent problems - not least the resource implications of the structures required to implement the post-qualifying system and a low level of programme approvals and awards - suggest the likelihood of further changes at this level. This is not an area which has received much attention yet in the academic literature, with the notable exception of Yelloly and Henkel (1995) (see also Jack, 1995; Youll, 1996).

Finally, with regard to the *scale of the enterprise*, the data from the 1994 survey showed considerable variation in the size of DipSW programmes, this being the area of core provision in terms of student numbers. A small majority (14, including five in the old university sector) were still relatively small (in current HE course size terms), with an intake of less than 40 students per annum; twelve programmes recruited 40-49 students; eleven recruited 50-59; twelve had intakes of 60-79; and eight had intakes of 80 or more students per annum. There was a marked difference between old and new universities in this respect, with nineteen out of twenty-three old universities having an intake of less than 60 while twenty of the new universities and remaining colleges (nearly half) had intakes of 60 or more.

The majority of institutions also had relatively small numbers of students on other courses, ranging from less than ten on postgraduate (research) programmes (at two old universities) to fifty or more part-time students, mostly on taught courses, in ten universities (9 new, 1 old). It has already been noted that CCETSW, in approving intake numbers for new qualifying courses and monitoring output, seeks to maintain a balance between supply and demand for qualified social workers and during the 1990s the total output averaged about 4,000 per annum.

Collaborative Activities

The other aspect of the structural arrangements in place by 1994, which has significant implications for the nature and work of the subject area, concerns the establishment of 'programme provider groups' required by

CCETSW to plan, deliver and monitor qualifying training programmes. These were to consist minimally of one institution and one agency and could be seen both as a formalising of collaborative arrangements which had often existed on an *ad hoc* basis between CQSW courses and representatives from practice, and as a restraint or steer on course content and the overall direction of social work education which academics might promote if left unchecked.

In the case of CSS courses, collaborative or partnership arrangements were already in place and this may explain the relative speed of change from CSS to DipSW in some institutions. However, in the case of former CQSW courses, the development of DipSW programmes required often intensive or protracted negotiations with local agencies to establish an acceptable size and form of partnership. It is interesting that CCETSW representatives, when pressed, for example at JUC SWEC meetings, for guidance as to how best responsibilities should be shared, declined to give a blue-print for 'programme provider groups', requiring institutions to work out their own arrangements. While this undoubtedly allowed a degree of flexibility in the system it was also a source of anxiety, conflict and mutual learning for many participants.

By the time of the 1994 survey, all institutions had partnership arrangements in place and only five respondents indicated the minimum collaboration required of one institution and one agency. All these consisted of ex-CSS courses with one Social Service Department partner. Just over a third of institutions (25) favoured a partnership including one SSD, one Probation Service, and one voluntary agency. This was certainly the preferred position of fourteen institutions in the old university sector where such arrangements were also usually associated with a DipSW award at post-graduate level. Probation agency participation was of course a requirement for courses offering a probation option but highly unlikely otherwise, because of the funding arrangements. This arrangement, where probation formed an important element in a relatively small and usually quite stable partnership, was to have particular consequences following the government decision to phase probation training out of higher education.

Another one third of respondents had partnerships with social services and voluntary sector agencies (22, 19 of which were in the new university sector), while twelve institutions had partnerships solely with statutory agencies (SSDs and Probation). A further thirteen had partnerships including Education Social Work/Welfare Agencies, but private agencies were mentioned in only four of the returns. Whether this had changed by the end of the 1990s is open to question. Only eleven of the respondents' 'providers groups' included more than one institution.

There is a possibility that some respondents misunderstood the question about collaborative arrangements and included as partners all agencies where students were placed. This may have given rise to some apparently unwieldy partnerships, for example, one including ten SSDs; another including twenty voluntary agencies; and another having ten private agencies, and reaching a maximum of 31 partners. However, given CCETSW's loose requirements in this respect and the provision for 'secondary partners' (whose responsibilities and level of involvement, such as in programme planning or review meetings, would be less than those of primary partners) it is conceivable that these were formally constituted agreements. CCETSW required contracts to be signed by all participants and included in documentation for validation purposes, increasingly also a requirement of HEIs.

A number of respondents also mentioned one voluntary agency acting as a representative in the partnership for other smaller NGOs. Omitting the small number of non-respondents to this question and the few large examples, the average size of programme providers groups in 1994 seemed to be about six, and to include agencies from two different sectors in the social work field.

There was no attempt in this research to evaluate the impact or functioning of partnership arrangements on the academic endeavours of social work educators, but there is impressionistic evidence to suggest that developing and maintaining provider groups in relation to DipSW implementation absorbed much staff time and energy, possibly at the expense, for example, of research activities. One example of this was suggested by a course handbook (of a medium sized, masters level course) which listed fourteen decision-making committees and advisory groups. Some of these would have been required or expected by the (old) university and the majority indicated some level of student involvement, but a number were a direct result of conformity with CCETSW requirements.

Certainly, the increased costs of staff time in establishing partnership arrangements were, to some extent, recognised by the allocation, via CCETSW, of development funds to individual programmes, for up to three years, around the implementation of DipSW programmes; and JUC SWEC lobbied for ongoing resourcing in this area (Annual Report, 1992). However, an early note of scepticism about partnership entered the literature following the 1993 Annual Conference of the Association of

Teachers in Social Work Education (ATSWE), which took 'partnership' as its theme. Thus, Payne (1994, p.53) argued that an analysis of CCETSW documents suggested that promotion of partnership 'stems from a struggle by agencies to control the definition of ideas and methods of social work and by universities to control placement resources' and put forward the view that personal networks and development of a new culture of social work education are more likely to be effective than the 'required' structural relationships embodied in programme provider groups.

This is an area about which many social work educators feel ambivalent - for a variety of reasons - and which raises pertinent issues for professional education more widely. It was not specifically asked about in the 1996 interviews and it is interesting that none of the respondents raised the matter themselves, although a number mentioned 'practice' (in the context of theory/practice debate or practice placements); and employers (for example, 'social work education reflects the tension between what the employers want and promoting a creative, critical approach'). It has, however, received critical attention in the social work education literature. For instance, Novak (1995, p.5) attributed the crisis in social work education partly to social work educators' adherence to CCETSW's requirements, including 'partnerships and bureaucratic procedures that are immensely time consuming and often of little benefit'.

Previously, Timms (1991, p.207) had identified joint programme provision as 'inherently unstable' and, more recently, another critic described DipSW arrangements as 'pseudo-autonomous programme providers operating as quasi-businesses, founded on semi-contractual mutual partnerships' (Webb, 1996, p.181), a view which assumed greater significance in the light of more recent changes in placement funding. Webb described the DipSW requirement for partnerships as being 'the linchpin in the strategy to bring colleges into line' not withstanding 'all the evidence about the cost and cumbersomeness of managerial structures' (p.180).

Collaborative arrangements were also to be the basis for developments in continuing professional education. Thus, in CCETSW's Paper 31 (1990) regarding post-qualifying and advanced awards, the principle was extended through regional consortia. These were responsible for approving programmes and administering registration of candidates for awards, including allocating bursaries. This devolution of responsibility from CCETSW to (initially) the largely voluntary efforts of academic and agency personnel represents another example of the bureaucratisation of the educational process and the diversion of academic (and agency) energies from their primary tasks. It also set up a system, the rationale for which may have been knowledge about and responsiveness to local conditions, but which has entailed significant levels of 'reinventing the wheel' as each consortium struggled to establish its own criteria and mechanisms for course approval. It has also, arguably, diminished rather than enhanced the likelihood of promoting national standards of excellence. These concerns were discussed by Jack (1995, p.81), who, from a position of social work educator with recent agency responsibilities, noted 'effective collaboration is extremely expensive to maintain for all concerned'.

Summary and Concluding Comments

This chapter has presented information about the social work subject area from data gathered in 1994 and 1996, augmented by JUC SWEC records and some literature. While social work educators clearly support the maintenance of social work in higher education (for reasons related to the knowledge base and nature of practice), some characteristics were identified which make its position vulnerable. These include the tensions inherent in a dual mandate, but also the epistemological nature of the subject. This can be described as 'interdisciplinary' and 'applied', both characteristics which have low status in the traditional hierarchy of knowledge.

The lack of clarity about the theoretical core, the competing disciplinary paradigms and the disputed nature of the professional territory, are reflected in the wide range of departments within which the subject is located. A minority of these are situated within Science Faculties, and the remainder in Arts, Human or Social Sciences. The subject has a low profile within HEIs, having departmental status in only a quarter of the cases in the 1994 sample, and its existence is not normally signalled in the title of its host department. It has a wide range of alliances, reported by 1994 respondents particularly, although about one third claimed association with social policy and a further third with health related subjects.

With regard to the range of courses offered, the qualifying programme, DipSW, forms the core of most subject areas, at either non-graduate or post-graduate level. The continued existence of qualifying awards at post-graduate level and evidence of some growth in the number of undergraduate programmes suggest unresolved questions about social work educators' views on the continuum of education and training established by CCETSW. There were relatively few examples in the 1994 data of additional programmes offering post-qualifying or advanced professional awards, with the exception of a small number of courses, mainly leading to practice teacher awards. DipSW course sizes varied considerably (with intake and output targets approved by CCETSW) and overall the number of students in the subject area was small, relative to some other subjects, such as law or education.

Information was presented about structural arrangements regarding programme provider groups required by CCETSW for DipSW programmes: these usually consist of about six agencies and an HEI. These arrangements reflect the necessity for the subject to have field links but have also increased the bureaucratisation of social work education. Concerns about the costs and instability of such requirements were identified. Some of the data in this and ensuing chapters seem to bear out an earlier prediction that management of the relationship with CCETSW would constitute a third sphere of activity (additional to HEIs and agencies) for social work educators in the 1990s (Harris, 1990).

6   Curricular and Pedagogical Characteristics

Introduction

This chapter considers the content of the subject area in the qualifying stage of training, (the DipSW). Introduction of DipSW requirements in the early 1990s had implications for both the curriculum and for teaching, learning and assessment, here referred to as pedagogical issues. While only a few respondents to the survey sent course handbooks or brochures with their completed questionnaires (6), others sent programme outlines or timetables, or added notes to the questionnaire (39) which gave clues as to curricula content. Further information was derived from course documents available to the researcher in other capacities and from CCETSW information for applicants (CCETSW, 1996).

Fifty-six DipSW programmes were analysed, although the level of detail available varied considerably. Additionally, there was some reference to curricular matters by some of the interviewees and in the social work education literature. For most respondents (with the exception of P/G diploma courses already mentioned) there was no change in the length of new programmes. However, the requirement (in the original Paper 30, 1989) to introduce an area of particular practice, to assess 'competences' *(sic)* demonstrated in practice, and to demonstrate values (for example, the 1989 requirements on anti-racism) all meant changes in curriculum.

In some cases, course changes in response to CCETSW requirements coincided with institutional moves to modularisation. This change, itself often a response to the declining resource base, had implications for the teaching and learning process. A traditionally high staff-student ratio in the social work area (CCETSW's norm of 1:10 had been eroded in the 1980s) and assumptions about the appropriate ways of transmitting knowledge, skills and values, were all increasingly challenged in the 1990s. Some departments have made radical changes in their mode of delivery to reflect this.

The 1994 survey results only hinted at some of the changes which were to become more apparent later, and in the 1996 interviews a question was asked explicitly about the implication of content and how it should be taught.

Material from JUC SWEC has not yielded much information for this chapter. An Information Sheet issued by the Joint University Council states that '...the Council has provided an important national forum for the discussion of academic issues such as the content of curricula, matters relating to resources and standards in teaching and research...', and there is ample evidence over the last decade or more that the Social Work Education Committee has taken seriously its remit to 'consult and co-operate with other [relevant] bodies' in pursuance of its goal of subject development (see Appendix 3). Considerable efforts have been directed to responses to various CCETSW proposals and to commenting on changes signalled in central government documents or experienced locally. Some working groups have had curricular concerns very much in mind, but have been more preoccupied with the overall structure and direction of the subject area and with resourcing.

Much of the work of the Committee proceeds on the basis of assumptions about the 'content' of the field and appropriate pedagogical approaches, assumed to be shared. These are occasionally made more explicit, for instance, in a regular concern about the place of research, a similar consistent concern to maintain 'work with offenders', and finding a place for comparative perspectives.

Curriculum Content

CCETSW Paper 30 did not specify a core curriculum, although prescription on outcomes virtually amounted to this: '... the regulatory framework and the specification of competences is doing no more than establishing a national curriculum in social work' (Webb, 1996, p.180). With some notable exceptions, this research indicated considerable conformity in the curricula components of college-based teaching. Paper 30 required programme providers to develop an explicit *practice* curriculum as the basis for practice teaching and assessment. However, this material is usually contained in separate placement handbooks not analysed in this research.

In addition to the college and practice curricula, Coulshead (1989) suggested that there is a *'process curriculum'*, which, while not very distinct within the material analysed, is in evidence. Holland (1988) identified an *invisible* curriculum concerned with integration of learning from three sources - academic disciplines, principles of professional practice, and practice placements - which poses pedagogical complexities for social work education.

Most handbooks contain a general statement about the philosophy or aims of the programme, and phrases such as 'preparation for a changing world'; 'reflective practice'; 'challenging discrimination (or inequalities or oppression)'; 'taking account of the current social, economic and political context' or 'resource constraints, or 'demands for accountability'; and 'recognising the impact of social divisions' or 'the powerful links between the personal and the political'. Programme providers aim to equip students with 'strategies for intervention' and to work in 'a wide range of agencies', though there was some indication of a gap between utilitarian courses tied to SSDs as potential employers, and more imaginative and academically ambitious programmes, unrelated to award level or type of host institution.

A minority of courses used client group or setting as the sole organising principle for curriculum construction, and two had moved exclusively to 'enquiry and action' or 'problem-based learning' avoiding divisions of the curriculum into units with separate syllabi. The great majority of course curricula consisted of a varying number of units (between 3 and 10 per year excluding placements), a minority of which suggested some degree of 'integration' or 'inter-disciplinarity', even if only in one unit. The following analysis categorised curriculum elements into *professional knowledge* (social work *theory*, *values* and *skills*); *theoretical underpinning* or disciplinary perspectives; areas of *particular practice* (APPs, subsequently renamed pathways); and a *miscellaneous* group of related studies which could be compulsory or optional.

Professional Knowledge

Core social work teaching (identified in 46 programmes) about models, methods and approaches used in the practice of social work, goes under many headings; 'principles and practice of social work', 'theory and methods', 'practice theories', 'social work intervention'. These suggest a lack of agreement or confidence about the *theoretical* core of the subject area, and tension between 'process' informed syllabi (concerned with the stages in engagement with service users), and those based on approaches for analysis and action in particular situations. The latter is more common but sometimes includes reference to the former and suggests an eclectic approach whereby students are presented with a range of methods or models to utilise as appropriate.

The traditional psychodynamic paradigm, which previously played a dominant and even exclusive role in the curriculum (Payne, 1991) may now be dealt with in one lecture, almost as an historical illustration, if at all. In 1991, Timms wrote about 'avoidance of the work of establishing theoretical foundations' (p.207) and this contributes to the perceived weakness of the subject. There is a small body of literature about the nature of social work theory and its relation to practice (for example, Sheppard, 1995; Elliott, 1995), but this area requires further work and some rethinking (Clark, 1995; Jones and Jordan, 1996).

'*Values* teaching' (identified as a distinct element in 36 programmes) also went under many headings, suggesting different aims and emphases. A minority of units were described as 'philosophy and values' or 'values and ethics', while over half included reference to 'anti-discriminatory values' (or principles) in the title. This teaching would sometimes take place as 'block' workshops or be related to practice situations, for example through seminar discussions, suggesting that the amount and level of theoretical input varied considerably.

Jones has suggested that 'values are crucial in defining a general orientation but in the absence of supporting knowledge can tend to lead to highly inappropriate and simplistic forms of intervention' (1996b, p.20). Macey and Moxon (1996) have also argued that it is necessary to draw on the social sciences to inform the value base, and Webb saw this lack as contributing to CCETSW's inability to rebut the attack on social work education's commitment to anti-discriminatory practice in the 1995 revision of Paper 30 (Webb, 1996, p.185). While there is relatively little literature about the teaching of values *per se,* there is rather more material about education for anti-discriminatory practice, one example including a taxonomy of stages in curriculum change in this area (Harlow and Hearn, 1996).

The third aspect of professional knowledge included units aimed at developing *skills*. Of 64 such units, 19 were concerned with work with individuals (sometimes subsumed under 'communication skills' or 'counselling' headings) and 18 with work with groups; 9 with families; and 7 with communities. There was some indication that these units are used as preparatory to or concurrent with placements, and assume that students should be able to work with groups of varying sizes and types, as well as individuals. There are discrete bodies of literature in relation to each of these fields. Such units sometimes provided an alternative to division of students on pathway lines, through a 'small group' forum where participation and peer learning could be maximised.

Other units mentioned included management (5), information technology (4), and child observation (2). The inclusion of management as a skills-based course partly reflects a tradition on CSS courses to cater for staff already in management posts, for example as heads of homes or day care units. Such modules might be expected to increase in relation to the 'care managers' and other posts where budgetary skills, 'people management' (staff, volunteers), and quality assurance are a requirement.

The relative lack of information technology skills teaching (despite its inclusion in CCETSW Paper 30, 1991) is of concern, though it may be offered in other units, for example 'research'. Apart from Glastonbury's work on computers in social work (1985, 1993), articles have appeared about teaching information technology skills (Bilson, 1993; Bates, 1995). Schwieso and Pettit (1995) confirmed the low priority given to this area and Rafferty (1997) has argued for increased education about, and use of, information and communication technologies (ICT).

The lack of (child) observation skills development is surprising, given some encouragement by CCETSW to (re-)introduce this following the Beckford Inquiry (Blom Cooper, 1985). It may be an aspect addressed by some courses in the placement context, as suggested by Tanner and La Riche (1995). There is a small amount of literature relating to child observation (Wilson, 1992; Baldwin, 1994), but Tanner and La Riche (1995) suggest that observation skills should also be developed with other groups and across a range of work settings.

Disciplinary Perspectives

The relationship of social work to the 'parent disciplines' of psychology, sociology, social policy and law has been mentioned; and there is evidence of continuing, discrete teaching in these subjects. Social policy could be identified in 33 curricula, psychology in 30 and sociology in 18, while a further 21 programmes have units with titles indicating integrated teaching about 'the personal and the political' or 'the individual and society' or 'life cycle and structural perspectives'.

Timms identified Paper 30's reference to 'the applied social sciences' but pointed out that their contribution would be weakened through a requirement that 'they be assessed in the mode of "know how" [rather than] "know that"' (1991, p.208). Jones suggested that 'Since 1975 CCETSW has made it clear that the contribution of the social sciences to the social work enterprise is both to be limited and controlled' (1996a, p.206), and elsewhere he referred to the 'stripping out' of social sciences from the curriculum in the most recent Review (Jones, 1996c). While the above figures do not support such a contention, it was unclear how the units might have informed the understanding or values of students. There is evidence (including the development and content of top-up or degree programmes) to suggest dissatisfaction by social work educators with the level or amount of social science teaching possible within a two year programme.

Finally, most programmes (42) demonstrate a discrete approach to the teaching of legal studies, or social work and the law, or the legal context, sometimes with explicit mention of a (sub-)unit on welfare rights.

Pathways

It was clear from the data that programme designers in the early 1990s were substantially influenced by organisational service delivery to particular client groups and by the needs of students in relation to prospective employment. This demonstrates a conjunction of the leanings (based on previous experience) of academic staff, the voice of the employer in curriculum design, and responsiveness to student demand. Thus, despite CCETSW's original view that APPs could be based on a method, approach, or setting (that is, did not have to relate to client groups), only a very small minority of programmes had such examples. These were community social work or work with community groups (3), residential care (12) (but nearly all specifically concerned with residential child care and the CCETSW initiative in this field), and the voluntary sector (1).

In 1994, all programmes surveyed had at least two pathways, one of which was 'Work with Children and Families' (or variations of such a title). In the majority of cases (48) the second was 'Community Care', sometimes called 'Adult Services' (which does actually cover users with a range of problems or conditions in many cases). Over half the programmes offered a third pathway of which the most likely title was 'Work with Offenders' (or Probation or Criminal Justice) (29), including one programme which offered forensic social work. As mentioned, a JUC SWEC working group worked with other groups and lobbied in an attempt to retain this pathway within social work education. The issue has also received attention in the social work literature, from both a policy perspective and a curriculum or pedagogical one (Williams, 1996; Eadie and Ward, 1995).

This group of programmes, where up to one third of an intake would be pursuing a pathway aimed at work in a setting/agency which now may neither offer placements nor require recruits to be qualified social workers, illustrates the vulnerability of social work education, if it develops too close a 'fit' with current organisational arrangements/employer requirements. The possibility of 'erasure', although raised by Pietroni (1995) in relation to community care developments, is also applicable in the criminal justice field.

Other specific fields for which pathways prepare students are 'Mental Health' (13), 'Ageing' (sometimes linked with disability) (8), Palliative Care (2), and work with people with learning disabilities (5) or addictions (1) or sensory loss (1). It is in the field of Mental Health work that literature relating to user participation is particularly in evidence, including reference to the educational role of people with experience of the 'client status' (Ramon and Sayce, 1993).

The pressure to include ever more 'subjects' as discrete areas of teaching is apparent, for instance in a survey which suggested that most students were only minimally prepared for work in relation to drugs and alcohol. The author saw this as constituting an increasing problem which cuts across most client group-based teaching (Harrison, 1990), but there was no evidence from this research to suggest an increase in this teaching on DipSW programmes.

Following the CCETSW revision of Paper 30, from 1995 it became possible to offer a generic instead of a particular pathway, and by 1996, 17 programmes had signalled their intention to do so alongside one or two other pathways. Possibly this decision was related to problems about securing appropriate placements, rather than a CCETSW commitment to genericism as opposed to specialisation (a term studiously avoided in Paper 30). But there have been debates about the extent to which a two year programme can equip students for a particular area of practice; the expectations of developments in the induction, post-qualifying and advanced stages of training; the extent to which early concentration may limit subsequent career choices; and the changing contexts within which students may seek employment.

Additionally, the above list of pathways does not apparently prepare students for established but minority posts or for employment in 'new' settings or with 'new' areas of need. Thus, for instance, social work in health care is barely represented in the curriculum of most programmes although it has a long established, albeit tenuous, place in hospitals, and is gaining a foothold in fund-holding general practices. Much more recently, the issue of genetics has come onto the public agenda, prompting a survey about the teaching of genetics in the context of social work education (Iredale and Cleverly, 1998): this area of teaching did not feature at all in the mid-1990s survey data. Finally, the word 'refugees' barely figured in most of the material examined. Burgess and Reynolds (1995) addressed this and also demonstrated a way of including changing concerns within a different curricular and pedagogical framework.

Other Elements

However, social work in health settings or with refugees was evident in a final group of units offered on about half the programmes, which can only be described as 'miscellaneous'. The most frequently cited unit in this category was 'research' (31 mentions). It did not seem appropriate to categorise this as core social work knowledge or skills, or a contributory discipline, given the wide range of meanings attached to this term. In some cases it was offered as a first level unit and was concerned with establishing study skills and introducing students to methods of enquiry. At another level it was concerned with research appreciation, while only in the final year of a few degree programmes or on post-graduate courses did it aim to explore research design and methodology relevant to students carrying out a small research project.

Another unit evident in over one third of the programme documents was 'working in organisations' or the 'organisational context of social work'. It was often not clear how far such units emphasised a theoretical basis for analysis of agency contexts or the development of skills required for work in particular types of organisation.

Eight programmes included a unit entitled *professional development* (or similar) which aimed to assist students in relating college-based teaching to practice issues, or in integrating 'the personal' (including values) with professional and academic development. There was some indication that such units are concerned with process rather than prescribed content and that they may be substitutes for earlier models of tutorial work.

Only one programme in this sample offered a unit in *interprofessional studies*. There seemed to be a lack of attention in the curriculum to 'working with others' (who may share concerns but have different perspectives and remits), despite frequent critical reference to this deficiency in social work practice, highlighted for instance in reviews of child abuse and community care 'scandals'. Such concerns might be addressed in units about health, disability or addictions offered to all students on five programmes; or in units about deviance/criminology (3) or poverty (1). The apparent lack of discrete teaching about poverty in social work education is disturbing given its recent increase and centrality in the lives of many service users (JFR Inquiry Group, 1995) and this has received only limited attention in the literature about social work education (Jones, 1995).

Finally, there was very little evidence of comparative perspectives through discrete units on European or international social work, only mentioned by four programmes. However, nineteen respondents reported involvement in ERASMUS programmes in 1994, including sending students abroad on placement, and four claimed other international links e.g. the TEMPUS programme. It is clear that ERASMUS programmes were not an integral feature of most DipSW programmes, though as a later survey noted, the scheme may have influenced mainstream teaching in less obvious ways on the estimated 20 per cent of courses which participated (Lyons, 1996).

Pedagogical Issues

An assumption predating this research is that one of the reasons for the vulnerability of social work within higher education derives from the relatively labour intensive teaching methods used. This has also been an issue in the 'banding' of social work (see Chapter 8). Some impressionistic evidence and literature (Coulshead, 1992) suggested that the area was under considerable pressure to use the change to DipSW to address this. Therefore, a direct question was asked in the survey about teaching methods, and followed up in the interviews.

Over two thirds of the survey respondents (43) said that they had introduced some pedagogical changes with the implementation of DipSW, aimed at more efficient use of staff time. The extent to which this was expedient, or consistent with traditional methods and assumptions, or with literature about how adults learn, or the nature of professional education, was not explored at the survey stage. Respondents were additionally asked to estimate time-tabled time which students would spend in lectures, seminars, projects (normally group activities), skills workshops or other types of activity.

Nearly a third of respondents (18) failed to provide a usable response, eight people expressing the time in 'blocks' which the researcher could not translate, and ten others saying that it was impossible or very difficult to calculate (for example because a range of methods was used within each unit) or that it would take too much time to calculate, or simply not answering. One of these responses came from a programme which had switched exclusively to 'Enquiry and Action Learning' (EAL, which eschews traditional divisions in the curriculum and timetable) with the agreement of their institution (Parsloe, 1996). Some of the other responses would have been a source of concern or irritation to HEI managers, or perhaps would have confirmed perceptions of social work educators as innumerate, or ignoring current realities. They would certainly not help educators win any arguments about the level of resourcing needed.

Of the remaining 46, nearly half (20) estimated that the curriculum was delivered through lectures for between 20 and 39 per cent of the time, with the same amount of time being spent in seminars in a higher number of cases (29). Only 11 respondents estimated that less than 20 per cent of the time was spent in lectures, while 13 estimated that it was 40 per cent or more (with similar proportions but lower numbers in relation to seminars). The highest proportions of time spent in lectures occurred on MA programmes in the old university sector, or on very large courses in the new university sector. About half (of the 46) estimated that less than 20 per cent of the students' time would be spent in projects and skills workshops (24 and 22 respectively) while slightly fewer said that this would account for 20-39 per cent of the time (20 and 18), with very few examples of more time being spent on these activities.

In response to other types of activity, 11 people mentioned tutorial work as accounting for up to 20 per cent of the students' time (it is not clear whether this would have included placement visits or not), while five identified 'experiential groups' as a separate activity and four mentioned independent study. The last form of learning, as opposed to teaching, suggests a number of possibilities; optimistically, that educators have taken seriously the idea of the student as an adult learner who can take responsibility for her/his own learning; but more cynically that, in the drive to resource efficiency, some of the learning is explicitly allocated to the student, and course units must indicate not just 'contact time' but also the time which the average student would need to spend to complete associated work.

CCETSW and post-qualifying consortia expect that proposals for validation of post-qualifying or advanced awards (which are often pursued part-time) should indicate the likely commitment in private study time as well as attendance. These suggest a mechanistic view of the teaching-learning process, since private study may also be guided learning and require the student to complete specified reading, exercises and tasks. It is clearly a response to the increasing pressures on academics and HEIs, and to a culture which requires students to achieve demonstrable goals and targets which can be described (for example in transcripts) and are readily marketable to employers.

A further question about the 'content' of the subject area, as demonstrated in its curricula and pedagogy, was whether respondents had participated in the Enterprise in Higher Education (EHE) scheme. Forty-three respondents said 'no' and four others failed to answer, but over a quarter (17) had done so, including four departments in the old university sector. The range of work carried out with this additional funding fell into two main types. The first was concerned with promoting 'agency involvement', or practice teacher development, or increasing the supply of placements (9 mentions); while the second was concerned with development of learning or assessment materials, including transcripts, records of achievement, portfolios, learning profiles, workbooks, use of 'competences' *(sic)* and means for approving prior learning (APL) (16 mentions). Most projects included more than one activity.

While EHE funding was undoubtedly timely and appreciated by a number of social work educators, it can also be seen as promoting developments of a particular kind; it 'emphasises operationalism and instrumental learning and increases employer involvement at the cost of professional control' (Taylor, 1996, p.158; Cannan, 1994/1995). It can also be seen as further fragmenting the range of resources to be bid for and then managed by social work educators.

The Relationship Between Content and Form

A number of respondents to the 1996 interviews, when asked about the subject area and about the pedagogical implications, prefaced their answers by consideration of the purpose of social work education. Some of these were reported earlier, but others are more directly relevant here. One respondent said that since 'what is brought to [social workers] is pain, anxiety, uncertainty, despair...the design of qualifying training should work from these [experiences] outwards to theoretical knowledge'. Another suggested that the kind of people who come into social work:

> want to do something practical in relation to [their] ideals. Therefore, education must deal with ideals and values as well as practicalities [but it] can't do things without knowledge and understanding...It's possible [to move from experience to understanding] by organising courses with formal teaching but also a structure which allows personal and interpersonal groups, and a lot of "lab work". The university underestimates this.

This was expressed slightly differently by a third interviewee:

> People coming into social work need to retain their excitement and enthusiasm to right wrongs and help people - and social work education must promote that through intellectual endeavour...[but education] works best when people also have first hand knowledge and the opportunity to integrate theory and practice, so the two must go together.

This view was echoed by a fourth person who also spoke of social work education as:

> trying to help people think on their feet, [and] use evidence based knowledge, not just intuition...[which requires an approach which will] marry experiential with more academic ways of teaching and learning.

The relationship between form and content was succinctly stated by another respondent as 'the medium and the message should be consistent', a view illustrated by the idea that, since the role of the social worker is concerned with developing (individual) potential - or empowering - 'students need to know what that means for them[selves]', in the context of the educational programme. These views are echoed in some of the social work education literature already cited (see for instance, Gould and Taylor, 1996).

Returning briefly to data from programme material, there was frequent reference in these to expectations of high levels of student attendance and participation or to responsibility for their own learning or involvement in active methods. Underlying these statements and the views expressed by the interviewees are assumptions about students as adult learners with important experience (of both a personal and practical nature) to contribute to the learning process. This is partly related to recruitment policies and practice (usually of non-standard entrants, often with prior experience) but also has its roots in literature, particularly in the education field a decade earlier, sometimes referred to as andragogy as distinct from pedagogy.

Knowles (1972) identified the difference as the increase in experiential techniques used with adult learners, both to draw on their experience and to involve them in its analysis. A number of British academics have since discussed the implications of this approach for social work education (Harris *et al.*, 1985; Gardiner, 1988; Henderson, 1994), and it has been explicitly related to the reflective practitioner concept (Gould and Taylor, 1996). Noting that social work education could not be about the 'didactic delivery of knowledge into empty vessels', one interviewee said that students had to take responsibility for their own learning 'within a defined framework...[and with] assessment landmarks in relation to legal knowledge, the application of social science knowledge and methods of intervention'.

Another interviewee advocated educational methods based on students 'finding out and understanding what they are doing and why, and [assisting them in] integrating the internal and external worlds'. However, a third respondent suggested that, while 'self directed learning should be at the core of social work pedagogy...[this had] been abused and reduced to "just sharing" and not helping students get beyond what they bring', another indication perhaps that social work educators themselves may have played a part in the current crisis.

Interviewees were not asked specifically for their ideas about curriculum content, but a number made reference to the contribution of particular subjects. One respondent said:

> There has been some attempt to make greater coherence (*sic*) of three different traditions, sociology, psychology and social policy...social work is beginning to think about interdisciplinary study...the antipathy between different traditions gets played out in social work education but they could be brought into healthy tension.

He advocated a curriculum built around the notion of psycho-social studies:

> because social workers are constantly crossing personal and political boundaries, so social work is caught [in] attempting to reconcile polarities.

Another respondent suggested that:

...the intellectual area comprises a discourse between a reflexive, therapeutic view of the world [where the goal is personal fulfilment]; a collectivist view of the world [where the goal is development of society]; and a reformist view [in which the goal is delivery of effective services within a state system of welfare].

Most respondents made some reference to the status or influence of particular disciplines within the curriculum. For instance, sociology was described as 'critical, self confidently theoretical', but there was some concern that its influence had declined with, for example, the loss from most curricula of community work as an approach. However, it has also been suggested that some of the thinking in the area of anti-discrimination and difference draws on sociological work and that a theoretically informed value base would demonstrate an appropriate 'use' of social science in social work education (Jones, 1996b).

Psychology was noted as being 'rooted in positivist traditions', and at variance with an increasing tendency in social work education to favour an interpretative paradigm. There have also been criticisms of the Eurocentric approach of much of the psychology research and literature (Robinson, 1993). However, there is a continuing value placed on psychology teaching, usually social psychology, but including also 'abnormal' psychology, even if this is then a site of tensions in social work courses.

Social policy was described by one respondent as 'empiricist...[and] imbued with corporatist traditions'. This view perhaps fails to acknowledge recent developments in the subject and its critical appreciation of the origins and directions of welfare, and of the role of 'welfare professionals'. It certainly holds a distinctive place in the majority of social work courses. Other subjects mentioned as having a possible contribution included philosophy, politics and economics, and, 'increasingly concepts from business and management'. With the exception of philosophy (very occasionally) and management (more often), these were not identified in the curricula examined.

The subject most in evidence in the surveys and interviewees was law, reflecting the emphasis given in reaction to employer dissatisfaction and public criticism in the 1980s (Blom Cooper, 1985). This resulted in the funding of a special working group (initially the Law and Social Work Research Group and then the Law Improvements Project) and production of literature (Ball *et al.*, 1988; Ball *et al.*, 1991; Preston Shoot, 1993) and more recently, the establishment of a Social Work Law Association. This can also be seen as a response to increased welfare legislation, related to personal social services, and a reflection of social work in the UK as a statutory activity, predominantly concerned with people experiencing poverty. Welfare rights is usually included within law teaching.

One interviewee said that social workers should have 'an understanding of the role of law in society, and...of legal rights and duties...', but, as another commented, 'Social workers need to know how to use the law as a resource and a tool - it's an interpretative matter', concluding that it should 'be taught in a more practice led manner'. Another said that 'thinking legally and being part of the system of law are different, ...[but social workers need to have] an understanding of the role of the law in society...including its relation to social policy and...of legal rights and duties and how these should be enforced'. However, Stevenson (1988) had warned that pre-eminence of law teaching in the social work curriculum could lead to a more technocratic and coercive form of practice, of which there was some evidence in the 1990s (Jones, 1992).

Questions were not asked specifically about the practice element in social work education but four interviewees referred to it: 'social work education might be possible on an intellectual basis only, but most students need well supervised placements'; 'Ideas can inform practice and practice must enliven theory'; and 'It is really important that this activity is integral ...but it must be prepared for, taught and assessed to the same standards as college based modules, as it's a key to subsequent development.' This respondent attributed the increased importance attached to social work placements to the CNAA's recognition of this area for accredited learning, predating more recent emphasis on the value of work-based learning in higher education policy.

However, one interviewee's (sole) comment of 'placements are an appalling drain in terms of staff time and resources. The placement model has virtually broken down' illustrates starkly the tensions around this area of work. Quite apart from issues of quality, agency control, or integration of theory and practice, there is a real challenge to social work (and other forms of professional) education to review the assumptions on which placements are based and the organisational arrangements and resourcing implications inherent in the current model.

Discussions in JUC SWEC meetings have indicated that CCETSW has been reluctant to reduce its requirements in relation to placements. There is also impressionistic evidence that courses have already cut to the minimum (2) the number of placements and days in each (50 and 80 respectively), and by the late 1990s some social work educators were reconsidering provision of qualifying training (or the size of programmes) in the light of placement problems. The professional press periodically report placement crises, but there is little academic literature specifically addressing this concern.

Returning to methods of teaching and learning, only two interviewees mentioned, spontaneously, the place of lectures: 'mass lectures are not too helpful although they have their place occasionally', while another said that in his department staff make relatively more use of lectures 'but with small [seminar] groups and use of case material'. There was rather more comment about tutorial work, a core 'method' in traditional patterns of course delivery and a contentious issue in reduced resourcing. Views ranged widely from adherence to traditional models (which have undergone significant modification since the 1980s in some places), to varying degrees of adaptation to current resource realities, sometimes also justified in pedagogical terms.

Thus, one respondent stated a commitment to a 'traditional model' of individual tutorials on the grounds that 'social work is situated on the boundary between the personal and the professional and the traditional tutorial addresses that...if we can't find some way to allow that process then social work is not just impoverished but placed in jeopardy'. He noted the possibility of group or peer learning as affording a similar opportunity, and admitted that his answer was coloured by his own theoretical orientation and strengths as an educator. Another respondent (manager) spoke of having 'retained the traditional model of social work education including skills workshops...and regular group tutorials and individual tutorials and placement visits by the tutor'.

At the other extreme, the most experienced academic and manager suggested that the traditional model promoted 'a 'mother hen' approach to social work education and had moved to the idea that people learn better in groups, with tutor 'support' 'reduced to a minimum'. Counselling or study skills, which tutors may previously have provided, should be obtained elsewhere if necessary. In support, another interviewee remarked that 'the demise of the traditional one-to-one tutorial may be no bad thing. It was very idiosyncratic and dependant on the quality of the teacher'.

Other responses suggested a range of compromises. One respondent acknowledged that the:

> personal consequences of difficult social work may require tutorial work or [help] from other sources, [while the] serious business of question and debate with oneself about practice and integrating knowledge can be better

done in pairs and groups, [facilitated] by tutorial support and a planned programme.

Others spoke of a reduced frequency of tutorial contact, 'but these need to be maintained as an opportunity to digest and integrate material [with] small group tutorials [being] probably OK for most'; and patterns of tutorial provision geared to different stages of the programme with more emphasis on group than individual tutorials. But one interviewee noted, 'the actual hours allocated is probably half of what it was ten years ago'.

There was general agreement about the need for small group work alongside more conventional pedagogic methods, and a recognition that 'these place real pressure on teaching and learning strategies'. This area has received little attention in the literature, but Coulshead suggested that tutorials counteract 'adult learning philosophies by encouraging dependence' and detract from the educator's other duty 'towards research and knowledge building' (1992, p.12).

One exception to the general adherence to a 'conventional curriculum' and 'mixed modes of delivery' revealed by the data was the move to wholesale adoption of 'problem based' or 'enquiry and action learning' (EAL). This was first developed at Bristol University in post-graduate level qualifying training and there are various accounts in the literature (Burgess, 1992; Burgess and Jackson, 1994; Taylor, 1996). It has since been introduced at the University of North London (autumn 1996) with a much bigger student group, pursuing qualifications at different levels, and is the subject of a monitoring and evaluation project.

Interviewees were asked specifically about 'enquiry and action learning' in 1996. Only one respondent was committed to 'a group-based, self directed programme' which characterises EAL, stating that it is 'based on a properly researched study into how people learn, [and that] it engages people and prepares them for life long learning'. Other respondents showed varying levels of interest in the idea. One questioned whether it was 'resource saving' (advocates say it was not a response to resource pressures), but thought that it was effective and was using it 'in a watered down version'. Another was 'favourably disposed...it emphasises the active role of the learner and his autonomy and capacity to link enquiry with processes of change'; but had not had experience of implementing it.

Other interviewees, except one, seemed to have introduced it in particular aspects of a programme; 'each module has student directed learning associated with it including some tasks, often in groups'; 'it is the principle used in project-based small work groups'. One respondent suggested that it had not been adopted 'wholesale' due to student anxieties and wanting 'more input', although again its exponents suggest it can be successful with students of a wide ability range. This may show the level of nerve, commitment or desperation motivating academic staff to introduce new methods (including the need to convince institutional managers and CCETSW) and security and satisfaction of using familiar and publicly accepted approaches is sacrificed. Social work educators have pioneered changes in various ways at institutional level, but it can be a high risk strategy for a subject area which is marginal, particularly if not supported by research evidence or wider changes in policy and perception.

Conclusion

This chapter has examined the 'content' of the area, as indicated in data about curricula and the teaching and learning methods used in course delivery. It has also considered the relationship between the social sciences and professional education and also that between purpose, content and pedagogical approaches. The findings do not suggest a wholesale rejection of social science as a legitimate and necessary part of social work education, though questions remain about how knowledge from this area is mediated through course design and delivery and adapted by students to inform their practice.

Findings also suggest some conformity in the models, methods and skills-based core of social work teaching, with little indication of theoretical developments, although there is evidence of research into the relationship between knowledge acquired in college and its use in practice. The research did not set out to inquire into the practice component of social work education (this constitutes 50 per cent of the students' learning experience and is often the part most appreciated by students themselves), and consequently discussion relating to this area is mainly about placements as a resource issue (see Chapter 9).

Responses about teaching suggest a move to more resource efficient methods, although there remains a strong commitment to the use of small groups, not least to address issues of process, important in the development of professional skills and practice. Traditional views of tutorial work have largely been supplanted by an educational rather than a therapeutic approach, and tutorials are now more likely to be in groups rather than individual. The role of the tutor in supporting placements was not explored and is an open question in terms of the models which currently operate or might be developed.

While some of the recent changes in curriculum or pedagogy might be attributed to external requirements or HEI resourcing pressures, some seem more rooted in the experience and values of educators themselves, including a widespread view of students as adult, and active, learners. There is some evidence that social work educators seek a research justification for approaches to teaching and learning; also of innovation in this field; as well as increased congruence between social work learning goals and methods, relative to the wider academic community. These may constitute strengths, or diminish the 'difference' sometimes attributed to the subject area, which can feed into its marginal position in higher education.

7   Research Issues in Social Work Education

Introduction

The extent to which social work has a body of research-based knowledge, and the role of social work educators in generating such knowledge, has been questioned. Social work educators responsibility could be three-fold; firstly, in undertaking research; secondly, in ensuring research informs their teaching and the wider enterprise of professional development; and thirdly, in teaching about research. To some extent the last of these has been addressed in the findings about curriculum and pedagogy. From the survey data it was apparent that there are divergent views about the need for research teaching, or about the priority to be given relative to other subjects in the curriculum.

This chapter explores how far social work educators are themselves involved in research, the priority which they give to this area, and the issues raised by its pursuance. There are also questions about how people who identify with social work might influence both the agenda and the conduct of research, with implications for the profession itself. While much of the literature in British social work journals is based on research, there has been relatively little material about the *place* of research.

Concern about this area flows from the poor showing and marginally improved positions of social work as a subject area in the 1992 and 1996 Research Assessment Exercises, (hereafter RAE) with implications for funding and status of the area, as well as its viability in individual institutions. A report to a JUC SWEC meeting (1/97) by two members of the Social Policy and Social Work Panel, noted that there were encouraging differences between the submissions to the two exercises. In 1992, social work as a subject area found itself ranked 68th in a league table of 72 subjects. By 1996 this ranking had improved to 57th out of 69 subjects (Lyons and Orme, 1998).

Some of the weaker institutions from the 1992 exercise did not submit again. There were some stronger submissions from new entrants to the 1996 exercise, and panel members noted that some departments with established research activities showed considerable improvement in the standard of submissions. In 1992, only 6 per cent of social work submissions were given the maximum ratings of a 4 or 5, while in 1996 this number had increased to 18 per cent (graded 4) and 15 per cent (graded 5).

Findings From the Survey

The survey questions related, in part, back to the 1992 RAE, which undoubtedly provided a stimulus to the subject area. Excluding four non-respondents, about one third of the departments or subject areas (21) had not participated in the 1992 RAE and slightly more (25) did not at that stage have a strategy regarding their participation in the next one.

Of respondents participating, numbers were fairly evenly divided between whether the subject area made an individual submission (18) or was part of a combined submission (20). In the case of the latter, respondents were subdivided between joint submissions with social policy (10) or with other subjects (sociology (4), health (2) and four respondents put 'social science'). Only thirty-one (of the 38) gave their research rating, with the majority (13) achieving a Three, ten a Two and only five attaining the highest rating (Five).

The decision about whether or not a subject area participated, and if so whether independently, seemed to be related to the size of the area (in staff terms) and the proportion of *active researchers* in a staff group. There were fourteen non-responses to a question about the number of active researchers on the staff, but other responses ranged between all (7) and none (9), with twenty-two respondents claiming two to five active researchers and eight claiming six or more. The report to JUC SWEC (1/97) concerning the 1996 RAE suggested that a department (subject area) would need a 'critical mass' of probably at least six active researchers on which to base a submission and that the overall number of people engaged in research (including assistants and researchers) would be an indicator of the existence of a research culture.

Predictably perhaps, both a higher number and proportion of research active staff were to be found in the old university sector. This was also true of *research fellows, research assistants and research students* of whom more than a third of respondents had none in the social work subject area (35, 28 and 25 respectively). Nine institutions had one research fellow, while six had two or more; seven had one research assistant while fourteen had two or more; and twelve institutions had less than four research students while ten had four or more (including five universities with ten or more).

It seems likely that the more people involved in the research enterprise, in whatever capacity, the stronger the position of individual departments (or subject areas) in attracting funding; new staff committed to developing research, or with established, research records; and research-oriented students. However, research participation and quality are clearly not a function of size alone. Other factors include the value placed on research by the host institution, and other indications of a research culture operating at the departmental or faculty level to encourage, legitimate or require research activity. There may also be dangers from a strong emphasis on research in a field such as social work, such as 'academisation' of the professional education programmes, and a research agenda determined solely by academic interests or availability of funding.

A question about the *funding* of research indicated that thirty-five respondents derived at least some of their funding from external sources. Amounts and sources of such funding varied considerably, from one respondent whose departmental research budget exceeded £5 million to three each giving figures in the region of £500,000 and £100,000 respectively. Other respondents gave figures of substantially less than £100,000 or no figures.

Sources of funding included central government departments (Education, Health and Home Office) (9); local agencies (8); 'charities' (Nuffield, Rowntree, Mental Health Foundation) (5); CCETSW (4); ESRC (4); and the European Union or United Nations (3). There is some concern about the low number of ESRC awards because the ESRC does not categorise social work as a separate subject area. Thus, applications are made under other subject headings and assessed accordingly.

An alternative way of classifying the scale of the enterprise suggests that of the thirty-five respondents (about external funding), nine had only small scale research activity (defined as only one project or locally based, low budget projects) while in seventeen institutions it was clearly an activity with quite a high profile (having a budget of more than £100,000, and/or a range of research projects in progress). In 10 cases the scale of the enterprise could not be deduced from the information available.

Finally, one question was asked about collaborative research and another about consultancy activities in the work of staff teams. Out of fifty-nine respondents to the first question, between approximately one third and two thirds of respondents reported collaborative research with colleagues as follows; outside the UK (22); in social work education elsewhere in the UK (24); in other disciplines (27); and in agencies (41). The high number collaborating with agencies seems to confirm a leaning towards the professional field and a degree of community involvement evident in some of the other research data.

Additionally, fifty-eight of these respondents said that staff were involved in consultancy and training activities outside the department/HEI, (although a sub-question suggested that eight respondents did not know how many staff might be so involved). Seven respondents thought that all or most staff would undertake this type of activity while the majority (21) thought that between three and five staff would be active in consultancy work. Questions remain about the scale and nature of this activity, and whether there has been any change during the 1990s, relative, for instance, to mainstream research.

A question was also asked about the availability and use of sabbatical time. In 1994, thirty-six respondents said that it was possible for staff to get paid sabbatical leave and twenty-one thought that this would be primarily for the purposes of undertaking/completing research, although ten thought it might be used for this purpose or to enable time to be spent updating practice.

The Place of Research in Social Work Education: Interviewees' Perceptions

Interviews took place shortly after respondents had submitted returns in connection with the 1996 research assessment exercise, and although rarely referred to directly, this is likely to have had some bearing on responses. Given the non-specific wording of this interview question it was hardly surprising that it was variously answered, relating both to research in the curriculum and research as an activity of social work educators.

Opinions varied as to the appropriateness or possibility of including *research in the curriculum*. One respondent said:

> it is very important for students to understand that knowledge comes from research as well as practice...[and] to get them into the habit of going to books and articles for knowledge when they need it. [But in relation to research methods] there is not time for students to learn them in two years and even at postgraduate level research exercises should be realistic in

scale...[although] they can do important pilot studies... It is more important for qualifying students to understand research appreciation.

Another interviewee claimed:

> All students, at whatever level, should have an understanding of critical social enquiry but demands are different [at different levels, so at non-graduate level, it is important] to read about, understand and value others' research [while] at post-graduate level they should have the capacity to carry out at least a single case design [project] and ability to critically analyse policies and their own work.

This theme, that research appreciation is important for non-graduate students but that a research-based component would be a requirement on a qualifying course at post-graduate level, was echoed by the majority of respondents, only two of whom did not comment on this aspect of the research issue. It is addressed in the literature slightly differently, as concerns about the content - paradigms and methods - appropriate to social work research.

Ironically, in redesigning a three year degree programme to include a DipSW rather than a CQSW, one respondent had substituted a practice study for a research-based dissertation 'to meet the requirements of a competency-based approach', changing the research element to one more concerned with appreciation. Another person commented that 'undertaking research as part of the placement would be problematic [since] practice skills take precedence'. In the former case, lack of research training at degree level would be compensated for by provision of a new masters degree (as an advanced award) with strong research methods and social work evaluation units, available to a minority of locally based workers.

Another respondent noted the improved opportunities for addressing research needs in the top-up degree year and the confidence derived from an individual project in which research issues are experienced first hand. 'Social work authority should come in part from research, not just from the agency base and statutory role of the worker'. Courses leading to *advanced awards* in promoting research skills were discussed by Youll and Walker (1995); and Bond and Jones (1995) described a one year project aimed at enabling the dissemination of research findings by practitioner researchers. Both discussions noted the costs of such training, and emerging evidence about opportunities for learning about research as part of post-qualifying or advanced awards is contradictory.

Three respondents saw a more integral relationship between research and professional development - 'good social work practice involves investigative and assessment skills, collecting data, weighing it up, drawing conclusions. It may not be academic research but research skills are an essential part of the social work repertoire'; and 'To practice social work is to engage in a form of research. They are so closely related we shouldn't think of them without each other'. This was echoed by someone involved with post-graduate level training, 'Good research skills are very relevant and very close to the practice of social work, including being critical of ones own methods'.

Schon's view of the reflective practitioner is someone who 'becomes a researcher in the practice context' (Schon, 1983, p.164). This has been applied to social work by Shepherd (1995), and Powell, 'Many of the skills involved in the collection of qualitative data can be developed through a reframing of many practice skills used by social workers on a day to day basis' (Powell, 1996, p.170).

With regard to the *research activities of staff*, there were some variations, but strong assertion that this is a responsibility of all educators and should not be split off from the teaching role. 'There is inestimable value in social work teachers being engaged in research and being able to bring that back into their teaching'; and 'you can't be a higher education lecturer unless you're testing yourself out against the profession and the knowledge base, so some form of enquiry and research is essential and it needs to be published'; or 'it's a contractual requirement that [academic staff] undertake research, though it is not necessarily funded'; or that '[social work] education needs to be informed and stimulated by doing research. If social work teachers are to be effective they need to do research themselves'; or 'It goes with the reasons for thinking that social work education should stay in higher education. We expect all staff to be active researchers - it is far more exciting to be taught by people doing research, talking about their own work, sharing their findings...'.

These views accord with those evident in the HEFC subject area review (1994/1995) where attention was paid in the evaluation of individual teaching to the citing of research and use of the teacher's own research experience. Universities with strong research reputations were graded 'excellent' in the subject review (though there were exceptions). Some respondents were less optimistic about research possibilities:

> There are pressures to do it but it's difficult to release staff to do it. We have managed to get a research assistant for one year with money from income

generation... Staff undertake personal interest based research. It's very small scale with a limited amount of local authority funding [£5,000 to £10,000]

or

There has to be a place for research in social work education, though we haven't been very good at it because of resourcing problems and the structuring of the academic year. You need clear time in which to carry out or write up research... There is a danger that only some people do research while others teach, that is a fragmentation of the role. There is an observable relationship between academic seniority and research, and a decrease in the teaching load.

Both these respondents from the new university sector indicated common concerns about resourcing, and the likelihood of tensions when the university overall may have a less strong tradition of research, and choose primarily a teaching mission.

Comments also related to tutorial work and placement visiting expectations placed on social work educators. The effects of a poor research profile in the research assessment exercise were also touched on:

Current rumours about the centres of excellence suggest that the situation could get worse. There are already practical problems about trying to carve out time for research and some departments are starting from a long way back. Is it worth keeping on trying? But the loss to staff and students would be enormous if [this university] became a teaching-only institution.

This echoed a wider concern among social work educators, subsequently taken up by JUC SWEC.

The interviewees' responses also revealed other motivations and concerns. One relates to the relative scarcity of social work educators holding doctorates. A subsequent survey (1998) by the Association of University Professors in Social Work (AUPSW) suggested that only 30 per cent of professors also hold doctorates. In 1996, two respondents made unsolicited points about this matter. 'I am currently discouraging staff from doing PhDs because it's really important to get ideas into the public domain...and the PhD detracts from time available for other forms of research [though the new approach by publication may make this more feasible]'. Another respondent said, 'The RAE sets the context for current research initiatives. You can't submit a PhD thesis so it's more important to write for publication. A PhD may form the basis for a significant publication, but a lot of research is *not* significant. But [nevertheless] it should contribute to our understanding and reflect the passions of the staff'.

Both these academics were managing social work departments (one with a PhD and one without, but both active researchers and writers themselves), one in an old university and one in the new sector. One specifically stated that research is 'important for the credibility of the academy'. These responses suggest that a dominant concern is with the status of the subject or, more parochially, the performance and reputation of particular departments (as encouraged by the RAE). It is likely, however, that there are individualistic motivations, as noted by Hardy (1941) who considered that the 'dominant incentives to research [are] intellectual curiosity, professional pride, and...desire for reputation' (cited in Becher, 1989, p.53). It would be naive to suppose that these are not also motivating factors for social work educators, and there will be more discussion about the relationship between career development, credentials, external influences and image in the next chapter.

Another motivation was that social workers and educators need to be researching the field *themselves*. 'People who are not trained as social workers but who research it may not tune in to the heart of it...so a research component is necessary to help social work understand itself better.' This was also related to the purpose and funding of research. Commenting on Department of Health funded research in the child protection field, one suggested that:

> it has been barking up the wrong tree...there is a radical shift taking place now that will completely alter our ideas about the work commissioned over the last twenty years and will endorse a concept of localism in child protection...a standardised corporatist model doesn't fit.

These suggest concerns about social workers/educators' influence on the research agenda and interpretation of findings. The researcher has a role 'not just in unveiling the facts but in constructing them' (Ravn, 1991, p.112). However, Becher (1989) also identified the susceptibility of the research agenda (of soft applied fields) to dictation by non-academic interests and cited Kogan and Henkle's view (1983) that the government promotes investigation of 'useful' topics (Becher, 1989, p.147).

The research agenda for social work was mentioned in passing by one interviewee who described social work as a 'research-rich field because it's so fast changing. The problems of practice - relationships, poverty, inequality - need to be more research informed'. However, a possible agenda has been suggested elsewhere (Statham, 1996), and is of concern to a recently re-established sub-committee of JUC SWEC.

Another concern of interviewees was that social work educators should promote methods and approaches compatible with the overall goals of social work (social justice and empowerment). This includes a wish to work collaboratively with the usual 'subjects' and users of research. One respondent thought it important to 'involve practitioners and users in a collaborative form of research, not just have an academic, selfish concern to publish...users and agencies must state their own needs'; and another emphasised the value of 'interactive forms of research, where people are participants in the research process, rather than objects'. Another described a particular model of 'partnership research', 'that is, a joint group sets the policy and the objectives and academic staff carry out the research, but through attachment to the agency...it works well, bringing out the implications for the agency of the research'; while a fourth said, 'I am interested in broadly based research and in alliances with users'.

In relation to the last point, Powell (1996, p.169) noted that, while the model 'of the researcher as actively engaged in the participatory process' is well established in the education field, it is less well developed in social work. The issue of involving users in research is represented in the literature in the work of Beresford and associates (for example, Beresford and Croft, 1986; Beresford and Trevillion, 1995), and the role of social workers as practitioner-researchers has also been addressed to some extent, including an early publication sponsored by CCETSW.

A few respondents said more about the *research paradigms* which might be appropriate, including 'the case study approach and feminist or social consultancy approaches'; or 'social work perspectives lend themselves to qualitative approaches'. These views were reflected more fully in the following statement:

> I don't want to get caught up in the view that social work practice must be "evidence based". The dominant ideology is that research must be functional. The implicit concept of evidence and the relation between knowledge and evidence, and ideology and practice is complex and obscured...A central problem is that social work has never clarified its core intellectual paradigm, so it doesn't have one for research, so different traditions are used. What it adds up to is a self-conscious pluralism...

Another respondent said 'approaches using consumer involvement have a value in social work research, but positivistic approaches also have a place'. This interviewee also suggested that 'if we take the idea of stakeholders seriously, then there are methodological issues about how best to involve users'.

The social work literature shows evidence of positivist traditions, notably in the work of Sheldon (1986), Sinclair (1992) and Macdonald and Sheldon (1998), and it has been suggested that this represents a growing body of empirical research which demonstrates the value of social work (Thyer, 1993). But this has also been criticised by Smith (1987) as inadequate on epistemological grounds and unlikely to prove generally feasible or helpful. It could be argued that the positivist paradigm has caused the ambivalence about, or lack of use of, research by practitioners. Apart from the possible dissonance with their own values, it could also be seen as requiring special technical skills beyond the reach of ordinary practitioners, and is possibly more accessible to other academics.

There may also be a gender dimension in this, and more recent literature makes explicit links between feminist thinking and research approaches (Wise, 1990; Orme, 1994). Powell (1996) clearly sees the appropriateness of research within the interpretive tradition, 'which gives prominence to the plurality of perspectives and understandings, ...[and is] conceived as an enterprise which involves all parties...in the research process' (p.165), but does not discount the value of seeking quantitative material within this approach.

Finally, there were a few comments about sabbaticals and consultancy work, although direct questions were not asked. On reflection this was regrettable as it might have given some indication of any changes between 1994 and 1996, even if only impressionistic. One respondent was clear that 'if staff have sabbatical leave this is expected to result in a publication'. A number of respondents mentioned the responsibility which educators have in 'interpreting research to the field'. One person specifically said that 'feedback to agencies, via workshops and training sessions is important'. This was an academic who had had a strong professional background in the locality, and whose work is respected for both its theoretical quality and its rootedness in 'real world' situations which practitioners, managers and students recognise.

A respondent, pessimistic about the amount of research possible within his institution, pointed out that 'We also undertake some consultancy and training work...including some policy development work', activities which sometimes gave rise to written material, though not necessarily publications. This can be related to Becher's view that 'in the social professions...it is possible to become an eminent academic consultant without having to write a great deal' (Becher, 1989, p.53). By 'write' he presumably meant publish in academic journals, also a concern to social work educators in the context of the RAE.

Respondents did not raise the matter of ethics in relation to research in the field of social work, confirming a view by Gallagher *et al.* (1995) that this is a neglected area. Perhaps this also reflects implicit assumptions about the similarity of ethical concerns between research and social work practice and the need for congruence in this.

The JUC SWEC Data and Outcomes of the 1996 RAE

JUC SWEC minutes and annual reports suggested a fairly consistent interest in research, at least since the mid-1980s and the Research Sub-committee was one of ten such working groups mentioned in annual reports through to 1990. A joint conference with BASW in 1985 resulted from a concern about the dissemination of research findings to practitioners, and this established a pattern for annual events, with a resulting publication, through to 1991. The 1988 conference was noted as having attracted 'more than 100 practitioners' (Annual Report, 1988) and, following the establishment of a steering group (in which JUC SWEC members were well represented), the inaugural meeting of the Social Work Research Association (SWRA) was held at the 1991 Conference. This was to provide a new forum where those doing research and those interested in its use in practice could meet, and JUC SWEC has since maintained a place on its executive committee.

On the political front, a letter from the Chair to the Director of CCETSW about the QDSW (three year) proposals expressed JUC SWEC's concern that papers showed 'no appreciation of the urgent need for practice-related research, to which educationalists are contracted to contribute...[which indicated] an imbalance between commitment to teaching and practice, compared with research'. By this stage some members of JUC SWEC were involved in the UGC Research Selectivity Exercise, and the inclusion of a Social Work Professor on the Panel was welcomed (Annual Report, 1989). However, since this only concerned a minority of the Committee, from the old university sector, and given other preoccupations at this time, it did not merit a high priority in JUC SWEC proceedings. This may have been one factor leading to the formation in

1990 of the Association of University Professors of Social Work, with membership restricted (at that time) to people holding Chairs in the (then) university sector.

In 1992, following the incorporation of the polytechnics into the university sector, this matter became of rather more pressing concern to many of the membership: the Committee was unhappy about the proposed criteria for the exercise and a working party was set up to draft a response, but to limited effect. The outcome of the exercise was disappointing, if not wholly unexpected for the subject area. The subsequent Chair's Annual Report (1993) noted that 'members expressed their concern [that] the model employed...seemed more relevant to subjects other than social work' and the Committee contributed to JUC's response to the Consultation Paper following the exercise.

A more pro-active approach to the 1996 RAE was evident in the 1995 Annual Report which noted that the committee had nominated assessors, suggested topic areas and offered views to the Social Policy and Social Work Panel about its criteria. In a long letter to two members of the Panel (9/95) the Chair had outlined various concerns and queries. She also expressed the view that, while the committee did not wish to 'engage in special pleading', the particular features of the social work educators' role - 'close tutorial support, long terms, the maintenance of field work and agency links, the demands of the national validating body...mean that research and publishing compete for diminishing amounts of available time'. Additionally, one of the Panel's members had been invited to make a presentation at the October meeting of SWEC and, notwithstanding some institutional rivalries, a shared concern was apparent in the debates (formal and informal) of termly meetings in the 1995/1996 period.

Other references to research in the 1990s documents included a reference to the high workloads of social work educators, 'undertaking research and teaching a vocational subject', evidenced by an AUT survey in 1995, apparently supporting the points made in the Chair's letter (but note also that AUT membership was traditionally limited to the old university sector), and a suggestion by the SWEC acting Chair in 1992 that the JUC should hold a combined annual conference. This should meet 'around an inclusive theme' and would address the 'need for a regular and larger scale conference structure in the applied social sciences, highlighted by the RAE'. The acting Chair saw this as an important means of generating theoretical discussion and published papers, and meeting 'a serious gap in the opportunities open to social work educators' to enhance their academic status.

This need has been met, in part, in the annual conferences arranged by the Association of Teachers in Social Work Education (ATSWE), which have recently addressed a number of issues important to social work educators. However, while the content is often of a high standard, these are modest and somewhat 'domestic' events to enable participants to engage across the college/practice boundary, rather than across disciplinary ones, and do not lead to the range of publications which a more ambitious or academic format would entail. Some social work educators present papers at non-social work conferences (for example, the Social Policy Association, the British Sociological Association, the Society for Research in Higher Education) and international social work conferences (following academic norms in the refereeing of proposals and the publication of proceedings). The 1994 meeting of the International Association of Schools of Social Work (IASSW) resulted directly in the publication of edited texts about British social work education (Ford and Hayes, 1996). The reasons for the lack of movement by the JUC on the 1992 suggestion is open to speculation and it was a theme returned to by the ex-Chair from the floor at the 1996 AGM.

Turning now to some further discussion of the outcome of the 1996 RAE, as described in the panel members' report to JUC SWEC (1/97), the criteria used in the grading of submissions were evidence of i) new theory or a publication which carries forward a particular debate and ii) 'user input' to the research process. Although the reading of material suggested that there was more research on policy than on detailed practice, there were particular strengths in research relating to probation and some good quality work in the child care field (including some which was critical of policy in this area despite being funded by government). Research in relation to social work education was described as being quite descriptive and not of a high standard, and 'a lot of the material on anti-discriminatory practice was lacking a theoretical base' (echoing a point made in the previous chapter). There was also a small amount of research related to international or comparative social work, with an emphasis on collaborative research. More formal reflections on the exercise were subsequently published (Cheetham and Deakin, 1997; Fisher, 1999).

The panel Chairs had reported that they had found it 'useful to have a single panel for social policy and social work because there is an overlap at the margins' and, should there be a further exercise, they would recommend the same arrangement (as has since been confirmed). While this indeed seems a logical alliance (for example, on the basis of data about alliances in HEIs) there is the drawback that not all social work subject areas are so aligned, and some social work research in both 1992 and 1996 was included in the submissions to other subject panels (such as sociology). This may be a reasonable institutional strategy in relation to small subject areas with only a few active researchers located in non-social policy departments. Also, sociology overall receives a better rating than social policy or psychology. But it renders invisible the social work research of some institutions, and fails to add to the collective body of social work research identified by the RAE.

This echoes the earlier point about the non-availability of a social work category in the ESRC classification, and both concerns were evident in the establishment of a working group (later a sub-committee) at the January 1997 meeting of JUC SWEC. Its task was to 'to identify and promote the particular nature of the research contribution which social work can make' (Minutes, 1/97). Subsequently, a successful bid to the ESRC for a research seminar series suggests that issues of the social work research agenda, the form (methodology) of social work research and the relationship between research and the development of the discipline can be further addressed in a systematic manner.

Conclusions

It is clear that considerable tensions persist regarding the place of research in social work education. However, there are some indications that it is being given a higher priority, both in relation to curriculum content and as a responsibility of social work educators. Doubt has been expressed about the very limited ability to equip students with research skills in the context of a two year course, although there is evidence of strong support among senior academics for attention at least to research appreciation and utilisation in qualifying programmes. In addition, the expansion noted, of degree level awards in the social work area, suggests a desire to increase the opportunities for some research input, and this is clearly a concern of post-graduate courses.

The question of research paradigms and methods which could most appropriately be taught has not been resolved, but there is increasing confidence in the interpretive paradigm and qualitative methods and there is also some evidence of the inclusion of users (whether practitioners, students or clients) in research design and execution. This may be related, in part, to the growth of 'feminist research' which might sit comfortably, because of the predominance of women in the area and the nature of the subject matter. The similarity in skills used in relation to social work practice and the research process has been noted and the principle of research-informed, if not evidence-based, practice is now widely accepted.

The 1992 RAE had provided a timely warning to the social work academy that, if it is located in HEIs, it is subject to higher education policies and evaluations. Some social work educators themselves had identified the threat to scholarly activity (and thus to the profession's knowledge base) in the changes required in the early 1990s. Indications from the 1996 RAE are of an increase in research-active social work educators. But the real pressures posed in universities to maintain (or develop) a coherent approach to professional education and to progress the research enterprise (including lobbying for funding), remain a significant challenge.

Apart from dilemmas about the focus of the research (and a possible tension between academically interesting or professionally relevant projects), there are methodological and ethical problems associated with researching social work practice and effectiveness, and a continuing need to communicate findings appropriately to students, the professional field and policy makers. Additionally, there is the constant responsibility to critically observe and comment on a fast changing scene in which educators themselves are also actors, but this is not peculiar to social work educators.

8 Identity and Careers of Social Work Educators

Introduction

One of the research questions was about the people who are social work educators and their part in the culture and state of the subject area. To what extent have they roots in professional practice or do they (now) see themselves as 'academics'? How far do their qualifications, titles and job descriptions facilitate the academic role; and does this then militate against credibility with the practice field? What might membership of professional organisations or academic bodies suggest about their priorities and identity? It has been assumed that for most people, social work education is a 'second career' or even a third, relative to social work practice and perhaps a management background. The career pattern is different from that of other academics, with implications for the systems of qualifications, recognition and rewards (Becher, 1989).

If entrants to the academic field are older and have prior experience, this has a bearing on the costs of such personnel. It might also be questioned whether the competing demands of two professions induce a sense of role confusion, or 'role strain' (Richards, 1985, p.26), or 'dual and conflicting role demands' (Collins, 1995, p.18) which inhibits role performance and confidence in one or both arenas. Differences in career patterns, and perhaps qualification levels, may contribute to feelings of marginalisation relative to 'mainstream' academic colleagues, and irrelevance to the field of social work.

With these questions in mind, data was sought from the survey in 1994 and interviewees in 1996. This constituted a fairly homogenous group of people who were nearly all senior academics responsible for departments or subject areas. However, there were differences in size of department or subject area, status of institutions, and individual variations in age and length of time in higher education and particular post. Some of the interviewees were professors of social work, but without managerial responsibilities. Initial findings were shared with a more heterogeneous

129

workshop group at an ATSWE conference (in 1996), producing a small amount of supplementary data. This confirmed the findings and has not been used here, with one exception.

The role, identity and careers of social work educators have not been discussed by JUC SWEC (as recorded in documents), other than in concerns about workloads and threats to the area. Ideas about professional roots and academic identity may be aspects of shared assumptions about the culture, without explicit reference or questioning. However, different levels of loyalty to professional expectations or to academic norms are sometimes apparent in discussions. There is little in the social work literature on this topic, although academic identities have received some attention in wider literature, particularly in recent higher education reforms (Halsey, 1992; Cuthbert, 1996; Henkel, 1997).

A high proportion of those entering social work education as students and then the profession itself are women, and women's role in the development of the occupation and of its education and training fields is significant. Questions arise about how women fare as senior academics in this subject area, and more generally about the relevance of this gender imbalance in perceptions and status of the area. A question was asked in the survey about the gender and race of respondents and the size of staff groups, but additional questions were not asked about the gender or racial composition of the latter.

There is considerable impressionistic evidence that women outnumber men as social work educators, but some suspicion that proportionately more senior posts are held by men. The evidence or otherwise for this and its implications, both for the careers and ambitions of individual women, and for the status of the subject area, are considered. First, biographical data about the survey respondents is described and related to 'identity'. Some additional biographical data about the interviewees is presented in Appendix 4.

Characteristics of Social Work Education Managers

Fifty seven (of the 64 respondents) completed the relevant questionnaire section, giving some biographical data about themselves as heads of departments or having responsibility for the subject area within a larger department. Women slightly outnumbered men (32:25), although this is not representative of the presumed gender imbalance of staff groups, which may be as high as 6:1 (guestimate based on staff lists from 8 institutions).

This can be compared with the gender composition of social work generally. For example, in separate surveys, women constituted 70 per cent of social worker respondents (Lyons *et al.*, 1995, p.177) and nearly 80 per cent of students entering the work force from qualifying courses in 1996 (Wallis-Jones and Lyons, 1997). All the respondents were white and predominantly British: this is significant in a subject area where up to 15 per cent of students may be recruited from ethnic minority groups (Wallis Jones and Lyons, 1997) and where the proportion of black students may average between a third and a half on specific courses (Lyons, 1996).

The majority of respondents (34) were in the age group 40-49 years, the remainder being over 50, with only one person over 60. From information about age and length of time in post it appears that the majority of respondents (28) entered social work education in their thirties, while a substantial number (25) were recruited in their late twenties, and the remainder in their early forties. There is some impressionistic evidence that early retirement (including on health grounds) may have reduced the figures for the older age group. There is very little evidence, with a few known exceptions, that older people had been promoted to more senior posts within the university (that is away from the subject area), or had moved from academic work (back) to the field (including management posts), although some 'leavers' have moved into freelance work (Collins, 1995).

All but two of the respondents had previous experience in social work before entering higher education as lecturers, and thus experienced a career change from direct practice or management to the academic role. There have been very few studies of the role of social work educators, but one carried out in the early 1980s noted the potential 'culture shock' of people moving from practice to academe (Richards, 1985, p.26). Fawcett and Featherstone (1994) reflected particularly on the transition from social work management to social work education and drew some useful comparisons between organisational cultures and their implications for workers. They cite the more individualistic values and behaviour of academics relative to the collaborative, supportive values espoused by social work and experienced in teams. However, some academics (notably in the sciences) have to work closely in project groups (for example to maximise use of expensive equipment) though inter-team rivalry may be intense; and competition, rather than co-operation, is an increasingly common feature of the academic environment as resources have diminished (Henkel, 1997).

Discussing stress in social work educators, Collins (1995) noted the need for this career change to be reflected in the induction and staff development of social work educators (and presumably other late entrants to higher education posts).

Most respondents had built up considerable experience in the higher education sector, exceeding 20 years in fifteen cases and with between 11 and 19 years for the majority (28). A further ten respondents had 6-10 years experience and only seven had less. This suggests substantial academic experience among social work education managers, but a considerable 'distance' from the field (in time terms) for many. This may be relevant to leadership of educational developments and research in a professional area, and could contribute to recurring criticisms of social work education as 'out of touch' (Richards, 1985; Collins, 1995) if not counter-balanced by participation of educators in practice-related activities, including research.

The majority of respondents (27) had only been managers for between 2 and 5 years, though a substantial number (16) had been in post for more than 10 years. Nearly one in five (11) respondents had been in post less than 2 years, which suggests some instability in leadership in the area, during a time of considerable change. A proportion of managers of social work education had experience of management prior to lecturing. But it is likely that career paths of social work educators follow a 'practice - (management) - teaching - (management)' pattern with research slotting in alongside, not the 'research- teaching-(management)' pattern identified by Henkel for bio-chemists (Henkel, 1997, p.8) and more common in other areas of academic life.

The majority of survey respondents (53) held a professional qualification in social work, a teaching force which has clear roots in the professional field. Of four not holding a social work qualification, all held first and masters level degrees and two held additional qualifications (DMS, CertEd). However, in line with non-graduate training in this area, only 36 respondents held a first degree (usually in the social sciences) although 38 held a masters degree (in 13 cases instead of a first degree). The majority (39) held at least three qualifications, usually one professional and two academic awards. While one of the academic qualifications might have been taken part-time, many people teaching social work will have spent a minimum of four or five years as full-time students themselves.

A relatively large number of respondents (32) held other qualifications, notably in teaching (11), law (3), management (4) and psychotherapy (3). While some of these suggest qualifications gained later to enhance professional or career development, some are indicative of career change at an earlier stage. Without fuller details of when qualifications were gained it is not possible to say which applies more often. The range of awards listed by respondents suggests individuals, if not a group, as being keen to enhance their qualifications and academic standing and/or committed to the values of life-long learning. While the former motive might indicate academic insecurities, the latter would signal notions of personal responsibility for professional development explicit in social work.

Less than one in five (11) respondents in 1994 held doctorates, confirming the relatively low level of research-based academic qualifications among this group. Of these, women holders outnumbered men (8:3) and numbers were more evenly divided between the old and new university sector (6:5). This represents a higher proportion in the old university sector (from which only 20 responses were received on this section). Unfortunately, questions were not asked about higher (research) degrees in progress, nor about qualifications of the staff group as a whole, nor about whether respondents themselves held professorships, so it is difficult to draw further conclusions from this data.

In relation to the last point, 17 respondents said that their department/subject area was represented at Association of University Professors in Social Work meetings. Given recent changes in the basis for award of professorships, this does not necessarily signify research excellence. The number of doctorates and professorships identified totals barely half the number of departments represented in this sample. This doubtless contributes to perceptions of an academically weak subject area and points up a further difference in entry to, and career patterns in, higher education. Henkel's paper confirms the 'apprenticeship model of the PhD' (Henkel, 1997, p.5) as the basis for individual academic identity and careers in higher education in a range of disciplines, as previously identified (Toulmin, 1972; Becher, 1989).

Various points confirm the priority given to practice, rather than research, as a prerequisite for entry to an academic post in social work education. Implications for the subsequent development of academic identity and career development are further explored at the interview stage of the study.

All the interviewees (7 men and 4 women, all white) had previous experience in social work and held professional qualifications. Seven had managerial responsibility for a social work section or a department including social work, and all except two principal lecturers in the new university sector were Professors of Social Work (or similar, see also Appendix 4). Nine had been in their current post for less than 3 years, though all had a minimum of 8 years experience in higher education and seven had 16 or more years. Four of the interviewees were based in the old university sector and seven in the new (with some evidence of movement between the two sectors), and all provided academic leadership in the subject area through research and writing and/or activities in professional bodies.

All clearly identified their career change from social work practice or management to academic posts, and sometimes also spoke about changes within the academic role at different stages in their careers. This usually related to a shift in emphasis from teaching to management or research, although all stressed the need to maintain or develop the research role in addition to teaching. For most respondents, careers in higher education did not start from a research base. The 'late flowering' of academics in terms of research and publications, which Becher (1989) noted in the social sciences, is also a characteristic of the social professions.

The management role was not seen as a way out of teaching or research, but as an additional area of responsibility. Some were not choosing management roles or had moved into positions where the management element had shifted from direct responsibility for social work education to a wider brief including research and development work with related professionals (2).

Membership, Representation, Roles and Identity

It was suggested earlier that role confusion might inhibit the development of strong academic identities and careers of social work educators. Two factors are relevant. The first is the extent to which educators feel constrained by one set of requirements and loyalties (to the field of social work) relative to another (academia). Secondly, how far can social work educators resolve the practice/theory tension in the development of educational programmes and their own academic roles and identities. This has been described as the 'emotion/knowledge' dichotomy by Fawcett and Featherstone (1994) who additionally identified 'process versus task' and 'team versus individual' dichotomies in moving from the field to academia.

Identity was explored by seeking information about the bodies which people join, or on which they have a representative role (asked of the survey respondents), and interviewees were asked for self-definitions and information about where they gain professional support and stimulus. It was thus hoped to tease out the extent to which social work educators have taken on an 'academic' persona relative to a 'professional' one. In the survey, questions were about membership and activities of all staff in the subject area or department, while interviewees were asked about themselves.

There was clearly allegiance to activity in the professional field alongside academic roles, as all but eight respondents to the survey said that one or more staff were involved in direct social work practice or management outside the institution. Of the interviewees, three also described themselves as having (some limited) current involvement with the professional field, one through direct practice, and two through membership of management committees and policy work. Two others indicated engagement through feedback of research, training or consultancy activities.

Responses about membership and representation suggested a continuing strong link with professional social work bodies. The majority of survey respondents (54) said that members of staff belonged to BASW, and five of the interviewees were BASW members, although two others had recently resigned. Membership of NAPO by staff was claimed by 28 survey respondents, and 18 listed other professional organisations to which staff belonged (for example SCA, ABPO, BAC). Fifty-one respondents indicated an involvement in regional post-qualifying consortia, confirming the high level of 'partnership' activity outside HEIs suggested previously.

In answer to an open question about 'any other forms of professional activity or representation', the majority of responses (20 relative to 9) suggested participation in 'social work' rather than 'scholarly activities'. These included membership of CCETSW and BASW committees, of the Mental Health Commission, of Adoption Committees, and of the managing bodies of local and national agencies. It is not suggested that any of the foregoing are inappropriate activities for social work educators or that they might not give rise to research or writing (and experience gained would inform teaching). But they all suggest an orientation, time commitment and search for recognition outside the university which is substantially different from that of other academics.

In relation to membership or representation on overtly 'academic' bodies, 33 respondents thought that staff were associated with research organisations, particularly the Social Work Research Association (17) and Social Services Research Group (13), although there were also a few mentions of the Society for Research in Higher Education (3) and the ESRC (1). Membership in this field was only mentioned by one of the interviewees, but they were not prompted by a list of possible organisations as the survey respondents had been. About half of the departments/areas (33) were represented at the JUC SWEC and over one third (24) on the Standing Conference of DipSW Courses, while, as mentioned, 17 were represented at AUPSW.

Of the interviewees, six represented their institutions at JUC SWEC and, while nine were nominally members of AUPSW ('they send me the papers'), only four normally attended meetings. An impression was formed of people as 'joiners/activists'; 'researchers/writers'; 'strategic activists and writers'; and 'would-be joiners or researchers but too busy'.

Nearly half the survey respondents claimed staff membership of ATSWE (also mentioned by two of the interviewees) although this organisation has a low membership relative to the total potential constituency. Twenty four of the survey respondents said that they or other staff members had been members of the HEFC panels for the subject area review. Other activities identified by survey respondents included membership of editorial boards (3), of external examination boards (3), and of the Open Learning Foundation (2), none of which were mentioned by the interviewees, although most were known to have current or recent experience of the first two.

Respondents were not active in any committees or Boards outside their own department or subject area in 33 HEIs. The remainder mentioned participation in Senate, Faculty Board, Academic Board, Faculty Research Committee or Equal Opportunities Committees. This would seem to support one of the interviewees who suggested that social work educators fail to utilise their professional skills within their own institutions (contributing to marginality if not invisibility of the area). There was some indication of the defensive isolationism sometimes adopted by social work educators, who can feel 'beleaguered' according to JUC papers and some of the literature reviewed in Part 1.

Responding to 'how do you think of or describe yourself?', interviewees used a range of terms indicating varying strengths in identification with 'social work', and different perceptions of the academic role. Eight people used the term *social worker* but in four cases this was no longer part of their identity: 'I can't really call myself a social worker, I've been out of practice for too long', or 'it's twenty years since I've done proper social work' or 'the rhetoric of practice can deflect us from the real task'. However, even among this group there was some recognition that social work education could be considered as 'a branch' of social work. Two others said their roots in social work were taken for granted and influenced their current activities, while the other two saw themselves as social workers with additional or different roles, 'more of a commentator'.

Three people described themselves as a *manager,* 'Now, in academic life, I might be seen more as a manager', while two related this role to their social work experience: 'you can ensure that there are resources to enable people to learn' or 'good management can make use of therapeutic principles'. Two people used their title, *university professor,* to describe themselves, while a third more recent appointment confessed a lack of ease with the title as yet. A fourth interviewee used the term *'academic leader'* and four others also used this term, one elaborating on the term 'social work academic', '...the notion of practice is played off against academic, but the university should speak to and across different spheres - practice, theory, research and policy'.

However, one respondent saw the word, academic, as 'a term of abuse' and another rejected it on the grounds that it 'has spurious connotations and is status seeking', echoing concerns about anti-intellectualism and egalitarianism, even of social work educators themselves, operating against the interests of the subject area in higher education (Jones, 1996a). Two people described themselves as (university) *lecturers,* one adding that social work lecturers 'have to demonstrate leadership capacity plus a level of research achievement and teaching abilities'. Three people described themselves as *social work educators,* though one qualified this as still having a 'substantial practice element, though now more in committees and an advisory role', and three people mentioned disciplinary identities (psychology (2) and social scientist).

Two people mentioned *writer* and *researcher* as being part of their identity, and three people mentioned the notion of *all-rounder* or the *holistic* nature of their role: 'my professional identity involves all these elements [academic leadership, teaching, managing and research]'. The range of terms used could be an indication of role confusion or of role overload, as suggested by Collins in his discussion of stress (1995). Some respondents pointed out that roles may vary over time, and it is likely that, if post-holders have a strong sense of identity and some control over the balance of work (as seemed likely in these cases), as well as public recognition (professorial appointment) they are less susceptible to stress.

None of the respondents described themselves as *tutors*, despite discussion of this role in earlier stages of the interviews. This suggests that, even where respondents advocate such a role in social work education generally, it is not a primary aspect of their own identity. Discussion with a workshop group of a dozen social work educators at different levels of seniority and careers suggested that use of the term *tutor* by some lecturers reveals 'a lack of academic confidence'; 'ambivalence about the academic role' and that it 'colludes with anti-intellectualism'; and none of them so described themselves in completing a short questionnaire. The significance of terminology was noted by Youll in the mid-1980s 'we needed to identify ourselves firstly as educators and secondly as...tutors...This shift in emphasis in role identification was...experienced as a significant turning point in the way people thought about their work' (Youll, 1985, p.70).

Perhaps in the context of mass higher education, the term *tutor* is anachronistic, and further shifts in terminology may even be appropriate. However, this raises questions about aspects of the social work 'tutor' role, particularly concerned with individual placement visits, which are further explored in considering resource issues.

Finally, interviewees were asked about support or stimulus in their professional lives, as a supplementary question to the one about professional identity (notified in advance). Perhaps it was the lack of forewarning or perhaps the question transgressed the personal/professional boundary, but it was not one that respondents seemed comfortable with and responses were brief. Four people clearly signalled academic colleagues as their reference point, including 'other heads of departments in the university' and 'friends and colleagues in the university sector, world-wide'; while three leaned more to the field 'support networks in social work' or 'people involved in the field. They are a key reference point in terms of values and objectives'.

Four people related to both the field and academe, for example, 'other social workers and researchers' or as one person said, enigmatically, 'other people in the same boat'. Overall, there was an indication that the most senior respondents were the most likely to look to the academy for satisfaction of their professional needs and, with two exceptions, there was no direct reference (in this context) to colleagues in other disciplines or fields of professional education. This concurs with literature which suggests a close relationship between personal and professional identities (Henkel, 1997).

Gender Issues and Reward Systems

The survey data demonstrated that women are relatively under-represented as managers of social work departments or subject areas. This is further illustrated in professorial appointments, although the survey data indicates that they are (proportionately) as well qualified as men. Interviewees were not asked about influence of gender on appointments, but one (male) interviewee in answer to the question about 'reward' said:

> Who do we think we value? Who in fact gets valued? Men get valued and rewarded more than women. Look at senior management in departments...there's still a glass ceiling. We do reward people who are academically productive, we don't reward...committed teachers...[but] we don't reward intellectuality in social work.

Data were not collected about the gender of active researchers or of successful research grant applicants, but scrutiny of the November 1994 membership list of the SWRA showed that there were 43 men and 57 women in membership, suggesting that men are relatively more active in this field (although not all the members are social work educators). There are also indications from the literature and editorial appointments that men are over-represented in publications. Under-representation of women at senior levels and lack of recognition might be expected in the wider field of higher education, and Fisher (1994) quoted research from the USA and Australia to confirm this, but it is more apparent and anomalous in an area where women are in the majority and are as well qualified as men. While there may sometimes be personal reasons for not seeking higher qualifications or more senior posts, it is also likely that lack of attainment (however defined) is in part attributable to an experience of 'organisations as gendered and as reflecting malestream discourse' (Fawcett and Featherstone, 1994, p.51; Carter *et al.*, 1992). If differences also relate to racial identity, experiences of discrimination are compounded (Mogissi, 1994; Francis Spence, 1995).

Turning to the gender composition of JUC SWEC and the distribution of roles and responsibilities within this organisation, men are in the minority but are relatively more likely to represent their institutions on the Committee than women. The distribution of post holders has varied. In 1990, the retiring chairman announced the establishment of the Association of University Professors of Social Work. It was suggested earlier that this arose from concerns about research and the place of social work education in the university sector, relative to CCETSW proposals/requirements about the direction of qualifying training. It is also possible that some professors were not happy with the representative role of JUC SWEC itself (personal communication) and this may have been related to the increasing role which people (particularly women) from the polytechnic and colleges sector were playing in JUC SWEC (personal conjecture).

Women chaired the organisation through much of the 1990s with men in the role of secretaries, and most of the sub-committees are convened by women, with the exception of Probation. This has always been an area where men predominated, conforming to its more overt 'control' role (Walton, 1975).

Witz (1991) suggested that the ascribing of professional status to an occupation is heavily influenced by 'patriarchal' assumptions and definitions from the traditional professions. This impacts on the field of social work, and by association, on social work education. This has included the perception that men lend intellectual weight or credibility to an area, and are more capable of developing theory, while women are better at practice, including a nurturing role in relation to students (Holland, 1988; Fawcett and Featherstone, 1994).

There is a strong tradition of a male majority among social science lecturers and in the management of higher education institutions. If an area, which is perceived as different and perhaps problematic, is staffed largely by women and often also led by them, it is conceivable that some of the usual mechanisms for resolving difference or promoting sectional interests will not operate, or that the observed differences are not valued, unless they become part of mainstream higher education policy and practice. There may also be differences in women's priorities and managerial style (possibly related to the values of the area) which may be particularly discordant with the managerialism evident in higher education since the late 1980s (Pollitt, 1990).

While the leadership of JUC SWEC by women may promote meetings where there is evidence of respect for others' views and collaborative initiatives, there may also be a lack of access to or influence in important policy-making arenas. This is speculative, and it is clear that, individually, particular women have achieved positions of respect within the academy or in the international arena; and that having a man in the senior position does not necessarily win friends or influence people. However, a question remains as to how far the fortunes of the area are bound up with its 'female' nature and whether the apparent increase of men in senior positions will improve either its intellectual capacity or its ability to defend or promote its position in higher education.

Some of the interviewees' responses to a question about 'what is valued or rewarded in social work education?' related to gender concerns, referring to the values of the profession and a commitment to ideals of social justice and equal opportunities. This question, despite prior warning, seemed initially obscure to respondents. Answers varied in the extent to which people thought in terms of professional as well as academic acknowledgement.

One (male) interviewee said, 'In one way we reward things that the academic system is prepared to reward' and told how he had been advised early on, by his (female) head of department in an old university, to write for academic journals rather than professional ones. However, he found it hard to identify rewards or recognition from the field.

> The social work profession is very ambivalent about its academy. It's quite disconfirming really, you feel irrelevant. Colleagues in the field...don't know or care what the academic world is like. [But] there is quite a lot of confirmation from students and I sometimes feel acknowledged in conferences or consultancies for being 'in touch'...but if you're not valued in the profession it's even tougher in the university.

This was echoed by other respondents:

> Practitioners have doubts about the value of academic activity...but they appreciate people who can make sense of things and develop...frameworks for practice. In academe, papers in refereed journals and bringing in research money are valued.

> [He was not sure that other academics value social work education but thought that they should] because of its mix of theory, practice and reflection; [or] ...Social service agencies reward us if we help with their problems through research and consultancy - we can be the respected outsider. In the university we're appreciated if we look good to the outside world through big research grants or gaining an excellent in teaching...we're seen as useful people...[and also valued in having] a high status woman [on the staff].

One analysis of the lack of value attributed to social work educators by the profession suggested that it is identified with theory and therefore difficulty. The respondent also thought that there was 'a legacy of problems around elitism' but hoped this was changing. Another respondent contrasted the position in two different institutions.

> In [x -an old university] social work education was seen as suspect and marginal because it doesn't deliver in terms which the university expects. The only reason it wasn't closed down was because of a social conscience and fear of a bad press because social work had links with the local community. The lack of valuation was reflected in the lack of resources and in effect the programme was staffed by teachers who were only tolerated rather than valued so this resulted in low morale'. [Social work education at this institution was headed by a woman professor, well respected in the professional field, at the time]. 'In [y -a new university] social work is seen as part of the university's mission. It pulls in students and money and its contact with the field is seen as positive.

Good relations with local agencies and the ability to 'pull in' funding for consultancy activities were apparently valued by other institutions as well, but social work educators might still be 'struggling to be seen as part of a proper academic group' in one of the new universities, while a colleague in another new university thought that his department 'could end up with both an excellent in teaching and a good research rating which would be unique within the university' (It did). Another respondent saw this as an area of change in a different way:

> ...being a good colleague, helping students, creative teaching [used to be valued, but now there is] pressure on people to...get funding, to publish. There is no hope of promotion unless you have a long string of publications. In this climate it's easy for students to be seen as a nuisance, we're losing care for the students which was one of the distinguishing features of social work education...[and constituted] an element of modelling.

Social work educators 'modelling' some of the skills and values of social work in their relationship with students, and the impact of the material on students (with concomitant demands on staff) are recurring assumptions held within the group, but not necessarily understood by other academics or managers (Collins, 1995).

There were three responses which alluded directly to a lack of value by social work educators for each other. One respondent simply said, 'We've allowed ourselves to be so browbeaten, we've not had recognition and we haven't given it to others'. Another said, 'I don't see social work education valuing or rewarding very much' and contrasted it with dental education where 'certain individuals are clearly respected and seen as authorities...on the whole social work educators are rather iconoclastic and sceptical. To some extent this is healthy but it doesn't help us to achieve security' and another said, '[We're] not very good at rewarding each other - we're very good at being critical and tend to pass this on to others. This affects our morale, our self-perceptions and our self-esteem. We're our own worst enemies'. But having said that, he thought that 'colleagues here are extremely supportive and unenvious'.

Some of these responses suggest an acceptance of increasingly academic but also increasingly managerialist reward systems which might reflect 'masculine' rather than 'feminine' values. But the emphasis given to acknowledgement from the profession (or desire for it) suggests an alternative reward system which distinguishes this from other disciplines. It reiterates the extent to which social work educators must address two audiences, with different and sometimes conflicting criteria for success or achievement.

Conclusions

Data discussed in this chapter confirm that social work educators enter academic life later than their colleagues in other disciplines, and that their career patterns are significantly different. Initial social work practice has traditionally been reflected in the weight given to professional experience and qualifications rather than academic awards or publications in recruitment to the educational role. This orientation persists in terms of continuing professional activities outside the university by educators and some hope of recognition from the field, though whether this is cause or effect in the face of a lack of recognition from within some universities is debatable.

Although the majority of social work educators represented here have achieved academic qualifications to masters level, in addition to professional awards, relatively few have attained doctoral or professorial status. This reflects an ambivalence about the relevance of research-based academic awards to the professional field, and/or a lack of academic confidence or role models, as well as demands on staff time in 'outside' representation and responding to change.

There is a view of the subject as lacking in academic credibility, and this may be compounded by the relatively high proportion of women in the social work education workforce, including some in senior positions.

Engagement with the field may detract both from research activities and from active involvement in the internal affairs of institutions. Participation in the former would enhance academic credibility, while participation in the latter might be beneficial to perceptions of the subject area, increasing its visibility, disseminating innovative educational practices, and building alliances with other subjects and professional areas.

There are changes in the identities and priorities of social work educators, suggested by the responses of interviewees, the concerns of JUC SWEC, and advertisements for appointments of social work lecturer posts. Adherence to academic values, with expectations about academic qualifications and rewards, may be strengthening. This is partly a response to increasingly competitive institutional conditions, norms and mission statements.

The active pursuit of stronger academic identities may also be of value to the professional field, where social work educators may provide a necessary and legitimate 'independent voice' in relation to practice and policy developments, on the basis of increased theoretical and research activity. This may be at variance with social work's 'anti-elitist values', or promoting an 'academic' education at the expense of more practically orientated courses, but such views may have contributed to the downgrading and destabilisation of the subject area.

Issues of dual responsibility or conflicting loyalties are likely to persist for social work educators. The subject will always be on the boundaries between education and practice. Explication of the tensions inherent in the role and in the subject area are important tasks of social work academics. Further examination of the part which gender plays in influencing perceptions and fortunes of the area also seems necessary.

9 Resource Issues and Change

Introduction

Key factors in the sense of crisis in social work education have been the pace and nature of change during the 1990s, and the growing sense of unease with its direction. Some of these changes have been at the behest of CCETSW, operating as a conduit for government policy. While CCETSW has made attempts to consult affected parties and relevant interest groups, the lead-in times between policy decisions, clarification, and required implementation have been short. This has been exacerbated by the different schedules of the academic year and the (central and local) government financial year.

Inextricably linked to the effective implementation of new policies, structural arrangements and practices is the resourcing of the subject area. This has both qualitative and quantitative dimensions. The first was considered in the previous chapter, in relation to the qualifications, experience and likely identities of people responsible for managing the change process. The second relates to the funding available to the area, the size and composition of the workforce, relative to student numbers and the roles and tasks to be undertaken.

Funding of social work education has been a periodic source of concern to social work educators as demonstrated in JUC SWEC discussions and representations to CCETSW. The low proportion of budget holders has been evidenced in this study, but, additionally, the often arcane, arbitrary or unclear basis for allocation of funding within institutions has sometimes obscured the relationship between costs and budgets, not necessarily to social work's disadvantage.

The subject area and institutions also lack control over an essential element in social work education - placements - and the funding of these has itself been contentious. Thus, resource issues can be examined in relation to both the level of resourcing to departments or subject areas, and also the resources available from agencies in the form of placements, practice teachers, mentors, and (usually senior) agency personnel who participate in partnership responsibilities.

Agency contribution to resourcing was addressed by implication, rather than directly in the survey, and was sometimes responded to in an open question about the area's strengths and weaknesses. There is also evidence about social work educators' concerns and CCETSW's role in this area in JUC SWEC papers. Interviewees were not invited to comment on resourcing in the same way, but made some relevant comments in response to a question about strategies for development.

Substantial changes are taking place in the nature of work, career and employment opportunities within and beyond the public sector, as commented on in the media and general literature (Crompton *et al.*, 1996). These are evident in the areas of both social work and higher education. For example, newly qualified social workers taking up temporary or locum posts doubled from 1993 (14 per cent) to 1996 (29 per cent) (Wallis Jones and Lyons, 1997). Specific questions were included in the 1994 survey to explore whether such changes are occurring in social work education and the implications of this are briefly considered.

Questions were asked in the survey about change in social work education in its institutional context and this is linked to relevant material from JUC SWEC papers and the literature. Interviewees were not asked a direct question about 'change' but, again, some respondents made relevant points. Overall, the chapter reviews both resource issues and changes, as perceived by social work educators.

Relating changes in social work to policy change in higher education, questions arise about how far the changes in social work education can be seen as efficient adaptation to changing environments, or as a fundamental redefining of the tasks of the subject area (March and Olsen, 1989). While changes in the area are largely the result of 'reform caused by the exogenous environment', questions arise about the part played by the actors in the system in instituting these or other changes (March and Olsen, 1994, p.33). The extent to which change has been imposed and out of the control of the actors has been the basis of individual and collective stress (Collins, 1995). But there are indications in some of the more recent data that social work educators are seeking to reclaim a role in defining the goals of the area and the most appropriate means of achieving them.

Resource Issues

Funding for the college element of social work education had been 'brought within the normal funding structures of higher education' following extensive consultations, but in somewhat piecemeal fashion, during the 1970s (Pierce, 1991). By the mid-1980s there were concerns that undertakings to safeguard the level of special funding for social work education, transferred from the Home Office and DHSS to the UGC in 1978/1979, were being eroded. JUC SWEC undertook a survey to compare the unit costs of social work education relative to students in social science, education, accountancy and psychology. The results of this were inconclusive, since responses from 34 institutions revealed wide variations and 'each institution seemed to have its own costing formula' (Chair's letter to membership, 14/5/86).

Perhaps this survey, representations about other resource issues (for example, the payment of placement travel costs) and the need for data to underpin the Council's proposals for QDSW, prompted CCETSW to commission a more substantial research study into the costs of social work education (Rustin and Edwards, 1989). This included both university and polytechnic courses at all academic levels, and drew some important conclusions not widely disseminated at the time but still relevant. Social work education managers had problems assigning financial costs to their activities; most courses 'required and received additional expenditures' of around 25 per cent (relative to social science programmes); the subject was wrongly categorised in both PCFC and UFC systems; the placement system was a source of difficulty and 'wasteful'; and costs per qualified social worker were highly variable, in part related to different patterns and levels of training. A unified system consistent with the four year B.Ed. degree was suggested.

Findings (submitted to CCETSW in November 1989) were overtaken by events and the hasty plans to establish the DipSW (rather than three year training) took precedence over immediate concerns about funding arrangements or more ambitious structural proposals. Meanwhile, a letter from the Director of CCETSW (30/6/89) to the DES requesting reclassification of social work from Band A (Social Sciences) to Band C (which included Education) or at least B, met with no immediate universal success, but laid the basis for individual institutional claims for what subsequently became Band Two funding (rather than Band One). Although this question was not relevant to about one third of the respondents (post-graduate courses), by 1994, 27 institutions were in receipt of Band Two funding with 17 receiving Band One, and there were indications that this situation improved slightly, prior to national changes in funding arrangements and allocation of the subject to (newly designated) Band C.

In the mid-1990s there were variations in how fee income was allocated within institutions and achievement of Band Two funding was not necessarily reflected in resourcing at subject area level. Thus, the answer of one respondent to the question about fee band status may still resonate, 'You may well ask! There is a good deal of confusion around this plus dispute within the institution. We are *supposed* to be Band Two'. This suggestion, that enhanced fees are not actually passed on to the subject area, for higher costs of particular teaching methods and administrative work, was compounded by contradictory advice as to how it should be used.

A letter from CCETSW to Vice-Chancellors in 1996, in the midst of a placement funding crisis, clearly indicated an expectation that institutions would receive this additional money and that it could be used to remedy a shortfall of finances for placements (of which many programmes were complaining). The potential 'switching' of money to part-fund placements (which were originally provided free of charge to institutions) caused further concern to social work educators, reflected in JUC SWEC minutes, an expanded Practice Learning Sub-committee, and a survey of members about the impact of the changed placement funding (Jan/Feb. 1997 minutes and correspondence).

Identifying the costs of social work education, and ensuring a rational and equitable distribution of resources in the subject area, is far from resolved. Should the profession, higher education or the consumers bear the costs of professional training within higher education? What might be the appropriate divisions and mechanisms for cost-sharing? In 1991, CCETSW produced an important consultation paper summarising the 'complex arrangements' pertaining to the funding of UK social work education. It also specified the objectives which funding should achieve and made a number of recommendations about how these might be met (Pierce, 1991).

Placements

The profession (as represented by employing agencies) plays a part in resource provision, via placements. Placements are an increasing source of concern within social work education, virtually outside the control of those responsible for course delivery (although DipSW partnership arrangements were, in part, intended to address this). Social work programmes at qualifying level must provide all students with two supervised practice placements (of fifty and eighty days) which provide the basis for assessment of the student's professional competence.

This area has undergone its own form of 'professionalisation' with new requirements since 1989 for training of practice teachers and accreditation of agencies. One effect has been an increased demand on both HEIs and agencies to contribute to training programmes, in which practice teachers themselves require supervision and assessment by mentors. This pattern of supervision and assessment in practice is also a requirement of any courses proposed for post-qualifying or advanced awards.

The basis of resourcing and rewards in practice teaching has long been contentious. Practice teachers have not normally received any direct payment for the work, nor workload relief. The Probation Service (with placements funded by the Home Office) has often been an exception to this. Payments, in the form of a daily supervision fee, have also been made to agencies providing placements in the voluntary sector (though not usually to individual practice teachers, except in the case of 'long-arm' arrangements which have become increasingly common).

The expectation was that Social Services Departments, the largest potential provider of placements, would meet the costs of placement provision internally through the Training Support Grant. However, there have been considerable claims on this diminishing resource in a period of rapid legislative and organisational change, including (re)training people providing front-line services, and development of courses leading to in-service awards at the pre-qualifying stage (NVQs). Placements were long made on a goodwill basis, with some recognition of the staff development potential for some practice teachers, and a concern to invest in future staff. This was already under strain in the 1980s and completely out of step with market-led provision of all services by the 1990s.

Concurrently, the reduction of places in the statutory sector, caused by internal pressures in SSDs and increased CCETSW requirements, had resulted in a large expansion of placements in the voluntary sector and concomitant rise in the placement budget (channelled from the Department of Health via CCETSW to agencies). This resulted in a radical revision of the funding provisions, such that, from April 1997, budgets available from CCETSW to programmes to support placements would be 'capped' and related to student intake; and would require institutions to negotiate contracts about the number of placements to be provided for an agreed sum, including the statutory sector. These changes led to the closure of some Practice Learning Centres (previously called student units), often located in the voluntary sector and providing a focal point for a network of placements in community organisations which might not otherwise be available. There was also a reduction in the infrastructure for placement organisation and support in statutory departments.

The Chairman of CCETSW wrote to the Chair of JUC SWEC (18/12/96 in response to a letter expressing concern about the new arrangements), suggesting additional funds, allocated (by government) since the early 1990s, had not resolved 'problems of quantity and quality'. The previous resource distribution, including a demand-led approach to the (voluntary sector) daily placement fee, 'was not sustainable'. Programmes varied in how they adapted to the reduced opportunities (compounded for some by the probation changes) and to the 'new' market approach. Setting up contracts to purchase placements from agencies has required investment of time and money, and deployment of negotiating skills in unfamiliar ways.

Placement changes have also had a direct impact in some cases on weak partnership arrangements, a further area in which small, unstable or poorly supported programmes are vulnerable. Educators are required to employ different skills from those normally expected of academics; and social work education generally is seen to have different concerns or make unusual claims on HEIs. In the words of one head of course about the placements contract process, 'I feel like a used car salesman' (JUC SWEC Meeting, 6/1/97). While his efforts paid off for one course, it further destabilised existing partnership arrangements of a neighbouring course, already hit by the loss of a Practice Learning Centre.

This overtly competitive mode, compared to previous collaborative efforts of social work educators and agency training officers (as in the London cluster system) demonstrated the extent to which political values have made inroads into the workings of this professional subject area. Recognition of the real costs challenges academics, agencies and CCETSW to re-examine the assumptions underlying placements.

Staffing

Questions arise about the availability and use of the academic staff resources within the institution to develop and deliver new programmes, and engage in other areas of professional and academic activity. Staff resourcing is a sensitive issue, as reflected in a reduced response rate or imprecise answers, to three questions at the survey stage. It has been common-place for a long time for people in both social work and higher education to feel under-resourced, relative to the goals, tasks and standards to be achieved.

Notwithstanding this caveat and the nature of the data, some calculation of staff student ratios (SSRs) in 1994 was possible. Such an indicator may be over-simplifying the picture, since it does not take into account how academic staff were supplemented by support staff of various kinds, or undertaking work other than DipSW programmes. Nevertheless, it provides some indication of favourable or unfavourable resourcing levels, and might suggest trends.

Thus, in 1994, nearly one third of the institutions seemed to have managed to maintain an SSR on the DipSW programme of between 1:10 and 1:12. It was notable that nearly half (9 out of 20) of these were in the old university sector and some of the remainder were courses at MA level which are differently funded. A further 22 institutions had SSRs in the 1:15 to 1:18 range, including most of the remainder of the old universities (7). Just under a third had SSRs of 1:20 or more (including 4 old universities). From this and other data gathered it can be deduced that institutions with lower SSRs were more likely to be doing most of their own teaching (that is without servicing arrangements from discipline specialists) and/or that they were engaged in a wider range of activities than DipSW delivery. This included provision of other courses, and research and consultancy activities.

Such units were not necessarily the largest, but were likely to have more varied activity and staffing profiles. A minimum departmental (or unit) size was two full time with one part-time colleague and inputs from two subject specialists to run one relatively small DipSW programme. A maximum size was seventeen full time and four part-time social work lecturers (with inputs from four sessional and six non-social work staff) offering the qualifying award to about 300 students at different academic levels, as well as other courses and research. Overall, there seemed to be no obvious relationship between fee band and staffing levels.

In only three institutions did the staff group consist of a nuclear group of *full-time, permanent* staff engaged exclusively in delivery of a qualifying course, though the impression is that this would have been a more common pattern in the 1980s. Two thirds of the respondents included at least one *part-time* lecturer in their work force (and many more in a few cases), and one third included people on full or part-time *temporary* contracts. A further 24 departments/units made use of *sessional* staff, and half included teaching by *subject specialists*. Although no question was asked about the nature of inputs by the latter, a few respondents volunteered that this was in law.

Only two respondents mentioned part-time *secondments* or specialist inputs from their partner agencies, or *joint appointments* (3), or additional staffing made possible by funding in relation to the placement provision or residential child care initiatives (PPI and RCCI, respectively). There is very little literature by social work educators relating to resourcing or workforce patterns, but Culkin and Thompson (1994) reported on joint appointments in relation to probation pathways, and Sleeman (1996) wrote about aspects of partnership arrangements including staff exchange.

A question about changes in level or deployment of staffing resources between 1990 and 1994 resulted in 55 responses. Some people said 'yes' but gave no details; fifteen claimed an improvement in resources (but in two cases stated that this had been achieved through a reduction in student intake) and a further fifteen said 'no change'. One respondent mentioned a new professorship, two mentioned the introduction of a joint appointment, and three said that new administrative or placement finding posts had been developed.

The findings suggest that the *pattern* of staffing was changing but it was not possible to say whether resourcing within institutions in relation to this subject area was improving or deteriorating; and, if the former, whether this was the result of permanent appointments or specially resourced and time limited ones. There were some indications of a move to a more flexible workforce, in line with wider trends, but as one respondent noted from an institutional perspective, 'the situation is too fluid to respond'.

The wide variations in the size and composition of departments or units obviously have implications for the nature and quality of the student experience as well as opportunities and constraints on social work educators and managers; and potentially for viability or development of the subject, in particular institutions. This has already become increasingly apparent in the changes to probation training. Probation Services had demonstrated more support for programmes in a number of practical ways, including joint appointments, relative to other agencies.

There is some impressionistic evidence of more efficient use of staff resources since the early 1990s, through increased role specialisation and the delegation of some responsibilities to non-teaching staff, including placement administrators. It seems that development grants, PPI funds (awarded on the basis of proposals, and time limited) and/or Band Two fee income were used in this particular way. As previously discussed, social work educators recognised the tensions between teaching, research, practice and management and the unlikelihood of individual staff being able to combine all these roles at the same time. But one interviewee said in 1996, 'within a team a combination is possible', and the value of some part-time, temporary or sessional staff may be apparent in this context.

Finally, mention should be made of the range of different sources from which *supplementary funding* has been available to social work educators during the 1990s, and the skills and values related to their procurement. Social work educators, in theory, have access to the same range of research funding as other social scientists and require similar skills to secure them. This also applies to funding from the European Union, particularly in relation to the previous ERASMUS programme, and now the SOCRATES scheme.

There are also similar inducements, or pressures, within HEIs to engage in income generation which accrues to both the institution and the area, or helps offset some costs (for example, placements). However, the market, including the voluntary sector and consumer groups, is itself limited and unlikely to meet high charges. This, combined with the not-for-profit ethic with which many social work educators are imbued, results in 'at-cost' projects - on altruistic grounds or in the hope of *quid pro quos* and future contracts.

The possibility of accessing funds within institutions, for example through the Enterprise in Higher Education scheme, has been noted, as has a range of funding opportunities from CCETSW itself. The latter have included funds which partly acknowledged the costs of new requirements, for example Development Funding, or which aimed to promote particular developments in line with government policies, of which the Residential Child Care Initiative and funding for Open Learning projects would be examples. However, these were available only on a competitive basis; the sums available were often relatively small scale (less than £10,000) and all required reports on how funds had been spent.

Funding procurement, budget management, project activity and evaluation processes constitute a further administrative drain on staff, with relatively little increase in subject area resources or autonomy. It exemplifies developments in the role of many social workers, and government policy for higher education and academics more generally, but hardly mitigates the sense of strain or difference experienced by social work educators.

The Changes

In 1992, the JUC SWEC Annual Report noted a busy year, but also expressed concern about falling attendance at its meetings, attributed to the heavy pressure on its members due to new social work programmes and other external factors. In the same year, Coulshead wrote that DipSW arrangements were proving to be 'administratively laborious in the extreme' (Coulshead, 1972, p.2) necessitating teaching economies. Frequent reference has been made already to change as a constant dynamic and to the cumulative effect in demoralisation of social work educators and vulnerability of the area. Data presented here reflects examples of specific changes revealed by the survey and about the impact and direction of change.

Major structural change occurred in higher education with the erasure of the binary divide (in 1992) and the incorporation of smaller colleges into the expanded university sector. This had already produced a direct impact on about one third of the respondents surveyed in 1994, and has subsequently affected nearly another third. This had implications for the balance of work, not least in increased expectations or opportunities to participate in research, which may be significant for the longer term staffing and development of the area.

Other changes within institutions were sometimes justified on educational grounds but could also be a response to external policy change, for example, on student numbers. Thus, modularisation and semesterisation had been experienced by about half the respondents (37 and 28, respectively) by 1994, and had been of sufficient concern to JUC SWEC for one of its members to produce a paper as a basis for discussion (4/6/94) on the implications for DipSW. Main concerns centred on the ability of programmes to 'fit' learning, including in placements, into discrete modules or units, assessed within semesters. Could a holistic approach to professional education be retained, including assessing how college-based learning, perhaps taking place the previous semester, might inform practice.

Modularisation is 'predominantly an aggregative model of learning' (Henkel, 1995, p.78) and whether this is best suited to the 'process' element and integrative intent of social work education has been questioned. Data from this research did not reveal how many respondents had been able to tie in restructuring of courses to meet institutional demands with redevelopment of programmes to meet CCETSW requirements. It is known that, for some, the timing of respective changes required consecutive rather than concurrent development and administrative work. It was also a change used as an opportunity by some educators, although the hoped-for benefits in terms of increased research time did not necessarily materialise (Wilson and Bradley, 1994).

Nearly half the survey respondents (28) had experienced organisational change in relation to departmental boundaries since 1989, and in two cases this had happened twice in three years. A further 13 respondents expected imminent change of this kind and seven others thought it was a possibility. One respondent referred to 'constant restructuring' and there is evidence that the experiences of many social work educators paralleled those of their colleagues in the professional field during this period (La Valle and Lyons, 1996a). These changes were being experienced predominantly by respondents in the new university or college sector (30 indications of departmental change, relative to only four in the old university sector) and may have been associated with institutional changes in status.

It is unclear from the data whether social work was more or less likely than other subjects to be affected by institutional changes, but a subject lacking clear boundaries and associations may be more vulnerable to such change. Since change in higher education is at least as much a response to economic considerations as to epistemological or pedagogical ones, the relative expense of social work education also makes it more vulnerable to changes aimed at economies of scale. But the mixing of social work and social science students (as may happen following modularisation) may have other costs.

Within the subject area, the major change was the introduction of the Diploma in Social Work in place of existing CQSW and CSS courses, which entailed 'running out' previous qualifications at the same time as bringing new ones on stream. There were no known cases of breaks between student intakes, and there were some cases where three different cohorts of students were operating under separate regulations for at least one year, with predictable 'teething troubles' for those on new programmes and demoralisation for those on old ones.

CSS courses were well represented in the first wave of approvals, with nine DipSW programmes being introduced in either 1989 or 1990 (only two of these were in the old university sector). The majority followed in 1991 (24 programmes) and 1992 (21). Ten new programmes were implemented in 1993. Eight of these were in the old university sector, and the majority were changes from one year post-graduate CQSW courses to two year masters level programmes. (The number totals 65 as one HEI introduced DipSW at non-graduate level in 1991, and at masters level in 1993.)

The revision of CCETSW requirements, not finally approved by Council until 23/2/95 but for implementation by Autumn 1995, was an example of further change, and also of the difficult timescales imposed on social work educators. The JUC Chair wrote to CCETSW (11/1/95) urging phased implementation over the 1995 and 1996 intakes, and this request, as well as representations from the CVCP, was heeded. Accounts of the change to DipSW and new requirements were contained in a number of texts (Jackson and Preston-Shoot, 1996; Vass, 1996; Webb, 1996) and, as previously cited, Jones (1996c) critically 'reviewed the review'.

Apart from the change to bring post-graduate diplomas into a two year framework, mentioned above, there is subsequent evidence of a trend away from masters level programmes towards degree level ones which represent about 22 per cent of DipSW programmes overall (CCETSW, 1996). This reflects the level of support among educators for a degree level award, and increased attempts to conform to institutional structures and norms, e.g. some programmes which had implemented two year non-graduate programmes after 1989, but taken the opportunity of the 1995 revisions to rethink their own provision.

In the post-1989 changes, there was some evidence that CQSW courses in close proximity were likely to change at the same time (needing to maintain their position relative to both partnership arrangements and student recruitment); and that courses in the London region changed later than elsewhere. The latter partly reflected the greater diversity of agencies and complexity of pre-existing placement networks, but also less stability and more strain within agencies themselves, making the establishment of new partnership arrangements more protracted. This was also a feature of the establishment of regional post-qualifying consortia, but less so of smaller consortia to deliver practice teacher training programmes. Both were examples of developments in which social work educators were involved during this period.

A question in the 1994 survey about further planned changes indicated that some respondents felt that change was being imposed and was outside their control, for instance, 'not our plans but government's'. But many responses also indicated an acceptance that this was an inevitable and necessary process and there were very few indications of 'no change'. A minority of respondents expected to reduce their social work education provision, including reducing numbers on qualifying programmes (16), and there were indications subsequently of a continuing trend.

In 1997 this might have been at variance with CCETSW's intention to maintain output at a level to meet demand, which was apparently still supported by the Department of Health (Riches, 1997). But a further review in the 1998/1999 period suggested less clarity about the level of demand and had an agenda to 'rationalise' social work education (personal communication). However, in 1994, three quarters of the respondents (49) expected to extend or diversify social work education in some way, particularly through the introduction of a top-up degree year (26, mostly in the new university sector). At that time, only four institutions had implemented a two-plus-one model (DipHE/DipSW plus optional degree year), but by autumn 1997 twenty three institutions had plans to develop this structure, virtually half of those awarding the DipSW at non-graduate level. (This continued to comprise half the provision of professional qualifying awards, overall) (CCETSW, 1996).

As in the case of three year programmes offering combined professional and academic awards, this may reflect a desire by social work educators to develop courses more consistent with institutional structures, but top-up degrees might also suggest a strategy to avoid CCETSW direction. There has been no general research into the extent to which students choose to proceed direct to a top-up degree, although the 1996 CCETSW Employment Survey showed that 40 per cent (44) of those respondents not in a social work post six months after qualifying had proceeded to further training or research (Wallis Jones and Lyons, 1997). Similarly, it is not known how far top-up degrees (or modules on them) have been developed to carry post-qualifying awards, and are used on a part-time basis by practising social workers, but in 1994, twenty one respondents had signalled their intent to introduce post-qualifying (and in a few cases, advanced) awards. Ten other respondents (8 in the new university sector) planned to introduce taught masters courses and four to introduce or expand PhD programmes.

Plans to introduce part-time or distance learning modes at the qualifying level were intimated by eight respondents and there seems to have been some patchy development in this area. It is a development favoured by some employers and for which there is a possible market among unqualified (or differently qualified) staff in the personal social services, and support from CCETSW (Cornwall, 1995). But there seems to have been some resistance to large scale development of this kind, partly related to ideas about the (group) socialisation process which some educators see as being part of the professional education programme. The only interviewee to mention this area noted in 1996, 'I am not convinced there is a huge demand...If the government sorts out student funding, most people want to go on a real course with human involvement', and that 'having the universities run things is actually cheaper for employers'. By the late 1990s, in view of the abolition of student grants and the resistance of the government to make exceptions for funding of social work students (at the time of writing), it remained to be seen whether lack of grants would increase applications to distance learning and work-based routes.

However, there is some impressionistic evidence of increasing use of 'approval of prior [experiential] learning' to give exemptions from some elements in DipSW programmes, and of links with agencies around 'in-house work placements', as a direct response to placement shortages and costs. CSS courses had already pioneered the idea of 'employment routes', and although few of these formally remain in DipSW programmes, it seems as if new patterns of provision are emerging in close collaboration with employers. Whether this is properly called 'part-time' or 'employment-based' (or work-based) is unclear. Similarly, only limited information exists so far about a new initiative by the Open University to offer a professional qualification by distance learning in conjunction with at least one large national voluntary agency, or about how far materials developed by the Open Learning Foundation, specifically developed for DipSW use, have been adopted (Adams, 1997).

With regard to other forms of diversification, mentioned by nearly half of the survey respondents, five expected to increase the research element; nine to develop part-time post-qualifying or advanced awards; and six to be involved in teaching on non-social work courses, or on joint or multi-disciplinary modules. One specifically noted 'change to social science if DipSW removed from higher education', reflecting either the mood of the moment or a wider concern about the direction of policy developments.

This theme of diversification was taken up by most of the interviewees asked about strategies for survival or development in 1996. Only one respondent specifically spoke against such a move 'Higher education is rapidly changing and frantically opening up more opportunities...it's not necessarily going to produce better education. Why should we abandon traditional social work education? It's succeeded reasonably well in being adaptive'. However, this was very much a minority view and six people mentioned diversification as a strategy which they themselves were actively promoting. One interviewee said, 'the key task is diversification', although another made it clear that this included *away* from social work education programmes, if necessary.

Specific areas of development mentioned by interviewees included post-graduate degrees of a specialist or interdisciplinary nature (for example, MSc in Community Care, MBA in Health and Social Care); submission of existing masters level units for award of professional credits; developing the research area, including through part-time opportunities for senior staff from local agencies, (fellowships); and integration of DipSW pathways into 'mainstream' degrees.

Additionally, by this stage some of the respondents were facing the impact of withdrawal of probation training and were mostly choosing to convert existing probation streams to criminal justice pathways, including juvenile justice, although one despondently noted that he was trying to 'salvage' the programme. Two respondents also spoke of participation in planning for new NVQ awards in the criminal justice field, one specifically saying he 'wouldn't have chosen to go this way...[but was] trying to keep all the options open'. However, developments in this area were again in question with the notification to JUC SWEC members (18/2/97) that the project to develop occupational standards and NVQ awards in the probation field, for implementation from 8/97, had been suspended. The impact on higher education provision of the subsequently announced Diploma in Probation Studies/NVQ Level 4 awards has yet to be assessed.

One interviewee specifically referred to the advantages of size in giving flexibility 'you can switch things around, and rebalance numbers [on different courses]...social work can never compete otherwise'. It seems increasingly apparent that *size combined with diversity* may be an important characteristic in the sustainability or development of social work as a subject area in higher education, coupled with the ability to carry out some of its work within the mainstream structures of higher education and to cross-subsidise its own activities within budgetary arrangements at basic unit level.

Summary and Conclusions

This chapter has reviewed the quantitative dimension of resources available to social work educators to initiate, respond to and 'manage' policy changes which have had structural, developmental and administrative consequences. It was not possible to demonstrate that shortage of resources, in the form of academic staffing, was a widespread problem in itself. There was evidence of variation in the resources available to social work in different institutions, with a clear indication of an increase from traditional SSR norms of 1:10 or 12, for about two thirds of the respondents.

There was also considerable variation in the number of staff available; and evidence of changing patterns of staffing in ways which might suggest more flexibility and responsiveness to the changing conditions, but which might also imply less continuity and stability in staff groups. This latter might impact on both development work and course delivery, with possible consequences for sharing of the administrative load and for staff-student relationships. Temporary, part-time and sessional lecturers do not necessarily have administrative or developmental roles, and may not be available for staff or student meetings. However, they may be part of a wider move towards specialisation of roles within staff teams (including in relation to research) and the issue is probably one of 'balance' rather than the appropriateness - or not - of a particular type of appointment.

Data suggested that a proportion of posts would be funded by time-limited budgets, the availability of which represented both a resource and a further demand on the time and skills of budget holders (often only one person in fairly small teams). However, such resources might give some staff groups a limited measure of autonomy, given the small number of units identified earlier as being responsible for departmental budgets.

The other aspect of resourcing discussed was placements and other resources under the control of agencies, rather than HEIs. This was an area in which exogenous policy change has had a particular impact on social work educators and where, although there is some evidence of the embracing of market values and approaches, it seemed likely that many social work educators were engaged in damage limitation exercises. These include cutting the numbers of students requiring supervised placements, and developing other courses which fit more easily with institutional structures, or which meet demands for other types or levels of education.

The recent crisis in placements had been precipitated by changes in the (CCETSW) funding arrangements, but also compounded by the withdrawal of probation training from HEIs, another policy change outside the control of educators, to which most are making a pragmatic response. While changes in the area have often been experienced as imposed, driven by political or economic agenda at variance with those of social work educators, there is also evidence of pragmatic and efficient adaptation to the changing environment, with some new initiatives.

A theme emerging in the management of change has been increasing diversity of course provisions and other activities within the subject area. This can be seen as both a reactive strategy, including the need to conform to changed structures within HEIs (modularisation and semesterisation), and an attempt to take a more proactive stance and reclaim some control over parts of the social work education enterprise (for example through top-up degrees or new post-graduate courses). The limited development of new modes of course delivery (part-time and distance learning) can be seen as attempts to maintain some of the values of educational opportunity, peer group learning and professional socialisation through full-time social work education and resistance to the 'commodification' of education.

It was concluded that area size, diversity and some degree of control over resources might all be important factors determining the viability or not of the subject area in particular institutions, although the strength and effects of policy changes outside the area may yet overwhelm the area as a whole. However, there did seem to be a qualitative difference between the responses received in 1994, when arguably social work educators were in the midst of, or exhausted by, changes, and those received from interviewees and evidenced in new texts emerging in 1996, and initial responses to the 1998/1999 review were more positive than might previously have been anticipated.

The view of one senior academic is apt here, 'I am more optimistic than for some time. More universities are considering the contribution which social work educators can make to courses other than CCETSW-approved ones...I am not happy about professional education but the area is developing and less reliant on CCETSW'. Although the demise of CCETSW has since been announced, it is likely that CCETSW itself had been seen by some as one of the problems in relation to social work education and views about CCETSW are therefore further considered in the next chapter.

10   Strengths, Weaknesses and Possible Developments

Introduction

The main aim of this research was to identify and clarify the characteristics which make social work education a viable or vulnerable discipline in current higher education. A related aim was to explore the impact of recent changes, and the threats or opportunities for development, as perceived by educators themselves.

The last section of the 1994 questionnaire invited social work educators to give their own views about 'problematic or concerning issues' and about possible strengths of the subject area. This was an open ended, two part question, answered by 61 out of 64 of the respondents in varying detail. Additionally, in 1996, interviewees were asked a slightly different question, about opportunities and strategies for development of the subject, and this produced further data.

In 1995, initial findings from the survey were shared with workshop participants at the annual ATSWE conference, after an exercise to investigate participants' views. The participants, a more broadly based group than those originally surveyed, mainly confirmed previous findings. There were, however, some variations in response and these are presented in conjunction with the original survey data.

Finally, JUC SWEC records indicate a strong motivation among social work educators to promote the development of the subject in higher education, and there are discussions of some of the themes raised.

The 1994 survey data demonstrated that weaknesses were more readily identified than strengths, suggesting a very demoralised group of respondents. Ten respondents answered only the question about problematic or concerning issues, leaving the other part blank. Another respondent said 'not sure what this is about' suggesting that the wording of the second part of the question was too ambiguous or global, referring to 'strengths or values which could influence developments in social work or higher education'.

It is possible that the wording of this question produced a particular emphasis on 'values' as a positive. One respondent suggested that more space was needed at this point in the questionnaire, although others added appending notes. Nineteen of the respondents, while answering both parts of the question, listed more concerns or problems than positives, and it was noticeable that these were predominantly from the old university sector. Only two respondents saw more strengths than weaknesses in the subject area, both from new universities. The remainder (majority) noted an equal number of concerns and strengths, although these were of a different order, and weaknesses might be perceived as more problematic. The majority of respondents cited more than one concern and strength.

Answers to both parts of the question were classified as follows. Problematic characteristics were grouped under five main headings - resourcing; change; value conflicts; survival; and research and relevance. Strengths were identified as relating to values; knowledge and theory development; teaching methods; and topical or pragmatic responses. These categories have also been used for presenting interviewees responses, and selected material from the ATSWE workshop.

In some respects, this chapter forms a reprise to the foregoing commentary. A degree of congruence with the researcher's own perceptions of the salient features is observable, although there were also some gaps. For example, structural arrangements and career patterns of social work educators themselves were not identified as either strengths or problems by the 1994 survey respondents (except occasionally by implication), although they were touched on by ATSWE workshop participants.

This chapter highlights the main themes from the research. In addition, particular attention is given to two subject area characteristics peculiar to social work; firstly, the role of CCETSW, and secondly, the nature and place of values in social work education. There is a further section on interviewees' responses about strategies for survival or development. First though, the problems and strengths of the area, as perceived by educators, are presented.

Problems and Concerns

Given previous discussion and data, it is not surprising that two thirds of the respondents (42) cited *resourcing* as problematic. Thirty responses were evenly divided between concerns about a lack of resources within the institution, and the shortage of placements externally. Respondents commented on 'inadequate resources to do the job' or 'funding', or noted the 'lack of stability in provision of placements' or simply, 'the placement crisis'. Eight people mentioned the administrative demands of the subject, including five specific comments about partnership arrangements, for example, 'the politics and costs of collaboration'.

A few people mentioned the conflicting expectations of individual or group performance in the three or four areas previously identified (research, management, teaching and practice), and the lack of resources available to address these sufficiently. Development work was not usually identified explicitly as a separate aspect of an individual or team role, but in view of the amount required in a limited time period might well have been.

The next largest category concerned the nature and pace of *change*, and was identified by half the respondents (32). This could be subdivided into change within the professional field (14), change in higher education(2), and change in social work education itself (16). In the first category, respondents were concerned about the nature of the changes, 'education for what?', and about the changes in local authority structures and agency roles, 'how many social workers will be needed?'. The limited responses about change in higher education related specifically to new monitoring systems, and modularisation and semesterisation.

Comments about change in the area of social work education were more common, and ranged from the general, 'constant change with no time for reflection or consolidation' to the more specific, 'the DipSW review', and indicated frustration about the direction of change by the validating body; 'the unrealistic demands of CCETSW' or 'the unworkable regulations for qualifying training'. These also indicated concerns about the (bureaucratic) arrangements for the continuum of training, the (inadequate) length of qualifying training and lack of preparation for work in particular areas, such as the residential field.

The length of social work qualifying training was given relatively more weight by the ATSWE workshop participants, who identified a lack of specialisation and concerns about standards of practice ('just about safe to go and practice') as a direct result of the limited training period (3 out of 22 workshop responses). This accords with some of the data previously discussed, which suggests an increasing concern and frustration about this issue by social work educators, resulting in new developments between 1994 and 1996 to address this.

One third of the respondents (22) identified *value conflicts* as a problem for the subject area, including the sense that both social work and social work education were operating in a hostile political climate (6), for example 'a political climate which emphasises technical and instrumental values and excludes critical analysis'. This was also expressed by others (9) as the difficulty of maintaining professional values relative to deprofessionalising tendencies in both social work and higher education, including the move to competency based assessment. A further third of this group noted the problem of maintaining anti-oppressive values in the political climate of the time or identified the teaching and assessment of anti-oppressive practice itself as problematic (at a pedagogic level).

An almost equal number of respondents (20) identified the threat to the *survival* of the subject area as the main problem. Not least among the reasons for this was concern about the survival of social work itself (7), 'will there still be a profession in 10 years time?'. A similar number wondered about the feasibility of social work education continuing in higher education, or made related points about who would decide the future of social work education, including two comments about the possible threat to CCETSW as the validating body. Three respondents mentioned the threat to probation training as an aspect of social work education, and one person queried whether the small size of some staff teams put it at risk in some institutions.

Finally, a small number of respondents saw the poor *research profile* as a weakness or identified concerns about the relevance of social work education to the professional field. Comments about research ranged from the pressures to produce it, to having no time to undertake it, and to the poor research record, quantitatively and qualitatively, of the subject area. This could be contrasted with respondents who were more concerned about the lack of relevance, and suggested either that a closer association with the field (rather than the academy) was necessary, or that research could usefully identify/support education in its attempt to prepare people for social work practice in a changing environment; 'Are social work changes being reflected in social work education?'; 'Is social work education too dissociated from the providers?'.

Some of the ATSWE workshop participants linked a concern about research with more explicit reference to 'inadequate theory', 'lack of academic rigour' and 'no agreed body of knowledge'. It was in this forum too, that reference was made to 'tensions and competition with other academic disciplines'; to the marginal position of social work vis-à-vis higher education and the profession; and to the lack of academic credibility accorded to the subject. One person also identified the self-critical role of social work educators and their deference to academics in other fields as a source of weakness in the subject area.

Some of the above points constitute criticisms from within about the nature of the enterprise, rather than a more analytical perspective on why social work might be viewed as a 'weak' subject and under threat. Not all the respondents share the same assumptions about what the weaknesses are and how they might be addressed, and this in itself constitutes a weakness; that is, some respondents explicitly or implicitly are in favour of strengthening the research base and academic credibility of the subject area, while others might want an even closer association with the field, and mechanisms to ensure 'relevance'.

Strengths

The possibility that responses to this part of the question were skewed by the wording is given some weight by the fact that, while nearly half the respondents to the 1994 survey (29) cited *values* as one of the strengths of the area, this was only one of 22 responses about strengths of the area suggested by ATSWE workshop participants in 1995. The wording used to describe these values by 1994 respondents varied from use of the terminology found in CCETSW documents (anti-racism, anti-discriminatory practice) (16 respondents), to more general references to 'social justice', 'equity', 'humanistic values' or 'upholding the rights and responsibilities of vulnerable groups' (or expressed as 'valuing diversity' by the ATSWE participant).

A further third of the respondents (21) thought that the contribution of social work educators to *the knowledge base* was a strength of the area. Some mentioned the carrying out of research relevant to practice, or the development of theory; and ten people specifically referred to the use of social science or multi-disciplinary perspectives to promote critical analysis of social work. This suggests a view of social work education which places it in a professional framework, rather than an academic one, although again the wording of the question might have encouraged a response about the contribution of the subject to development of the field. Only two respondents suggested that the strengths of the subject (in the area of values) could benefit the institution.

Nearly a third of the respondents saw the *teaching and learning approaches* of the area as a positive attribute, noting an emphasis on student-centred and participative learning; attention to the personal, to process and to 'empowering' approaches; and 'innovative' teaching methods. Given the problematic nature of resourcing, this may suggest a principled adherence to some approaches which are currently in question or imaginative attempts to circumvent them. However, some of the approaches common to social work (and other forms of professional education) are now being adopted more widely in the pursuit of 'relevance' of graduate skills to the world of work. In this sense, social work might be in the vanguard of educational developments within institutions, or at least in step.

Finally a 'catch-all' group of responses (8) identified *pragmatic or topical strengths*. These included 'an ability to change'; familiarity with vocational education; managing and educating for diversity; a high level of recruitment and 'expertise with non-standard entrants'; and, not least, 'our students get jobs!'. One of the participants in the ATSWE workshop also noted the pragmatism of social work education as both a strength and a weakness. What might be seen as a positive attribute in some circumstances, could also be dysfunctional in others. This reflects again the Janus-like character of the discipline and the need to engage appropriately with two systems.

Although not commented on in the survey data, it was clear from the HEFC Teaching Quality Assessment Exercise (1993/1994) that in many HEIs the subject area 'performed well' in relation to institutional criteria and mission statements. If good performance occurs in both teaching and research assessment exercises, institutions may see the subject area as having real value. Fifteen (out of 75 English) institutions gained an 'excellent' rating in the 1994 TQA, of which eleven were in the old university sector (HEFCE, 1995). Of the fourteen (English) institutions awarded a rating of 3a or higher in the 1996 RAE, seven had previously gained an 'excellent' in teaching. It is difficult to make precise comparisons, since some of the institutions rated as 'excellent' in the TQA may not have made a research submission or it may have been included in another subject area's submission.

If above average standards are achieved in both teaching and research, and combined with positive relationships with local communities, good recruitment, low wastage rates and good employment statistics, institutions may well view the area favourably, notwithstanding possibly higher unit costs and the potential for value conflicts. However, the likelihood of the subject area meeting all these criteria in all institutions is not great, and in some places there is evidence of the predominance of weaknesses or problems over strengths.

CCETSW

Views about CCETSW were not explicitly sought, nor necessarily addressed, in the 1994 survey. However, it became evident from developments in 1995, (when an *ad hoc* conference of social work educators was convened at Liverpool University) and from subsequent literature, that an increasing number of social work educators saw adherence to CCETSW's requirements (and the values and assumptions reflected in these) as itself a weakness of the subject area. Even before 'New' Labour's proposals in 1998 heralded the demise of CCETSW, there were dissatisfactions with its role and functioning.

It was clear from interviewees' responses, JUC SWEC records and some of the literature, that social work educators held somewhat ambivalent or negative views about the organisation and the part it has played in recent developments. CCETSW's role in, for instance, pushing for uniformity, or of not withstanding pressure to dilute particular values, has received critical attention, as has its insistence on formal partnership arrangements and apparent favouring of the employer interests in content and assessment. CCETSW's style and its role around the turn of the 1990s were also the subject of critical commentary by a former social work education adviser (Brewster, 1992).

In 1996, over half (7) of the people interviewed spoke about the organisation in varying tones of frustration or resignation, usually on the question about strategies for development. The opening statements on this topic by five interviewees were unambiguously negative. 'I am very unhappy about CCETSW's role and the structure of the DipSW'. 'CCETSW is not good news. It has attempted to deskill, compartmentalise and devalue training'. 'CCETSW is irrelevant: it's a paper tiger'. 'One way forward would be getting out of CCETSW. It's a terrible nuisance, and has held standards down rather than putting them up'. 'CCETSW has no powers to deal with placement issues'. At the extremes, one of the interviewees continued, 'It's a nonsense and should be got rid of', while another said, 'I don't see how the organisation can be sustained. There is no need for a validating body as such'.

The focus of people's criticism of CCETSW varied and related both to the requirements which CCETSW placed on social work education and to its use of power, or even lack of power. One person commented particularly on the difficulty of developing and sustaining partnership arrangements, 'There has been no consistent effort in relation to education and training [locally]. Agencies can't commit resources, and some Directors have been experienced as quite hostile'. (He contrasted this with probation, 'Probation has been a wonderful support', and with positive experience of the Health Service). This can be linked to CCETSW's lack of power in relation to placements, 'Placement opportunities · are diminishing rapidly, despite more money and work being poured into the voluntary sector. CCETSW is under so much pressure itself it can't see local problems so it can't help us'.

This respondent also resented the increased expectations of CCETSW in relation to participation in other areas of work, 'I am active in local PQ developments, ...but why can't CCETSW do this centrally?' Another also saw the post-qualifying area as symptomatic of CCETSW's failings, 'I am not impressed by their P/Q developments. They're very unclear and bureaucratised, with the educational component minimised'.

Other interviewees were more concerned about the lack of an intellectual basis and holistic perspectives in CCETSW's requirements, 'The notion of competencies suggests that social work can be broken down into discrete areas. It denies the complexity and creativity of the work': other comments, illustrative of the concern about the knowledge base and assessment methods, as implied or prescribed in CCETSW requirements, have been cited in previous chapters, and some of the literature (Webb, 1996; Jones, 1996b; Jackson and Preston Shoot, 1996).

However, two of the respondents were more measured in their response, and four of the critics tempered their views with some appreciation of either CCETSW's position, or speculation about what the alternatives might be. One interviewee saw 'CCETSW as being in a very difficult position between government, the employers and the universities, and as having given in to one party rather than achieving a consensus'; while another thought that 'CCETSW has been under enormous strain from the government to come up with things'. One interviewee, pursing the theme of CCETSW's lack of power said, 'Social work education is going to go its own way and what is CCETSW going to do about it? It has a statutory responsibility to turn out social workers; they need us more than we need them', but conceded 'we can go too far unless there is a responsible head of programme'.

Another respondent explicitly saw the need for a validating body, 'and it's good that there's only one body, but it should have more representation from social work educators as well as students and clients, and it should be more detached from government'. A critic said 'I am publicly not a knocker of CCETSW because it is necessary for the credibility of the profession that there is a central validating body', and contrasted the UK situation with the 'anarchy' of the American social work education scene. But this was also mentioned in more positive vein by another respondent who had 'some sympathy for the USA Council on Social Work Education, but running our own validation system is hard to imagine'.

Four respondents speculated about the possibility of a radically different role for CCETSW or a General Social Services (or Social Work) Council. In relation to the first, one interviewee said, '[CCETSW] could administer a national test which students could take, but the universities should be trusted to set their own course standards'. His preferred option was for a General Council of Social Work or Social Services, responsible for registration and professional qualifications, 'we've waited too long for this'. However, another interviewee had 'fears about a General *Social Services* Council. It would attempt to incorporate everyone and would be a force for deprofessionalisation', but two people explicitly favoured a General *Social Work* Council, similar to the General Medical Council. From the foregoing it can be seen that, while criticisms of CCETSW were considerable, there was no consensus about the possible alternatives.

Turning to data from the JUC SWEC, it was clear that this organisation had had a long-standing relationship with CCETSW, as one of the stakeholders whom CCETSW regularly consulted. A CCETSW representative normally attended the termly committee meetings, and the organisation was proactive in raising matters with CCETSW as well as reacting to new proposals and developments. Additionally, JUC SWEC put forward nominations to CCETSW Council and, while the representation of social work educators had declined dramatically since the mid-1980s, someone from JUC SWEC was on the Council or National Committees throughout the 1990s. In addition, a number of members were involved, on an *ad hoc* basis (and not necessarily formally as JUC SWEC representatives), in a range of steering and development groups.

Annual Reports of JUC SWEC and other documents up to 1997 testified to the organisation's efforts to represent the views of educators on a range of issues, either through written responses or through 'consultative meetings' (sometimes including representatives of other groups such as ATSWE). An analysis of Annual Reports showed that the following concerns were the subject of consultation or lobbying over a decade or more:- proposals for or revisions to qualifying training, including probation (every year); placements (annually); post-qualifying training (1987, 1989, 1990, 1991); the costs of collaboration (1989, 1991, 1993); competencies (1989, 1994); funding arrangements (general, 1991); clearing house arrangements (1991); the increasing burden of monitoring and evaluation (1993); and transcripts (1995). Additionally, there were periodic collaborative ventures with CCETSW, including two conferences about 'Euro-developments' (1989, 1990) and one about the HEFC's Teaching Quality Assessment Exercise (1993).

While some respondents acknowledged that, in operating as an agent of the Department of Health (primarily), CCETSW's powers to promote social work education interests were limited, others thought that its role of late had been more pernicious, or at least more concerned with its own organisational survival than the good of the subject area. It was noted that its role in relation to qualifying education was primarily concerned with professional *training* without any responsibility for research; and its remit extended increasingly from qualifying to pre-qualifying and post-qualifying levels in the wider social care field. This meant that the *education* of a professional group, generically called 'social workers', was less central to its operations, and its influence in the 1990s extended in ways which were of more concern to employers.

An earlier role of giving advice and undertaking development work increasingly seemed subordinated to its statutory duty to approve programmes and, in so doing, to regulate the numbers of people embarking on social work training and the standards of those subsequently entering the profession. Overall, the data suggested some agreement about the need for a body independent of HEIs, which represented the interests of the profession as a whole, and which had some responsibility for maintaining professional standards. But it had become a debatable question among educators as to whether CCETSW was an appropriate body or able to carry out its remit effectively.

Values in Social Work Education

Turning to the area of values, CCETSW Paper 30 (1989) codified a development which had been taking place during the 1980s in piecemeal fashion in social work education. It required that attention should be paid by *all* DipSW programmes to the combating of racism and other forms of personal discriminatory behaviour and structural exclusion or oppression of minority groups (including women, a minority in the political sense of having less power than the dominant male group).

Since the early 1980s, a number of courses had given attention to the personal aspects of prejudice which give rise to discriminatory behaviour and sought to enable students to examine their own attitudes and see where change might be necessary in their dealings with other students, clients and future colleagues. This was a response to commitment among staff to develop feminist and anti-racist perspectives in a radical critique of social work (Langan and Day, 1992), but was also prompted by demands of increasingly diverse groups of students, exposed to the messages of wider social movements.

This stage of 'consciousness raising', particularly in relation to race and gender, gave way to more insistent concerns that students should learn how to identify situations in which other people's behaviour or the operation of institutions and policies discriminated against individuals and groups seen as 'different', and the development of strategies to address the causes and consequences. This required an analysis of power differentials at individual, group and societal level.

Courses and student learning were informed by theoretical material and empirical studies from psychology and sociology, and policy developments and legal frameworks could be analysed to demonstrate how they perpetuated or sought to address particular forms of discrimination, exclusion or oppression. At best, the onus on social work students to examine critically themselves, the organisations within which they operated, and the policies they were required to implement, would be placed in a wider philosophical and ethical framework and be integrated at a personal level to form a secure professional value base.

From the late 1980s some social work educators, often women, have been readily identified by their writings as promoting anti-discriminatory values; and have sought to apply feminist or anti-racist perspectives to social work theory, education, policy and practice (for example, Humphries, 1988; Dominelli, 1989; McNay, 1992; Carter et al., 1992). However, not only was one of the interviewees concerned how particular values were being adopted, but some of the literature has questioned equal opportunities and related values espoused by social workers, and the role of social work academics in the 'construction and legitimation of such discourses' (Sibeon, 1991/1992, pp.194/5). Sibeon suggested that teaching and learning about values within social work education was 'susceptible to an authoritarianism that is simultaneously silly and sinister' (p.189), and cited the concerns of Rojek et al. (1988) that liberatory social work dogma is 'repressive because it won't tolerate diversity or aberration' (Rojek *et al.*, 1988, p.144).

A similarly critical article by Webb (1990) had sparked an unusually heated debate in the social work literature (Webb, 1990; Dominelli, 1991; Webb, 1991; Smith, 1992) and was followed by a public denouncement of CCETSW's requirements in relation to values, in the wider educational press (Pinker, 1993).

Teaching about anti-racism and feminism, in the 1980s and early 1990s, had its roots in civil and democratic rights and personal 'liberation' movements. Its operationalisation in British social work policy and practice occurred when political and societal values were shifting in favour of individual responsibilities and against the recognition of collective needs or redistributive policies. Social work educators were perceived by some as being increasingly 'out of step' in promoting these values, or naive or inept in their attempts to do so. Hence, criticisms from within the academy in the early 1990s were mirrored by criticisms of social work practice externally and by 1994 the government was requiring CCETSW to review Paper 30, including reference to this area of work (Jones, 1996c).

Nevertheless, about a third of the respondents to the survey saw the values concerned with anti-discrimination and social justice as a strength of the area, notwithstanding the conceptual and emotional difficulties facing those teaching and learning (where sensitive attention by staff to group processes and intra- and inter-personal dynamics are essential). The extent to which social work sees itself as an occupational group which should address inequalities and injustices may set social work education apart from other disciplines. There is impressionistic evidence to suggest that both social work students and staff can be perceived within HEIs as raising awkward questions, pointing out home truths or simply being assertive about their own and others rights. At least two of the survey respondents who identified this area as a strength saw the value base as an opportunity to contribute positively to the policy and ethos of higher education (as well as to social work practice).

The contradictory position of 'values', as both a strength and weakness, was identified by at least one of the survey respondents and one of the interviewees. Those seeing it as a weakness were sometimes more concerned about 'how to do it effectively' than the political consequences of doing so. Some respondents seemed to be thinking about how social work presents itself to others as suggested in the identification of 'Managing and educating for diversity' as a strength. Given use of this term in current organisation literature, this may be a more acceptable way of framing a traditional concern with inequalities than some of the 'anti' language. It may also reflect a stronger concern with tolerance of and valuing 'difference', than with action aimed at redressing social injustices.

Only two of the interviewees in 1996 made specific reference to anti-discriminatory values, both in ways which indicated support for their inclusion in social work education. One person, generally critical of CCETSW, qualified his remarks, 'I disagree with the political attack on CCETSW. I don't think that work in the ADP area was over the top'. Another interviewee said, 'I think it is a remarkable achievement that social work is the only profession which has a written clear political commitment at the core of its curriculum, that is anti-racism and anti-discrimination'. However, this was qualified, 'I don't endorse everything that has gone on under this - but at least a dialogue has been started. Normally, the hallmark of a profession is its basis in scientific knowledge, but social work is based on an ideological commitment'. Two interviewees referred to attempts to demonstrate the values of social justice through action research aimed at empowering users and saw this a definite strength of the subject area.

Turning back to the literature, Jones (1996b, pp.19-20) identified 'a cluster of so-called social work values' as having replaced the social science knowledge base in social work education, and a means by which CCETSW has paid lip-service to the needs of clients relative to the interests of agencies. However, he also suggested that (anti-discriminatory) values 'now remain one of the few tangible sites where it is still possible to glimpse the wider purpose of the activity', and it can clearly be seen as a site of resistance to the dominant ideology of the day. Webb (1996) also saw anti-discriminatory values, at least as expressed in a list of oppressions, as a substitute for the social sciences, and pointed to the superficiality of rhetoric in this area. He suggested that an approach to anti-discrimination framed around competence to the exclusion of analysis and knowledge is epistemologically unstable (Webb, 1996, pp.184-5).

The weak theoretical base of some of the literature, noted by Macey and Moxon (1996), and research in relation to anti-discriminatory values has already been mentioned, including feedback from the 1996 research assessment exercise. As Langan (1992, p.7) wrote, 'The question of whether the principles of anti-discriminatory social work will prevail over the vocationalism currently in vogue remains to be resolved', and arguably, this may be determined in part by the extent to which research and teaching can be informed by more sophisticated understanding and communication of the complexities of the area.

Opportunities and Strategies for Development

The more concrete plans which 1994 survey respondents and the 1996 interviewees had for developments in the area have already been recounted. However, many of the responses of the 1996 interviewees were of a more general nature and can usefully be presented here with some supplementary material. Some people were concerned primarily with relations with the profession, 'We should play to our advantages. ·We should value successful work within the university as long as it doesn't degrade our other activities. We must maintain successful public activities with local agencies as a basis for research and publications'. This outwardly directed view was echoed in 'We have important servicing and consultative roles as teachers and researchers, and the agencies continue to want this'.

There were also responses influenced by academic considerations. The development of a more flourishing research culture was a common aspiration, as in responses about post-graduate developments (5) and specific references to research: 'There's a growing sense of the social work academy with an interest in research and teaching and learning...our research base is expanding but we must find time to create and plan and involve as many colleagues as possible'; or 'Research and writing are important in terms of how we are perceived as a department...We need to organise ourselves better...people need space and time to do things'.

Other responses emphasised the particular contributions which social work can make to higher education. One interviewee stated that 'the overall strategy is to work from our strengths...so for instance we should make use of work-based learning, our relationships with outside agencies...portfolios and mentoring. We should go out and 'sell' them!' This view was shared by others, 'There are very few areas of academic activity where some of the aspects we emphasise are not taken into account. Given current trends, social work education should begin to feel more comfortable in higher education'.

This was related to whether respondents saw the area as under attack or relatively secure, and by 1996 these respondents were mainly positive in their responses: 'In some ways social work education is well placed. It is recognised that education needs to equip people to work in the real world, but it's important not to allow this to turn education into a purely instrumental activity'. 'There is no particular hostility to social work education in higher education - it is highly regarded here. It is effective in a difficult area'. However, as the same speaker acknowledged, 'One of the things happening locally is that some first year degree work and basic training is being shifted to Further Education, so we must ensure that all of social work isn't shifted. ...Social work must be a strong academic activity which the universities are happy to have in their portfolios'.

This threat was apparent in another interviewee's response, 'The university has other professional schools and is quite well disposed to them. But if social work is being redefined at NVQ level we have no part to play in it'. Anticipating this scenario, the area at this institution was rapidly extending its range of activities and courses and 'Social work teaching might become a second string rather than a first string to ones bow'. Another interviewee suggested that 'There is a danger of social work being marginalised in ordinary academic institutions, but if there is no institutional commitment to an applied discipline then social work should be elsewhere [for example in professional schools]'. Another person spoke of the need to 'be part of the ordinary degree and post-graduate system, rather than different and special'. However, he also floated the idea of creating 'departments more like teaching hospitals, including alliances with local agencies where research is done and we make a real contribution to the community'.

Three of the interviewees spoke of existing or potential alliances with other professional areas. One person said, 'The university is still relatively positive to social work education but it's partly because of our alliance with health'; or 'Currently we're seen as odd animals, half in and half out of the institution, but there are also other examples of professional training [which we need to relate to]'. A third spoke more speculatively about a possible move to the development of professional schools, 'We need to establish broad multi-disciplinary alliances. Nursing can gain from social work and social work from research in education'. A possible alliance with social policy was not viewed so favourably by the same person, 'It's an applied discipline, yet it's seen as more academic and allied with the managerialists. In America, social work and social policy co-exist rather than social policy taking over'.

A need to promote the area more positively was also expressed by a number of the respondents; 'We need to develop a more political role within the institution, to be more astute and anticipate things more, to be pro-active rather than reactive. We need to build alliances and give the area a higher profile. Social work will thus be a more valued activity, and...morale would be improved'; or 'We need to have pride in what we're doing and push the message that communication and demands are not just one way. Higher education may not be very responsive but we have things to say about how the outside world operates, and we should be more assertive about this'. This was linked by another interviewee to the need to strengthen social work education networks and representations, 'to engage in strategic thinking and not just be reactive'.

Other possible developments mentioned were the strengthening of links with European social work education, not least because 'they still have a community work component', and the possibility of forming a special interest group for social work educators in BASW. However, despite a relatively positive response overall, the likely contraction of social work education, in the form of its demise in some institutions, was also mentioned by a couple of respondents and in the light of other data and developments this remains an imminent likelihood. One respondent saw this in institutional terms, 'Undoubtedly there will be university mergers. Some of the present divisions and duplications are untenable', but another was more concerned about the viability of individual courses, 'some will go under - this one?'

Particular strategies for survival or development were identified - maintaining the qualifying stage of social work education as a manageable part of a larger enterprise, and increasing control over the volume and nature of workloads. However, a reduction in the number of institutions offering social work education and its concentration into bigger units, as has happened with probation streams in the early 1980s, early 1990s, and more recently, seems inevitable, at least in the short term. In the light of the further review of DipSW in 1999, whether a subsequent downgrading of education and training provision occurs is still an open question.

Finally, possible future threats and opportunities, as perceived by social work educators, can also be identified from the priorities for the activities of JUC SWEC in 1997. Thus, a long standing Practice Development Sub-committee was being reinvigorated and urgent representations made to CCETSW; the Probation Sub-committee continued to monitor, lobby and encourage on-going involvement in the criminal justice field; the International Sub-committee was operating as an active information network with effective representation at European and international level; and a newly established Research Sub-committee began mapping out an ambitious agenda for future work.

Three of these are predictable areas of national concern, but the interest in European and international links during a period of intense local change and pressure can be variously interpreted. Some may see it as 'flight' from a difficult area, or a distraction from local concerns. But another possibility, identified in an evaluation of the ERASMUS programmes (Lyons, 1996), was that such activities have provided some educators with an important source of stimulus and perspective, enabling British concerns to be placed in a wider comparative framework and contributions to be made to international debates, as happens in other disciplines.

Conclusions

This chapter has presented the findings on social work educators' perceptions of the strengths and weaknesses of the area, and possibilities for its development, and has recapitulated several themes identified in earlier chapters.

A number of factors related to teaching and learning, the knowledge and value bases, and student characteristics, were identified as strengths, while questions of resourcing, speed and direction of change, values, threats to survival, and research were all perceived as problematic by respondents to the main survey. The overall tone of responses in 1994 was judged to be demoralised.

By 1996, a selected group of interviewees gave some impression of a more confident mood, although evidence of criticisms and concerns remained. It is not possible to say how representative of the wider field this latter small, selected group were in this respect. However, their range of backgrounds and differences in perception on specific issues, coupled with material from JUC SWEC and the literature, suggested that reliance could be placed on their views.

Social work educators' views on two particular topics, CCETSW and values, was examined in some detail, not because these had been identified as core areas of inquiry in the research design, but because it became increasingly clear that the workings of these two 'institutions' have had a major bearing on recent stresses within the area, and on how it might be perceived externally. In relation to CCETSW, there seemed to be some agreement that an external professional body was necessary, but less consensus that CCETSW was the most appropriate or effective mechanism. The main criticism related to the extent to which it has been influenced by government and employer interests, to the near exclusion of the educators' voice. With regard to values, this remains a contentious area, but there are indications of a shift in language and a more critical approach (internally) to an area which must remain central to the conduct of social work as a professional activity.

Among the conclusions which can be drawn from the data are the diversity of situations vis-à-vis the field and institutional contexts experienced by respondents, and the range of perceptions of the causes and solutions to problems of the subject area. There was evidence of a continuing, strong orientation to the field, and concerns to maintain professional qualifying training in ways which are relevant and appropriate. However, there was also an indication of an increasing commitment to academic values and a wish to be more integrated into mainstream structures. There was further evidence of role strain among social work educators and a perceived need to develop the subject area in ways which reduce workloads and enable more strategic and proactive developments. This would include the development of alliances and seeing the social work education enterprise in the wider context of professional education and international perspectives.

The possibility of the 'downgrading' of qualifying social work training (and its wholesale removal from higher education) remained a risk identified by some respondents, and a few responses referred specifically to the likelihood of reduction in the number of social work departments or subject areas (on the basis of size and cost). However, other respondents were more optimistic about the adaptability of social work and its viability within HEIs. Some saw this specifically in relation to wider changes in higher education, and increased congruence between the goals and approaches of social work and host institutions.

Part 3 of this book relates the characteristics of British social work education, as identified in the foregoing data, to the framework initially elaborated and reconsiders the relationship of the subject to its professional field and to the wider area of professional education.

PART 3

BACK TO THE WIDER CONTEXT: ISSUES AND PROSPECTS FOR SOCIAL WORK EDUCATION

11 Social Work: The Discipline and the Profession

Introduction

Chapter 2 identified the over-arching issues of socio-economic and cultural change in society which have impacted upon social work, including an actual or perceived rise in violence in domestic and public life, and the effects of political and ideological changes on the organisation and practice of the profession.

Conflict was perhaps inevitable between an occupational group committed to respect for individual and group difference, social justice (redistribution) and anti-discriminatory policies and practice, and a government intent on re-establishing more traditional, individualistic and market principles in public life. The statutory and organisational changes of the early 1990s reflected both these contextual issues, and an earlier preoccupation with professional status was overtaken by concern about social work's continued existence.

Many of the developments in social work education and characteristics identified in Part II are linked to concerns of the field. Concerns about relevance were evident in the changes to qualifying training signalled in 1989 and 1994, and also in the establishment of a new structure for the development of post-qualifying and advanced awards. These changes combined to impose pressures on both educators and organisations to establish and maintain programmes of a prescribed kind in a period of need for (well) qualified social workers, but also of decreased resources and significant change. There has been evidence of government intent to discredit values central to professional formation at the qualifying stage and to 'shift' the values of social work educators regarding management and delivery of social work education; for instance, in the marketisation of placements.

There are inherent tensions in the nature of social work and its relationship with the state, and it is perhaps inevitable that these will be reflected in social work education. This may even be a test of its relevance.

Social work educators have strong roots in the professional field and many retain a close association with it, arguably to the detriment of developing the discipline and their own academic identities. Additionally, too close a 'fit' between education and current employment patterns may make the subject vulnerable and may not be in the longer term interests of the profession and service users.

The relationship between the professional field and the educational process is not a concern unique to the UK. Social work educators and researchers elsewhere also struggle to maintain relevance and credibility with the profession while establishing academic credibility. Such tensions have been noted in countries with a variety of traditions in social work and in educational models, including Sweden (Svensson, 1994), the USA (Rice and Richlin, 1993) and Australia (Hartman, 1989). This chapter reviews changes and characteristics of social work education in England and Wales, with particular reference to the identity and biography of social work educators.

Sites, Purpose and Relevance

Lack of consistency in the departmental location of social work education mirrors a long-standing struggle about the siting of social work as a professional activity in the UK. Social work's 19th century origins as an ancillary activity in institutions concerned with punishment, rehabilitation, health care and schooling are still evident in the marginal position of probation officers, hospital social workers and education social workers. These social worker roles (quite specialised, by client group and setting, if not by level of work), are always open to redefinition by others and need to be constantly negotiated.

Similarly, in non-social work departments the subject may be rendered invisible (for instance in the research assessment exercise) or may be perceived as so different or resource inefficient as to be problematic. Thus, social work educators in HEIs need to engage energetically with others in a position to influence objectives, content, structures and resourcing. But this research suggests that social work educators' energies are more likely to be focused on external activities and reference groups than on engagement within institutions. While dual accountability is recognised, educators may continue to see themselves as specialists within social work rather than as 'academics'.

Social work also had its roots in 19th century Poor Law provision, where the central concern was the relief of poverty and encouragement of personal morality as the basis of social order. The post-war establishment of local authority welfare and children's departments, and their successors, social service departments, continued a tradition of care for people 'in need' in the community or in residential establishments. While it seemed, in the post-Seebohm years, that social workers had now secured their own base where they could control their own resources and determine their own agenda, this proved to be illusory.

The social work element within social service departments became smaller and also less significant in terms of the overall work and values of departments. This may be less true of Social Work Departments in Scotland, where the very name signifies the core activity. Additionally, the public identification of social work with social services, the role of social workers in relation to people perceived as deviant, damaged and disreputable, social workers' apparent failure to cure, contain or remove them, and their attempts to understand and 'accept' them, have not enhanced the status of the occupation.

From the data presented, social work educators are not generally employed in large, 'autonomous' departments within HEIs. Current trends towards diversification, rationalisation and a reduction in qualifying training as the core activity cause social work education, at least at the qualifying stage, to become a minority and lower status activity, less involved in more academic pursuits. Qualifying education could be removed from higher education (as has happened, in part, with teacher education), just as an increasing range of social work provision has been removed from social service departments. Recent developments in probation training may, however, suggest an alternative scenario.

The third strand in the history of social work development was its roots in charity organisations, settlements and philanthropic activities. These have experienced a resurgence in rethinking of the roles of established voluntary agencies, the development of new forms of community and self-help organisations, and the more recent impetus given by government and society to private practice and provision (though philanthropic effort may be unplanned and idiosyncratic).

The relationship of social work education to this third strand is less obvious, since social work education has been substantially determined by the requirements of the largest employer of newly qualified social workers, SSDs. However, the spur to changes in placement funding was the increased use of the voluntary sector, and NGOs often form a numerically significant element in DipSW partnership arrangements. The separate development of youth and community work courses and the near demise of community work in both social work and youth and community programmes testifies to increased pressures to individualise assessment and responses to people presenting problems.

There is no obvious 'privatisation' parallel yet in the private provision of social work education, though the employment of sessional staff ('freelance' trainers) or the development of open and distance learning routes to qualification suggest marketisation of labour and education which could become more prevalent. It is also likely that relationships will be developed with a growing private care and therapy sector, if existing placement models continue.

Educators have experienced increased bureaucratic, technocratic and managerialist pressures, familiar to social workers in the statutory sector (and sometimes in large voluntary organisations). These are partly processes within higher education institutions, but can also be attributed to the requirements placed on providers of qualifying, post-qualifying and advanced awards. It can be argued that, except for the Teacher Training Agency (TTA), CCETSW has taken a more prescriptive line than most validating bodies relating to partnership arrangements, course content, assessment and monitoring, all impacting on social work education, and on the agencies involved.

Qualifying programmes tend to be highly geared to the needs of social service departments, with (previously) about one third aiming to equip students for the probation service, and smaller numbers offering specific training related to education, health, psychiatric or other fields. Changes in the role of social workers in SSDs have implications for the focus of social work education, as do shifts in responsibilities to the voluntary and private sectors. Social work education has not adequately addressed more broadly-based concerns, for instance about poverty and about particular client groups or settings. Moves to problem-based or enquiry and action learning signified in some of this research suggest more flexible curriculum construction and programme delivery methods, linked to the shifting nature of social work.

The 1990s have seen a renewed focus on informal care by family, friends and neighbours, and the consumer role in shaping services, most strikingly reflected in the proposals for the composition of the General Social Care Council. These trends have implications for the numbers and roles of social workers, and for 'consumers', including informal carers having a say in the design and delivery of education programmes, as well as social work services. The notion of partnership comes to the fore again. There was little evidence that this has yet been seriously addressed by social work educators, although occasional references to 'empowerment' and collaborative forms of research suggest some patchy development.

Professional groups tend to demarcate territory and erect barriers to outside 'interference', and institutions 'protect their boundaries'. There is evidence that social work organisations and academics are not much different. The involvement of service users in social work courses, in ways which are not tokenistic or exploitative, would have resource implications and require negotiation with the host institution. However, the picture looks rather different if one regards the consumers of social work education as students; it is at this level that modelling of staff attitudes and course systems, to promote participation, responsibility and feedback, was more in evidence and capable of further development.

Boundaries and Alliances

The concern here is with the content and functions of social work rather than its organisational form, and again parallels can be drawn between what happens in the field and what has been observed in social work education. Despite various attempts to demarcate the social work territory, the occupational boundaries of the social work role are frequently unclear.

Other groups may share an overlapping knowledge base, but they are unlikely to have the same goals, values or powers. Conflict (or lack of contact) rather than co-operation, between social work and other agencies, has been well documented in the profession's failings (previously in the child abuse field, but more recently in 'community care'). The implications for social work education are two-fold. It mirrors some of the territorial disputes and difficult relationships between social work education and adjacent academic and professional subject areas. It also suggests that far greater emphasis needs to be given in courses to the development of particular skills (such as networking and negotiation) and to 'inter-professional work' than was evident from the data.

Some of this input might be at the qualifying stage, but it is perhaps more important and feasible at the post-qualifying and advanced stages of professional education. One reason is the current length of social work training, in which there are issues about overcrowded curriculum content and about socialisation into professional role and identity which qualifying training should provide. Conversely, post-qualifying training is essentially concerned with consolidating learning, and this stage or the next (concerned with extending knowledge and expertise in particular directions) are appropriate locations for learning about inter-agency practice. The need to address systems and policies at a higher level, which this usually entails, is also better addressed when personnel have more experience of, for instance, organisational roles.

Many factors impact on the development of good working relationships between allied professionals, not all of them amenable to change by social workers. Improved understanding of the factors militating against inter-professional work, as well as innovative attempts to engage professionals in shared learning, need to be addressed locally through in-service programmes as well as more formal continuing education. Course design and delivery are influenced by the biographies of social work educators, and limited attention to interdisciplinary work may result from insufficient experience in their prior roles and agency culture. This may be compounded if there is little encouragement of inter-disciplinarity within higher education itself (Barnett, 1994) and locational factors militate against collaborative efforts.

Levels and Length, and the Continuum of Training

The length and level of training has already been indicated as a source of status problems compared with other professionals and social work outside the UK. The historical development of courses at post-graduate level in the old university sector excluded many from an occupational group which was largely untrained, in favour of an elite group (in class and educational terms) in positions of relative power or status. This adversely affected both external perceptions of the profession into the 1960s and early 1970s, and aggravated internal schisms about status and elitism (in the later 1970s and 1980s), manifested in BASW's open membership policy and resistance to the ASW award.

Currently, a two year course at post-graduate level may be appropriate and sufficient as a conversion course for those who already hold a first degree and enter social work later. But in this case, the adoption of the American term 'MSW' would distinguish this qualification from other masters level courses being developed sometimes in conjunction with advanced professional awards. The persistence of half of the qualifying training at non-graduate level is of concern at a time when 'qualification inflation' is widespread in other areas and when there are problems of unemployment for well qualified graduates. It seems a greater anomaly, given that social work students tend to enter university at a later stage, with relevant work experience.

On the other hand, in the face of student poverty, some social work educators regard a two year non-graduate route as a commitment to open access. Such routes were favoured by employers using secondments to increase qualified staff numbers (Wallis Jones and Lyons, 1997). However, in the late 1990s this position is under review and the increased use of APEL and exemptions could accommodate two-year (or part-time) routes through three year degree awarding programmes (whether or not these are directly modelled on probation training). Indications in the data suggest that social work educators have been implementing such change on an *ad hoc* basis. This must have the tacit approval of the field, since rules about partnership in course design and delivery apply and there is no evidence of increased demands on agencies (for example through a third placement). There is no guarantee that graduate qualification in itself ensures status of the occupation or freedom from government intervention (as shown in teaching) (Becher, 1994), but it would bring the occupation into line with teachers, nurses and counterparts in many other countries.

The question then remains about the nature, level and status of post-qualifying awards (including those for ASWs and practice teachers) which CCETSW 'pitched' at degree level. This may have recognised the likely level of qualification held by potential candidates or a too ready acceptance of the government veto on three year training. It seems that this was not an appropriate level of qualification for people with at least two years experience intending to take on more specialist roles, and who may have initial qualifications at degree or post-graduate level.

This research suggests that the post-qualifying awards should be seen as essentially concerned with consolidation, including induction to the workplace, rather than extension into specialist roles in the mental health and practice teaching or other roles, such as management. Professional awards in these areas could reasonably be part of post-graduate diploma courses, unless undertaken in the context of more theoretical studies and research based dissertations, meriting masters level awards.

The foregoing discussion presumes the relating of professional awards to academic levels, about which there was much discussion in the operationalisation of the requirements of Paper 31. Qualifying training is but a beginning in terms of professional development. It seems consistent with wider societal and professional trends, and personal aspirations, to include the possibility of academic as well as professional credits in an approved system of continuing education. The evidence suggests support from educators for this development. The design of the requirements reflected encouragement of improved availability and standards, including recognition of in-service training programmes. Universities were minimally included in the assessment and validation of such programmes, but sometimes in more overt joint planning and delivery.

The imposition (and acceptance) of the continuum of training could be viewed more cynically alongside CCETSW's role in the Care Sector Consortium of establishing pre-qualifying training at NVQ Levels 1-4 and the concern, not least among educators, about the incorporation of the qualifying stage of social work education into this framework. While there has been some development of the new post-qualifying and advanced awards as college based programmes, many more are in agencies and there were protests from well established academic courses (which had CCETSW recognition under former post-qualifying arrangements) that previous funding had been allocated to regional consortia to meet a wider range of demands.

Given the current uncertainties about student funding, including postgraduate level and part-time awards, the implications of these developments for student numbers and resourcing of the area are considerable. This may explain both involvement in post-qualifying activities by social work educators (as an attempt to retain some share in resource allocation) and also diversification into other forms of academic work, not dependant on CCETSW for approval.

There is relatively slow progress in getting regional systems 'up and running' and (as yet) limited output of people holding post-qualifying or advanced awards under the new system. This probably reflects the cumbersome nature of the system, the new learning needed by both educators and trainers to agree levels and standards, and the sheer weight of other demands on personnel, rather than resistance to the idea of continuing professional development. The area is under review at the time of writing.

Establishment of a continuum of training was an ambitious move by CCETSW. Although most countries have social work education more securely located in the university sector and minimally at degree level, there is less evidence of agreed frameworks within which continuing professional development (CPD) takes place. The extent of collaboration required between the field and institutions in programmes for post-qualifying education in British social work might be viewed as appropriate by advocates of more 'integrated' forms of professional education (Curry *et al.*, 1993), although arrangements seem more elaborate than in some other professional fields. Attitudes and developments in relation to CPD could usefully be further researched.

The possible 'up-grading' of qualifying awards to degree or post-graduate level, and extension of advanced courses, have implications for the profile of social work educators. While professional qualifications and experience have previously been valued in the recruitment and promotion of social work educators, this research suggests there is also a need for more emphasis on academic credentials and leadership in research and theory development, albeit rooted in the concerns of practice.

The Regulation of Social Work and Social Work Education

Literature and data sources indicate that some of the 'blame' for the state of social work education in the 1990s was laid at the door of its regulatory body, CCETSW. This has partly been attributed to its status as a QUANGO, heavily subject to government and employer interests, as opposed to having defence and promotion of the profession and users as its core purpose. Additionally, social work does not have a powerful voice in the form of a strong professional association, and Becher (1994) noted the inability of the occupation to establish a credible 'collective image'. Nor had social work, to date, shared the apparent advantages of other occupations in operating a degree of self-regulation through professional Councils, although evidence from this research suggested that social work educators were not unanimous about the advisability and appropriate form of any such regulatory body.

Employers could reasonably be assumed to be primarily concerned about and responsible for practice standards. But the growth in BASW's Advice and Representation Service (in defence of members in dispute with employing agencies) and the role of other professional bodies in guarding members' rights, suggested general support for establishment of a General Council (Parker, 1991; Brand, 1997). Lack of a protected title had been seen as one of the factors putting British social work out of step with most European Union neighbours at the time of the 1989 Directive on Professional Training (Barr, 1990). However, a protected title is not in itself a sufficient guarantee of good practice and professional conduct (Henkel, 1994), and regulatory bodies also specify requirements about professional updating and development, as well as taking disciplinary action against members whose conduct falls short of public and professional expectations.

These responsibilities in relation to social workers have become part of the brief of the recently announced General Social Care Council (GSCC). Its wide scope and the high representation of service users are novel features relative to other Councils. They accord with the rhetoric of partnership and consumer voice, and signal that the Council will be more concerned with the protection of the public than with promoting a narrow professional project.

Funding such a body through registration fees will be in line with practice in other fields, and is consistent with an approach to education and training which assumes that those who enjoy the benefits should incur an increasing proportion of the costs. However, it raises the possibility of exclusion of some people from educational and employment opportunities (already observable in some fields such as law) on the grounds that they cannot meet such costs.

Theory and Practice

A frequent criticism of social work education and a tension around the changes in DipSW alluded to earlier, has been the lack of relevance between what students learn on qualifying courses and what they are expected to know in practice. This is not a criticism restricted to UK social work education, nor to this form of professional education. This 'lack of fit' (as more recently termed, for instance in the TQA exercise) has various facets. These include the level of job-related specificity expected of college-based elements in the programme; the pedagogical approaches and assessment methods used to enable students to learn for practice; and the contribution of the practice placement element itself.

Data from this research suggested that curricula are overcrowded and heavily influenced by employers in the statutory sector. However, it also seemed that there were large gaps in particular areas of knowledge or skills-based learning; for example, in relation to ill-health and disability, child observation or research. It can also be suggested that merely extending the length of courses by a year may not create enough space to cover the ever increasing range of 'things' that social workers are expected to know about.

Additionally, 'training' people for specific roles, for instance to undertake child care work in a statutory agency, may result in people being qualified, but not to do jobs which have changed (even while they have been training) and not to do 'new' jobs or similar work in different circumstances. It seems necessary, therefore, to think in terms of greater generality in some of the curriculum content, but with more emphasis on process aspects (learning to learn, researching resources) and greater clarity about the particulars to be learnt in the placement context.

It can be argued that social work education should be providing students with broadly-based social science knowledge (perhaps in a more integrated 'psycho-social' framework); more focused and comparative knowledge about social work principles, methods and organisation; and professional skills and values (for example, through use of experiential learning workshops and practicums). The aim would be to produce people capable of critical analysis, applying problem solving and other skills, and reflecting on their actions and developmental needs (Kennedy, 1987). It seems likely that increased numbers of qualifying students will enter 'new' roles in the voluntary or private sectors, and that past experience in professional practice of educators will have less relevance to the changed conditions.

Regarding social work principles and practice, the extent to which programmes should continue adherence to the casework paradigm (even if reframed as care management) can be questioned. In the USA, Midgley (1995) identified the need for a social development approach, described as social interventions that are compatible with economic development objectives. He sees this approach as appropriate in a wide range of societies, including those where consensus about the welfare state and role of social workers has broken down (or not been achieved). It is also an approach requiring intervention at the social planning and policy process level, reasserting the need for social workers to engage at 'macro' as well as 'micro' and 'mezzo' levels. Both community and social development models might be regarded in the British context as simply 'new fashions' or out of step with current assumptions about scope and focus of social work intervention. But they might also offer useful counterpoints to traditional and individualised methods, at a point where social work roles are in question and where 'persistent poverty in the midst of economic affluence' (Midgley, 1995, p.3) should be reinstated as a central concern of the occupation.

American literature is a rich source of research and theory about methodology and fields of practice, but there have been strong concerns to 'indigenise' social work education and reduce the reliance on externally produced material. British social work education does not need to 'import' concepts or teaching material, but the data suggested a motivation among some educators to engage with international networks and develop comparative perspectives. This may assist a more academic and critical appraisal of UK developments.

Curriculum content is closely related to pedagogical considerations and resourcing issues. There was little evidence in this research of radical change in pedagogical methods; for example, adoption of enquiry and action learning. However, the data suggested that social work educators were concerned to ensure some congruence between the medium and the message, and the concept of andragogy has had some influence on the style and delivery of the curriculum, however constructed. The idea that 'modelling' of behaviours and relationships might be important, given the nature of the work for which students are being prepared, has quite widespread support, but may suffer from reduced resourcing and other priorities within the subject area.

Traditional ideas about the tutorial role, still evident in some of the data, are being challenged both on pedagogic and pragmatic grounds. It is suggested that social work educators' adherence to tutorial work may reflect a need to retain a form of practice akin to social work and prevent development of more secure academic roles. It seems increasingly out of step with the new realities of the field and higher education.

Assumptions underpinning DipSW requirements were that more and better placements would result from changes to the college curriculum, the increased training of practice teachers, partnership arrangements, more placement documentation (including learning contracts), and the use of competencies assessment. The current research did not set out to test these assumptions.

However, some of the data and literature suggest that, while placements play an important role in professional training, they constitute a very variable element in the student experience and an expensive, even 'wasteful', element in the educational process. One respondent suggested that a culture shift was necessary so that students on placement are seen as the norm in agencies and part of a healthy culture of professional development and organisational learning, rather than being exploited, envied, ignored - or simply refused a placement.

This may represent a utopian view of the future, but indicates that the anti-intellectualism of the profession, coupled with the pressures and constraints on agencies, bring existing assumptions and arrangements into question. Questions might relate to the number, length and expectations of placements; their purpose and the role of practice teachers relative to college-based social work educators. For instance, if practice teachers are now better trained, are the placement visits by college 'tutors' still appropriate or might there be other ways of arranging liaison between college and the field which would be more efficient and as effective?

While UK training in relation to placements is respected by colleagues abroad, the current amount of time spent in placement, the specialist qualifications of practice teachers, and the amount and form of assessment, are unusual outside the UK. In a useful 'comparative overview' Rogers (1996, p.21) confirms concerns about the status and resourcing of the practice component 'on both sides of the Atlantic' and also relates these to 'the deeper debate about professional education versus technical training' (p.27) apparent beyond the UK. However, it seems likely that the need for exposure to real world problems will continue to be seen as an essential element in professional education for social work.

Biography, Values and Power

One of the defining features of social work and of its educational enterprise has been its image as a female occupation, which has also informed perceptions about the intellectual and value bases of the occupation. Even with the long-standing involvement of men in most areas of social work, a stereotype persists that women, in some forms of social work, are concerned with care, and that men, in others, are concerned with control, although the establishment of unified social services departments fundamentally challenged this.

The Seebohm Report signalled a shift in expectations about the management of the task, and current evidence demonstrates the predominance of men in senior positions, in both agencies and educational programmes. Gender differences are compounded by class and race differences (social work education having been relatively open to non-standard entrants), which has added to how social workers may see themselves - or be seen - as 'different' and excluded from the networks of power open to other professional groups.

How gender, race and class of social work educators might impact on the nature and status of the discipline was not fundamental to the research design or methodology. It is therefore not possible to say how far the biographical characteristics of social work educators replicate those of the broader professional field (Lyons *et al.*, 1995) or other academics. But there seems to be a greater likelihood of men achieving senior positions in education (as in practice) and of a relationship between perceptions of the subject and its female image.

It was partly an adherence to anti-discriminatory values which led the occupation to be viewed as 'out of tune' with public attitudes and to policy developments affecting its funding and legitimacy in the early 1990s. As has been noted, status (and therefore power) is partly related to public trust (Becher, 1994, p.166). Quite apart from a more general diminution in public confidence in professionals, it is clear that British social work has suffered from negative public perceptions with a knock-on effect to social work education. It can be argued that the very subject matter of social work will always involve uncomfortable associations and have the potential for public criticism and blame. The centrality of 'ideology', identified by one interviewee as a strength, may also constitute a significant weakness if it is at variance with the dominant social values, and even be discounted by potential allies if it is not supported by an accepted knowledge base.

The wider the gap between social work aspirations of a political rather than a technical nature and the governmental concerns of the day, then the greater the likelihood of conflict. The period researched illustrated government intervention aimed at de-emphasising the professional nature of the role, increasing demands for technical skills (with associated expectations of educational providers), establishment of alternative training frameworks, and differentiation and isolation of workers who might otherwise share similar concerns.

Social workers' (and educators') articulation of unpopular or minority views and needs, and enabling have-nots to get greater access to resources, power and knowledge, makes the occupation 'subversive' by definition and liable to be silenced or ignored if concerns do not match the agenda of those in power (Lukes, 1974). It might also be an unwelcome player on the wider professional or disciplinary stage. Such perceptions may feed into the very behaviour for which social work can be condemned - more strident and confrontational approaches, or more isolationist and defensive ways of operating - both evidenced in criticisms of social work education.

But social workers are not the only people concerned about equity or justice, or challenging male or white domination; and, as suggested earlier, building alliances is possible and necessary. Developing a healthy relationship with other disciplines and occupations, consumers and institutional and political systems, while maintaining commitment to the value base, is surely one of the most significant challenges facing British social work and social work education in the new millennium.

Questions remain about the association between workforce characteristics, the value base, and the power position of both the occupation and its associated subject. It seems possible that recruitment to social work education posts has been less influenced by academic status than by other considerations, including professional experience. This, and the lack of apprenticeship into the discipline (conventionally provided through PhDs at an early stage in other academic careers) could further contribute to limited perceptions of social work educators as academics and the vulnerable status of the subject area in HEIs.

Summary and Conclusions

This chapter has revisited some of the debates and concerns of social work as an occupational field and argued that, in many important respects, social work education mirrors the insecurities and conflicts of the wider profession. Similarities were noted between the difficulties of 'defining' the purpose, core tasks and appropriate organisational forms of social work relative to educational content, with inherent risks in preparing students for roles which are too job-specific.

Further parallels were drawn between the imprecise boundaries of the field and the subject area, and the implications for the educational task at qualifying and post-qualifying levels. Issues about the status of social work were related back to questions about levels and length of qualifying training, as well as to broader issues of public perception and trust. Criticisms about the relevance of social work education to practice, and insecurities about the status of both the occupation and the discipline, apparently have many causes and extend beyond Britain.

Continuing debates about the level and length of qualifying awards remain problematic for UK social work, although the implementation of a continuum of training could be viewed as an ambitious and probably unique initiative. However, there are anomalies in the 'pitching' of some professional awards and the academic level at which they should be located. The general principles of a close association between academic and professional awards, and between educators and employers, are supported, but the specific organisational arrangements of the 1990s have been viewed as resource intensive and not necessarily effective. Some of the literature about post-qualifying awards suggests that the costs were too great for all but a very small minority of people to benefit, and that institutions and employers might be increasingly unwilling or unable to bear the costs.

The further review of the system in 1999 suggests some acknowledgement of these concerns. This, together with reshaping of the regulatory and training frameworks (with the establishment of the GSCC and TOPSS - Training Organisation for the Personal Social Services), heralds a period of further uncertainty and change.

The knowledge, skills and values of social work were considered. Although some of these are not particular to social work, the contexts and purpose of application are. It is suggested that social work education should provide more generalist and principled *education* as well as skills training, including attention to process. Social work education should equip students for more varied and changing employment opportunities, suited to the concept of 'portfolio careers' (increasingly evident in social work) and to continuing professional development and life-long learning.

Placements play an important part in the educational process as a way of 'grounding' theoretical and generalist principles, and enabling assessment of 'know-how' as well as 'know that'. However, the question of resourcing suggested that this is an unresolved issue for social work educators and employers, which needs radical review in the light of current realities and possible alternative models.

Finally, the place of values and biography were considered. These also play a part in the perceived weakness of social work as an occupation and a subject area. This has been a conflictual area, periodically, and played a part in the increasing efforts by government to control the occupation and curtail its educational goals. It seems likely that there will be constant tension around this area, possibly to a greater extent than is evident in other occupations.

A further question was raised about the biography of individuals in the workforce of both the field and the subject area, contributing to an (over) identification with people who experience disadvantage and discrimination, and feeds into a lack of power. In such circumstances, it is predictable that some attempts will be made to raise the academic status of the subject and to engage in other strategies to advance the professional project. However, social work's own capacity for internal dissent has been evidenced in the past and can be as damaging as external criticism.

The implication for social work education is that the education and training process needs to aim at producing social workers who are confident about their professional role and identity; whose values are well rooted in a sound knowledge base and can be rationally articulated; and who have the skills to access and win allies in networks and systems which are invariably bigger and more powerful than the social work enterprise.

Evidence from this research suggested a continuing strong commitment to the professional field by social work educators, but some exhaustion with imposed change and disillusionment with the direction of change from CCETSW earlier in the decade. There was also some evidence of an increasing recognition of the role which social work education itself could and should be playing in the wider field of professional and academic research and development. The extent to which a more proactive response to recent events accords with developments in other parts of professional education and the higher education system is considered in the concluding chapter.

12 Professional Education in Higher Education

Introduction

Recent literature presumes a generic field of professional education within which subjects share similarities and there are grounds for learning from each other (Bines and Watson, 1992; Becher, 1994; Eraut, 1994). Earlier literature had identified disciplines as having distinct cultures related to the interplay of epistemology and the biographies and action of academics (Toulmin, 1972; Becher, 1989). This research supports a view that professional education is culturally different from academic disciplines, not least in the extent to which its form is shaped by external forces. Moreover, professional education is not homogeneous and can be differentiated according to a range of characteristics and cultures.

Traditionally, the culture (organisation and values) of HEIs has favoured disciplinary knowledge over professional education (Hixon Cavanagh, 1993), although recent trends in UK higher education policy suggest this may be changing. Externally, there are different assumptions about which occupational groups constitute professions; different histories, including their place in higher education (Friedson, 1986); and continuing status differences. These are reflected in the associated educational enterprises.

Some models of professional education are considered next, followed by a discussion of the implications for the place of social work in higher education.

Models of Professional Education

Bines (1992) adapted a typology of professional education, related to the history of professions as a progression from an apprenticeship model through a technocratic model to the current position where more sophisticated notions of the relationship between theory and practice are being developed. She relates this to the shifting locus of control from the occupational group to the academy and now to the development of a partnership between the professions and higher education. This 'progression model' is recognisable in social work although there has always been a relationship between the field and academy and it is the nature of the relationship, the relative power balance, which has been contentious.

An alternative formulation was presented by Jones and Joss (1995) who considered the likely outcome of particular types of training for resulting professionals. They identified professionals who would be practical, technical, managerial or reflective, with concomitant variations in their relationships with clients. They also included 'operatives', or deprofessionalised workers, 'subject to ever more prescriptive rules...managerial imposition...increasingly hierarchical structures' (p.24). In this scenario, professions might evolve from the managerial stage into either 'operative' or 'reflective practitioner' types.

Historical development, the current locus of control, the likely outcomes of education are important dimensions of models developed, but there are other dimensions on which patterns and cultures of professional education can be compared. Some of these are now discussed in relation to the institutional context and generic field of professional education.

The Organisation of Professional Education

Characteristics of social work education identified in Chapter 5 throw into sharp relief some of the contrasting assumptions and organisational arrangements underpinning other forms of professional education. There is a general assumption that professional education *should* take place at higher education level but other occupations afford examples of education and training outside HEIs (medicine, teaching) and/or following an academic degree (law, psychology).

Locating responsibility outside normal HEI structures suggests the power of a 'strong' profession to determine content, boundaries and values of a subject. This is unlikely to be so in the case of 'weak' professions, where the state seeks to define the roles, skills and goals of the group, for instance, through imposition of a national training curriculum (Graham, 1996) as in teacher education. It is this latter model to which social work would conform if removed from higher education. The resultant loss of an independent and critical role (encouraged by higher education) concerned respondents to this research.

The alternative model offered by psychology or law, where professional training follows an undergraduate (theoretical) course, postpones decisions about 'suitability' and controls entry to the profession at a later stage than social work (academically, though not necessarily chronologically). The academic ability of applicants is proven and the professional education stage is closely linked to employment (through limited availability of training places), with varying expectations about the extent to which students/trainees will be self-financing.

The post-graduate model of training for social workers was rejected in the 1960s (when the tide was turning against experts in society and elitism in higher education), and more overtly in the early 1990s, with CCETSW's implementation of the training continuum. The issue has been revisited in the late 1990s with the capping of bursaries and calls for evidence about the 'added value' of post-graduate outcomes relative to non- or undergraduate routes. Advocates of different academic levels of qualifying education have focused on opportunities for entry to the occupation ('open access') rather than outcomes, and have stressed the maturity and prior experience of applicants rather than their academic attainments. However, this emphasis, and the resulting age profile of British students (as well as level of qualifications), is strikingly different from social work education in most other countries. This perpetuates concerns about academic standards in a subject seen as 'weak' for a number of other reasons.

It is possible to envisage a development where institutions choose to promote post-graduate routes, possibly at the expense of maintaining non-graduate or undergraduate programmes, other than, for example, through degrees in social welfare or psycho-social studies. Development of part-time routes closely linked to employment (as in the psychology model) might be in step with wider developments in higher education and employment patterns, and would reduce the risk of 'closure' of the occupation to people on grounds primarily of income (as tends to happen in law). There was no evidence at the time the data was collected of widespread support for such a move, although it may be implicit in some developments taking place. It raises afresh issues of professional accreditation (of programmes) and funding, and would require a radical shift in current assumptions, but it could constitute an alternative form of 'rationalisation' of current provision. Whether the profession as a whole and various stakeholders, including HEIs, would see such a move as in their interests is an open question.

Knowledge, Research and Practice

Concerns about the knowledge base of social work identified in the data may have parallels in other forms of professional education. General issues about the nature of knowledge; its presentation in specialist or generic forms; the relative weight given to theory, skills and values (ethics); and the place of practice learning are germane to all forms of professional education (Jones and Joss, 1995). Additionally, 'new' knowledge within particular disciplines, and changing requirements in the professional field, require a dynamic concern with curriculum design and content, as well as particular approaches to teaching, learning and assessment.

There are substantial differences between the nature of knowledge utilised by different professions and the corresponding research paradigms. Application of Becher's (1989) theoretical framework does not explain the status differences (in academic and professional terms) between medicine and engineering (both falling within the 'hard applied' knowledge quadrant) or between law and social work (both categorised as 'social professions' within the 'soft applied' knowledge quadrant) and other explanations are offered later. The wish to make professional subjects more academically credible through research and theory development (Brown and Gelertner, 1989; Hartman, 1989) has widespread relevance, and the tensions noted by social work educators around the creation as well as the transmission of knowledge are not unique.

Walker (1992) divided professional knowledge into content (theoretical core), process and practice knowledge: this has relevance to subjects other than social work, including the attention to 'process'. While interpersonal and group dynamics are a particular feature of social work curricula, other professional groups also require skills in establishing relationships and communicating. Some of the differences, therefore, relate to emphasis and purpose rather than to specific knowledge or skills. Concerns about the integration of tacit knowledge with learning (in college and practice), and the development of professional identity, also need to be addressed in the curricula and pedagogy of other forms of professional education.

The shift from knowledge as process to knowledge as product (Scott, 1984), typified by the move to outcome-based evaluation and the use of competencies to assess learning in practice, has not been peculiar to social work, nor limited to the generic field of professional education. There are wider concerns to ensure that elements such as the new frameworks of 'knowledge organisation' (including modularisation) and assessment of learning do not detract from goals of academic coherence and holistic understanding (Barnett, 1994).

Becher (1989) noted that personal values are likely to impact on the 'social professions' (widely defined to include also teaching and nursing) more than other disciplines and this research has suggested that 'values' have assumed a particular prominence in social work education. The nature of social work places unusual demands on students (and therefore educators) in terms of integrating their individual experience and attitudes with their learning and practice. However, even this characteristic, the linking of the personal and the professional, may be seen as a question of degree rather than absolute difference relative to other professional groups.

Professional educators are likely to be involved in the selection and utilisation (presentation) of knowledge and ideas from other disciplines in ways which are relevant to their particular field. This entails the integrating and synthesising of knowledge, and there are variations in the extent to which this is undertaken by professional educators themselves or by 'specialists' from other disciplines. Medicine, for instance, draws heavily on the knowledge fields of other disciplines (for example, pharmacology), suggesting that it is not the lack of an exclusive knowledge base in itself that determines the academic strength of a subject. However, some forms of knowledge may be perceived as having a more theoretical or conceptual basis, as opposed to deriving from experiential or practice learning, and the valuing of an interdisciplinary approach to knowledge creation may also be at odds with the wider culture of higher education (Barnett, 1990; Hixon Cavanagh, 1993).

Professional educators have called for a reconsideration of what constitutes knowledge and valid research, and of how different forms of knowledge are organised and ranked (Rice and Richlin, 1993). But the ownership, control and ranking of knowledge is still a contested issue within the academy as well as between the subject and the field. Professional educators, including social work educators, have been weakly placed to challenge established hierarchies of knowledge, but significant changes now taking place in higher education give scope for a shift in traditional relationships and assumptions about knowledge, research and pedagogy.

There are considerable variations in the extent to which professional educators engage in research; the research profile of specific subjects; the sources and level of research funding; the research paradigms used and extent to which they are taught to students; the nature and degree of collaboration within and between subjects; and the existence of 'practitioner research'. The last RAE did not reveal any consistencies in performance of professional subjects relative to academic disciplines (*Times Higher Education Supplement*, 20.12.1996) but four of the subjects ranked in the bottom third are ones identified as 'female orientated' (Becher, 1989). Other factors, such as the public perceptions of the *need* for, or credibility of, research (affecting funding), have a bearing on research quantity and quality, as well as the aspirations and capacity of the relevant academic community.

With regard to pedagogy, some of the recent initiatives and concerns of social work educators have been paralleled or prefigured in other forms of professional education. Problem based education (EAL) originated in medical education in Canada. Schon's ideas developed in education and management and were tested in architecture and music. Research and literature about how students learn originate from psychology and teacher education. Training for supervisors (practice teachers) was realised in nursing well in advance of social work.

It seems as if the belated or patchy adoption by social work of some approaches has been related to a preoccupation with developments in its external field or a defensive concern that social work is different and must find its own solutions. But in a time of rapid change, learning and research across disciplinary and professional boundaries could be in the interests of professional education as a whole (Bines and Watson, 1992), and social work educators have contributions to make within the academy as well as externally.

Status, Power, Regulation and Resources

Location of professional education within higher education places subjects on boundaries between different systems, and under pressure to conform to different norms and expectations. In this respect social work is no different from other professional education (Hartman, 1989). Disputes between the academy and professional bodies have arisen in relation to curricula and assessment in a range of professions (Hixon Cavanagh, 1993; Vang, 1994) The pre-existing status differentials between professional groups are mirrored in their regulation and the resources available to them to protect or promote their interests in higher education.

Burrage (1994) suggested that the interest groups with a legitimate concern about the form, content and standards of professional education are the individual professions, employers, government and consumers. The professions are usually represented though accrediting bodies, the power and credibility of which vary. The last two decades have seen an increase in intervention by governments in the regulation of education of occupational groups undertaking state sanctioned activities. This shift in power between the professional accrediting body and the government was well illustrated in the case of social work, and the research identified concerns about the extent to which CCETSW was able to represent an independent professional voice, relative to both government and employers.

The development of collaborative work with employers has also been formalised in social work and could be seen as reflecting similar moves in other forms of professional education, as well as being in line with wider moves to promote active relationships between HEIs and the world of work. The opportunities, pressures and risks which such 'required' relationships entail are thus not peculiar to social work, although it can be speculated that the pressures and risks may bear more heavily on professional courses relating to hard pressed areas of the public sector (including teaching and nursing), than on areas where there is a greater degree of choice and commercial opportunity.

The impact on professional educators of arranging placements also varies - in mentoring or supervision in the field; in the form and emphasis of assessment; and in the role that teaching staff play in making and monitoring such arrangements. In some subjects the responsibility for gaining relevant practice experience rests with the student or is automatically available through employment in a trainee post. Teaching and nursing share with social work expectations about the close involvement of academic staff in securing and visiting students 'on placement' with concomitant resource implications (Bines and Watson, 1992).

The individualised nature of this task contributes to the labour intensiveness of professional education and the extent to which it is seen as expensive by institutions, however the placements themselves are funded. This particular aspect of the role may extend outside normal teaching times and breaks into what might otherwise be 'quality' or 'clear time' which academics need to produce good teaching and research (Johnstone, 1996).

It also adds another dimension to the role and tasks of professional educators and may contribute to role strain (Collins, 1995). However, as Collins himself identified (1994), the argument for continued involvement of academic staff in social work placements relates to continuity and a wider frame of reference in the students' professional development, and to responsibilities for ensuring equity and educational standards.

Biographies and Career Patterns

This research indicated that social work educators enter academic life later than their disciplinary counterparts. This is likely to be true of some other forms of professional education, where it is also the case that entering lecturing means leaving the professional field. The extent of the split between the teaching role and practice is varied and in some occupations, such as medicine, there is clearly less of a split and more of a shift in the focus of work at different stages in individual careers.

In the case of teaching, nursing and social work, at least, it is likely that entering academic work means relinquishing professional practice (or management). In current conditions, much work (in schools, hospitals and agencies) is reactive and prone to crises which militate against continued (part-time) employment, other than in occasional specialist posts. Impressionistic evidence suggests that people who try to retain 'a foot in both camps' are likely to feel most acutely the differing expectations of employing institutions and to experience role conflict and disadvantages in career progression.

While the move into academic work may be perceived by some as a 'flight from the front line', one set of expectations and pressures are replaced by another and a change in mode (for example, from relatively reactive to proactive behaviour) is required. It seems that the effects of this career change, both for individuals and for the development of subject areas, have not been fully explored or addressed in higher education. Warner and Crossthwaite (1995) suggest that attention to staff development and human resource issues generally have been relatively underdeveloped. Issues about 'legitimacy' of the educator role, as well as of subjects, play a part in wider debates about individual and collective confidence, performance and continuance in higher education.

If, as in the case of social work, a measure of anti-intellectualism exists in the profession of origin, this may compound the marginal position of professional educators, relative to the field of practice, and require more effort in establishing collaborative arrangements, whether for programme delivery or research ventures. However, wider developments in higher education suggest that requirements regarding external credibility and joint work are impacting increasingly on all academics, and educational policies and institutional missions may give increased legitimacy to this type of activity.

With regard to gender, there are clear imbalances in favour of men in some of the traditional professions, including the academic field, relative to the predominance of women in less prestigious or secure professions. Despite earlier assumptions that women are not discriminated against in the academy, this is not the case (Brooks, 1997 and more recent statistical evidence from HESA). The forms which such discrimination might take however are subtle and more actively addressed in some institutions and disciplines than others. If discrimination exists in relation to individual careers, then it may also operate in relation to subjects where women are in the majority, and possibly in leadership roles. Just as individuals may feel undermined or unacknowledged, groups of staff may also feel marginalised or disregarded, or have less expected of them - and respond accordingly.

It can be questioned whether changing conceptions of knowledge (and its relationship to experience) and the changed work context (portfolio careers) will shift the negative effect of (female) gender in particular occupations. It seems more likely that new working patterns will impact differentially on men and women, such that there is little real change in the distribution of power. If, as was suggested in relation to social work, gender differentials in the workforce are compounded by race and class differences, the consequent perceptions of the subject may be further affected. It seems likely that nursing and teaching have also been used as avenues of social mobility, adding to the factors contributing to low status accorded to these subjects.

Future Prospects?

Some of the evidence in Part 2 has identified the extent to which social work education has experienced rapid change over the last decade, and the position of individual courses - if not the whole enterprise - in higher education may still be vulnerable. Nevertheless, while demise remains a possibility, there are also reasons for thinking that there may be scope for development. Barnett (1994) located a responsibility to analyse, question and comment on existing arrangements and assumptions with *all* academics, and this would seem to support the rationale for the maintenance of social work in higher education, rather than in an exclusively employment-based framework. The feasibility of, or support for, the latter position was not examined in this research.

Data gathered in the mid-1990s suggested continuing differences in the experiences and perceptions of social work educators, partly according to their location in the new or old university sectors, and it remains to be seen whether current changes in higher education enhance these differences, as universities seek to establish distinctive missions and identities. Conversely, the forces of national monitoring arrangements and league tables could exert pressures for conformity, in which case existing advantages are likely to be rewarded and disadvantages compounded.

Characteristics have been identified in this research which clarify some of the reasons why social work has been seen as a weak subject within higher education, and vulnerable to a range of pressures within and outside higher education. The macro-elements of these pressures can be represented diagrammatically as forces pulling social work education apart or at least in opposing directions (see Appendix 5). Thus, higher education policies, institutional arrangements, academic values and student interests may pull social work education in one way while welfare policies, the particulars of social work organisation, professional values and the needs of service users may pull it in a different direction. Alternatively, there might be *push-pull* factors at work, with strong pressures from government and employers *pulling* social work into the field and the resource-intensive nature of the subject *pushing* it out of higher education. Inevitably, its position on the boundary of two systems requires dual accountability and constant negotiation.

It is possible to observe trends in higher education which might suggest a more comfortable place for social work and other forms of professional education in the academy. Using the 'new vocabulary' identified by Barnett (1994) as characterising higher education, social work has 'vocational relevance' and aims to equip students with 'communication skills' (and others) relevant to 'employment'. Curriculum design is now clearly related to (required) 'learning outcomes' and assessment is substantially based on 'competencies'. Design and delivery of the majority of social work education is carried out 'in partnership' with employers. Many social work academics have long seen themselves as educators and have been concerned to promote student 'responsibility for their own learning'. Specific approaches, such as experiential and problem based learning, have been used to develop students' knowledge and understanding, and development of particular qualities, such as 'flexibility'.

The subject area scores well on some of the performance indicators used to assess quality in higher education (reflecting, usually, a close association with institutional mission statements), but the very prevalence of the 'new language' and associated regulations and arrangements, may have inhibited the development of the discipline and the maintenance of a critical perspectives on social change and the role of social workers in particular. This echoes Barnett's concern that, in the face of utilitarian conceptions of knowledge and the commodification of education, higher education itself will cease to operate a critical role in society.

Additionally, it may be that concerns about the nature of the subject have arisen at a time when disciplines themselves may be 'losing their potency' (Barnett, 1994, p.136). Just at the point where social work may be defining its own research agenda, as befitting a discipline (Toulmin, 1972), this and other ideas about academia seem less relevant. But as higher education expands, so new subjects are developed and social work may be more compatible with a concept of problem based domains (Trist, 1972) than traditional disciplines.

The findings also suggest that social work educators may not have taken sufficient account of their higher education context and of potential benefits of alliances with other subjects. The strong sense of professional identity evident in social work educators can be seen as a strength relative to the professional field. But the biographies of social workers and the culture of the discipline may have militated against the development of a more robust subject which, while engaging with the field can also step back from it, and which can meet academic demands of theory development and research. There are however, recent indications of an increasing capacity both to satisfy academic norms *and* to contribute to professional knowledge and practice through research activities, though issues about disciplinary identity and funding of research remain. It is suggested therefore that establishment of the subject on a more secure basis requires renewed negotiation of the subject's relationship with higher education, with the professional field and with other forms of professional education.

Potential for development might also be assisted by wider shifts in society, which could be more open to Habermas' (1978) advocacy of values located in communicative action rather than instrumental rationality. Such a shift might assist in the revaluing of different forms of knowledge and also support academics, including social work educators, in providing students with a critical perspective on their world and equipping them for change.

Toulmin (1972) suggested that a role of academics was to give continuity to ideas (as well as developing new ones) and to trace the 'genealogy of problems' in a discipline (p.142). Such a rationale for the continued existence of social work in higher education was echoed in a response to the 1994 survey, which suggested that one of the strengths of the subject was its capacity to maintain 'its history and a vision for social work'. Additionally, the 'civil' role which Barnett (1994) suggested as a feature of academic responsibility (in relation to the ethical and communicative dimensions of society) is clearly also applicable to social worker educators and the professionals they are training.

In conclusion, there is no clear cut answer to the question 'can social work survive in higher education?' Its future is bound up with the future directions of the professional field and of higher education. This research has identified a number of characteristics and circumstances which make social work vulnerable, but also some which could contribute to its continued viability in HEIs. Social work educators' responses to this exercise (and in other ways) have demonstrated qualities of resilience and adaptability, and the capacity for 'reframing' problematic situations which, it is suggested, could be combined with greater confidence in their academic role (as well as professional identity) and in their contribution to current debates.

Social work as a change-oriented subject has developed strategies with regard to teaching, learning, assessment and research which have wider relevance. It is thus well placed to participate in current and potential changes within higher education and society, and professional skills and knowledge can be used to form alliances within and across institutional boundaries. The decision regarding the future location and shape of social work education itself does not rest exclusively with social work academics. However, they constitute a legitimate interest group and bear a significant responsibility to critically examine and articulate the issues pertaining to future development of the subject and the profession.

Bibliography

Abel Smith, B. and Townsend, P. (1965), *The Poor and the Poorest*, Bell, London.

Adams, R. (1997), 'Potentials and Pitfalls of Open Learning: Initiatives in Health Care and Social Work', *Issues in Social Work Education*, vol. 17, issue 1, pp.30-48.

ADSS (1985), *Sixth Survey of PSS Expenditure, Staffing and Activities*, ADSS.

ADSS/CRE (1989), *Race Equality and Social Service Departments*, Commission for Racial Equality, London.

Bailey, R. and Brake, M. (eds.) (1980), *Radical Social Work and Practice*, Edward Arnold, London.

Baldwin, M. (1994), 'Why Observe Children?', *Social Work Education*, vol. 13, issue 2, pp.74-85.

Ball, C. and Eggins, H. (eds.) (1989), *Higher Education in the 1990s: New Dimensions*, OUP/SRHE, Milton Keynes.

Ball, C., Harris, R., Roberts, G. and Vernon, S. (1988), *The Law Report: Teaching and Assessment of Law in Social Work Education Paper 4:1*, CCETSW, London.

Ball, C., Roberts, G., Trench, S. and Vernon, S. (1991), *Teaching, Learning and Assessing Social Work Law*, CCETSW, London.

Balloch, S., McLean, J. and Fisher, M. (eds.) (1999), *Social Services: Working Under Pressure*, The Policy Press, Bristol.

Bamford, T. (1982), *Managing Social Work*, Tavistock Publications, London.

Barclay Report (1982), *Social Workers: Their Roles and Tasks*, Bedford Square Press, London.

Barker, H., Benington, N., Corrigan, P., Davies., B, Dominelli, L. and Ginsberg, N. (1978), *Preparing for Social Work Practice: A Contribution to the Unfinished Debate on Social Work and Social Work Education*, Department of Social Studies, University of Warwick.

Barnett, R. (1988), 'Limits to Academic Freedom: Imposed or Self-imposed?' In Tight, M. (ed.), *op cit.*

Barnett, R.A. (1992), *The Idea of Higher Education*, SRHE/OUP, Buckingham.

Barnett, R.A. (1994), *The Limits of Competence: Knowledge, Higher Education and Society,* SRHE/OUP, Buckingham.

Barr, H. (1990), *In Europe: 1, Social Work Education and 1992*, CCETSW, London.

Barrett, S. and Fudge, C. (eds.) (1981), *Policy and Action: Essays on the Implementation of Public Policy*, Methuen, London.

BASW (1980), *Clients are Fellow Citizens*, BASW, Birmingham.

Bates, J. (1995), 'An Evaluation of the Use of IT in Childcare Services and its Implications for the Education and Training of Social Workers', *Social Work Education*, vol. 14, issue 1, pp.60-76.

Bebbington, A. and Kelly, A. (1995), 'Expenditure Planning in the PSS: Unit Costs in the 1980s', *Journal of Social Policy*, vol. 24, issue 3, pp.385-411.

Bebbington, A. and Miles, J. (1989), 'The Background of Children Who Enter Care', *British Journal of Social Work*, vol. 19, issue 5, pp.349-368.

Becher, T. (1989), *Academic Tribes and Territories: Intellectual Enquiry and the Culture of Disciplines*, Society for Research in Higher Education/Open University Press, Milton Keynes.

Becher, T. (ed.) (1994), *Governments and Professional Education*, SRHE/OUP, Buckingham.

Becher, T. and Kogan, M. (1992), *Process and Structure in Higher Education* (2nd edn.), Routledge, London.

Becker, S. (1997), *Responding to Poverty: the Politics of Cash and Care*, Longman, London.

Beresford, P. and Croft, S. (1986), *Whose Welfare: Private Care or Public Services?*, Lewis Cohen Urban Studies, Brighton.

Beresford, P. and Trevillion, S. (1995), *Developing Skills for Community Care: A Collaborative Approach*, Arena, Hants.

Bernstein, B. (1971), 'Primary Socialization, Language and Education: Class, Codes and Control', in Vol. 1, *Theoretical Studies Towards a Sociology of Language*, London: Routledge.

Biglan, A. (1973), 'Relationships Between Subject Matter Characteristics and the Structure and Output of University Departments', *Journal of Applied Psychology*, vol. 57, issue 3, pp.204-213.

Bilson, A. (1993), 'Applying Batesons' Theory of Learning to Social Work Education', *Social Work Education*, vol. 12, issue 1, pp.46-60.

Bines, H. and Watson, D. (1992), *Developing Professional Education*, SRHE/OUP, Buckingham.

Bines, H. (1989), 'Issues in Course Design', in H. Bines, and D. Watson (eds.) *op. cit.*

Birch Report (1976), *Working Party on Manpower and Training for the Social Services*, DHSS, HMSO, London.

Blackstone, T. and Fulton, O. (1975), 'Sex Discrimination Among Women University Teachers', *British Journal of Sociology*, vol. 26, issue 3, pp.261-275.

Blom-Cooper, L. (1985), *A Child in Trust: A Report of the Panel of Enquiry into the Circumstances Surrounding the Death of Jasmine Beckford*, London Borough of Brent, London.

Bolderson, H. and Henkel, M. (1980), 'Public Accountability, Responsibility and the Personal Social Services', Brunel University, unpublished.

Bond, M. and Jones, J. (1995), 'Research in Practice: Promoting the Dialogue', *Social Work Education*, vol. 14, issue 2, pp.85-100.

Bowlby, J. (1951), *Maternal Care and Mental Health*, WHO, London.

Boyer, E.L. (1990), *Scholarship Reconsidered: Priorities of the Professoriate*, Carnegie Foundation, Princeton, New Jersey.

Boys, C.J., Brennan, J., Henkel, M., Kirkland, J., Kogan, M. and Youell, P. (1988), *Higher Education and the Preparation for Work*, Jessica Kingsley, London.

Brand, D. (1997), 'Rowntree Steps up Support for GSSC Work', *NISW Noticeboard*, Spring, p.7.

Bray, S. and Preston-Shoot, M. (1992), *Practising Social Work Law*, Macmillan, London.

Brewer, C. and Lait, I. (1980), *Can Social Work Survive?*, Temple Smith, London.

Brewster, R. (1992), 'The New Class? Managerialism and Social Work Education and Training', *Issues in Social Work Education*, vol. 11, issue 2, pp.81-93.

Brooks, A. (1997), *Academic Women*, SHRE/OUP, Buckingham.

Brown, G. and Gelertner, M. (1989), 'Education: Veering from Practice', *Progressive Architecture*, issue 3, pp.61-67.

Brown, P., Hadley, R. and White, K.J. (1982), 'Appendix A: A Case for Neighbourhood Based Social Work and Social Services, in Barclay Report, *op cit.*

Burgess, H. (1992), *Problem Led Learning for Social Work: the Enquiry and Action Approach*, Whiting and Birch, London.

Burgess, H. and Jackson, S. (1990), 'Enquiry and Action Learning: A New Approach to Social Work Education', *Social Work Education*, vol. 9, issue 3, pp.3-19.

Burgess, H. and Reynolds, J. (1995), 'Preparing for Social Work with Refugees Using Enquiry and Action Learning', *Social Work Education*, vol. 14, issue 4, pp.58-73.

Burrage, M. and Torstendahl, R. (eds.) (1990), *Professions in Theory and History: Rethinking the Study of the Professions*, Sage, London.

Burrage, M. (1994), 'Routine and Discrete Relationships: Professional Accreditation and the State', in T. Becher (ed.) (1994) *op cit.*

Campbell, B. (1993), *Goliath: Britain's Dangerous Places*, Methuen, London.

Campbell, D.C. (1969), 'Ethnocentrism of Disciplines and the Fish-Scale Model of Omniscience', in M. Sherif and C. Sherif (eds.) *Interdisciplinary Relationships in the Social Sciences*, Aldine, Chicago.

Cannan, C. (1992), *Changing Families, Changing Welfare: Family Centres and the Welfare State*, Hemel Hempstead, Harvester Wheatsheaf.

Cannan, C. (1994), 'Enterprise Culture, Professional Socialisation and Social Work Education in Britain', *Critical Social Policy*, Vol. 42, winter, pp.5-18.

Cannan, C., Berry, L. and Lyons, K. (1992), *Social Work and Europe*, Basingstoke, Macmillan.

Cannon, T. (1993), 'Public Knowledge', *The Times Higher Education Supplement*, 14.5.93.

Carter, P., Jeffs, T. and Smith, M. (eds.) (1990), *Social Work and Social Welfare Yearbook 2*, Open University Press, Milton Keynes.

Carter, P., Jeffs, T. and Smith, M. (eds.) (1991), *Social Work and Social Welfare, Yearbook 3*, Open University Press, Buckingham.

Carter, P., Everitt, A. and Hudson, A. (1992), 'Malestream Training: Women, Feminism and Social Work Education', in M. Langan and L. Day (eds.), *op cit.*

CCETSW (1987), Paper 20.6 *'Three Years and Different Routes'*, CCETSW, London.

CCETSW (1987), Paper 20.7 *Better Education and Training for Social Workers*, CCETSW, London.

CCETSW (1989), Paper 30 *'DipSW: Rules and Requirements for the Diploma in Social Work'*, CCETSW, London.

CCETSW (1991), Paper 31 *The Requirements for Post-Qualifying Education and Training: A Framework for Continuing Professional Development*, CCETSW, London.

CCETSW (1993), *Standards on CCETSW Approved Programmes Annual Report From the Education and Training Committee: an Overview*, CCETSW, London.

CCETSW (1993), *How to Qualify for Social Work: 1994-5*, CCETSW, London.

CCETSW (1996), *How to Qualify for Social Work: 1997-98*, CCETSW, London.

CCETSW/LGTB (1987), *Workforce Planning and Training Needs*, CCETSW/LGTB, London.

Centre For Human Rights (1994), *Human Rights and Social Work: a Manual for Schools of Social Work and the Social Work Profession*, United Nations, Geneva.

Cheetham, J., Fuller, R., McIvor, G. and Petch, A. (1992), *Evaluating Social Work Effectiveness*, Oxford University Press, Oxford.

Cheetham, J. and Deakin, N. (1997), 'Assessing the Assessment: Some Reflections on the 1996 RAE', *British Journal of Social Work*, vol. 27, issue 3, pp.435-442.

Clark, C.L. (1991), *Theory and Practice in Voluntary Social Action*, Avebury, Aldershot.

Clark, C.L. (1995), 'Competence and Discipline in Professional Formation', *British Journal of Social Work*, vol. 25, issue 5, pp.563-580.

Clark, C.L. (1996), 'Competence, Knowledge and Professional Discipline', *Issues in Social Work Education*, vol. 16, issue 2, pp.45-56.

Clarke, J., Cochrane, A. and Mclaughlin, E. (eds.) (1994), *Managing Social Policy*, Sage, London.

Clarke, J. (ed.) (1993), *Crisis in Care? Challenges to Social Work*, Sage/Open University Press, London.

Clunis Inquiry (1994), *The Report of the Inquiry Into the Care and Treatment of Christopher Clunis*, HMSO, London.

Cohen, P. (1990), 'Teaching Enterprise Culture, Individualism, Vocationalism and the New Right', in I. Taylor (ed.), *The Social Effects of Free Market Policies: an International Perspective*, Harvester Wheatsheaf, Hemel Hempstead.

Collins, S. (1994), 'Placement Visits by Tutors from College Based Programmes', *Social Work Education*, vol. 13, issue 3, pp.4-23.

Collins, S. (1995), 'Stress and Social Work Lecturers: Dreaming Spires, Ivory Towers or Besieged in Concrete Blocks?', *Social Work Education*, vol. 14, issue 4, pp.11-37.

Collins, S., Lyons, K. and Sears, M. (1987), 'Possible Steps Forward to Aid Practice Placements', *Social Work Today*, 19/1/87, p.12.

Colvin, D. (1995), 'The Social Work Diploma: a Question of Degree', *Professional Social Work*, 9/95, pp.13-14.

Connelly, N. (ed.) (1996), *Training Social Services Staff: Evidence From New Research*, NISW, London.

Cooper, L. (1992), 'Managing to Survive: Competence and Skills in Social Work', *Issues in Social Work Education*, vol. 12, issue 2, pp.3-23.

Cornwall, A. (1995), *Making Better Use of Open Learning*, CCETSW, London.

Corrigan, P. and Leonard, P. (1978), *Social Work Practice Under Capitalism: A Marxist Approach*, Macmillan, London.

Coulshead, V. (1988), *Social Work Practice: an Introduction*, Macmillan, Basingstoke.

Coulshead, V. (1989), 'Developing the Process Curriculum', *Issues in Social Work Education*, vol. 9, issues 1 and 2, pp.21-30.

Coulshead, V. (1992), 'Transcending Dip.S.W.: Making Teaching Economies', *Issues in Social Work Education*, vol. 11, issue 2, pp.2-13.

Crompton, R., Gallie, D. and Purcell, K. (eds.), (1996), *Changing Forms of Employment: Organisations, Skills and Gender*, Routledge, London.

Culkin, M. and Thompson, J. (1994), *A Study of the DipSW Probation Stream Joint Appointments*, CCETSW, London.

Curry, L, Wergin, J.F. and Associates (1993), *Educating Professionals: Responding to New Expectations for Competence and Accountability*, Jossey Bass, San Francisco.

Cuthbert, R. (1996), *Working in Higher Education*, SRHE/OUP, Buckingham.

Deakin, N. (1994), *The Politics of Welfare*, Harvester Wheatsheaf.

Department of Health/Welsh Office (1998) (December), *Consultation Document on Post Qualifying Education and Training*, Department of Health, London.

DES (1989), *Student Numbers in Higher Education, Great Britain 1975-87*, HMSO, London.

DES (1991), *Higher Education: a New Framework*, Cmnd. 1541, HMSO, London.

Dewey, J. (1933), *How We Think: a Restatement of the Relation of Reflective Thinking to the Educative Process*, Free Press, New York.

Dews, V. and Watts, J. (1995), *Review of Probation Officer Recruitment and Qualifying Training* (The Dews Report), Home Office, London.

DHSS (1968), *Report of the Committee on Local Authority and Allied Person Social Services* (the Seebohm Report), HMSO, London.

DHSS (1976), *Working Party on Manpower and Training for the Social Services* (the Birch Report), HMSO, London.

Doel, M. and Shardlow, S. (eds.)(1996), *Social Work in a Changing World: an International Perspective on Practice*, Arena, Hants.

Dominelli, L. (1989), *Anti-Racist Social Work*, Macmillan, London.

Dominelli, L. (1991/2), 'What's in a name? A comment on Puritans and Paradigms', *Social Work and Social Science Review*, vol. 2, issue 3, pp.231-235.

Eadie, T. and Ward, D. (1995), 'Putting a Scenario Approach to Teaching Social Work Law into Practice: One Years Experience on an APP', *Social Work Education*, vol. 14, issue 2, pp.64-84.

Eastman, M. (1994), *Old Age Abuse: A New Perspective*, Chapman Hall, London.

Eggins, H. (ed.) (1988), *Restructuring Higher Education*, OUP/SRHE, Milton Keynes.

Elliot, N. (1995), 'College Reflections on Practice Theory', *Social Work Education*, vol. 14, issue 3, pp.5-24.

England, H. (1986), *Social Work as Art*, Allen and Unwin, London.

Eraut, M. (1994), *Developing Professional Knowledge and Competence*, Falmer Press, Brighton.

Etzioni, A. (1969), *The Semi-Professions*, Free Press, New York.

Fawcett, B. and Featherstone, B. (1994), 'Making the Transition from Social Work Management to Social Work Teaching: It's the Same Difference', *Social Work Education*, vol. 13, issue 1, pp.47-59.

Ferguson, R. (1994), 'Managerialism in Education', in J. Clarke, A. Cochrane and E. McLaughlin (eds.) *Managing in Social Policy*, Sage, London.

Fisher, M (1999), 'Research Note: Reassessing the Assessment', *British Journal of Social Work*, vol. 29, issue 1, pp.173-174.

Fisher, S. (1994), *Stress in Academic Life*, SRHE/OUP, Buckingham.

Flood Page, C. (1989), 'Review of Tight, M. (ed.).' *op. cit.*, *Higher Education*, vol. 18, issue 5, pp.629-631.

Ford, P. and Hayes, P. (1996), *Educating for Social Work: Arguments for Optimism*, Avebury, Hants.

Ford, P. (1996), 'Competences: Their Use and Misuse', in P. Ford and P. Hayes (eds.) *op cit.*

Foster, E.E. (1989), 'Review of Eggins, H. (ed.) (1988)' *op cit.*, *Higher Education*, vol. 18, issue 5, pp.624-626.

Francis Spence, M. (1995), 'Reflections on Black Lecturers in Social Work Education - Finding the Boundaries Between Roles and Responsibilities', *Issues in Social Work Education*, vol. 15, issue 2, pp.35-50.

Freidson, E. (1986), *Professional Powers: A Study of the Institutionalisation of Formal Knowledge*, University of Chicago Press, Chicago.

Froggett, L. (1997), 'Containment, Connection, Creativity and Competence', *Issues in Social Work Education*, vol. 17, issue 1, pp.65-68.

Gallagher, B., Creighton, S. and Gibbons, J. (1995), 'Ethical Dilemmas in Social Research: No Easy Solutions', *British Journal of Social Work*, vol. 25, issue 3, pp.295-311.

Gardiner, D. (1988), 'Improving Students' Learning: Setting an Agenda for Quality in the 90s', *Issues in Social Work Education*, vol. 8, issue 1, pp.3-10.

Gardiner, D. (1989), *The Anatomy of Supervision: Developing Learning and Professional Competence for Social Work Students*, SRHE/Open University Press, Milton Keynes.

Geertz, C. (1995), *After the Fact: Two Countries, Four Decades, One Anthropologist*, Harvard University Press, Cambridge, Massachusetts.

Gibb, G. (1988), *Learning By Doing*, Further Education Unit, London.

Glampson, A. and Goldberg, E. (1976), 'Post Seebohm Social Services - II: The Consumer Viewpoint', *Social Work Today*, 9.11.76.

Glastonbury, B. (1985), *Computers in Social Work*, Macmillan, Basingstoke.

Glastonbury, B. (ed.) (1993), *Human Welfare and Technology*, Assen, Van Corcum.

Glennerster, H. (1995), *British Social Policy Since 1945*, Blackwell, Oxford.

Goldberg, E. and Fruin, D. (1976), 'Towards Accountability in Social Work: A Case Review System for Social Workers', *British Journal of Social Work*, vol. 6, p.1.

Goldberg, E.M. and Hatch, S. (eds.) (1981), *A New Look at the Personal Social Services*, Discussion Paper 4, P.S.I., London.

Gould, N. and Taylor, I. (eds.) (1996) *Reflective Learning for Social Work*, Arena, Aldershot.

Graham, J (1996), 'Closing the Circle: Research, Critical Reflection and the National Curriculum for Teacher Training, *Higher Education Review*, vol. 29, issue 1, pp.33-56.

Habermas, J. (1978), *Knowledge and Human Interests*, 2nd edn., Heinemann, London.

Hadley, R. and McGrath, M. (1984), *When Social Services Are Local: The Normanton Experience*, Allen and Unwin, London.

Hall, P. (1976), *Reforming the Welfare*, Heinemann, London.

Hall, P., Land, H., Parker, R. and Webb, A. (1975), *Change, Choice and Conflict in Social Policy*, Heinemann, London.

Halpern, S. A. (1985), *'Professional Schools in the American University'*, Working Paper No. 6, Comparative Higher Education Research Group, Graduate School of Education, University of California, Los Angeles.

Halsey, A.H. (1992), *Decline of Donnish Dominion*, Clarendon, Oxford.

Halsey, A.H. and Trow, M. (1971), *The British Academics*, Faber, London.

Hanmer, J. and Statham, D. (1988), *Women and Social Work: Towards a Woman-Centred Practice*, Macmillan, London.

Hardy, G.H. (1941), *A Mathematician's Apology*, Cambridge University Press, Cambridge.

Harlow, J. and Hearn, J. (1996), 'Educating for Anti-Oppressive and Anti-Discriminatory Social Work Practice', *Social Work Education*, vol. 15, issue 1, pp.5-17.

Harris, I.B. (1993), 'New Expectations for Professional Competence', in Currey *et al.* (1993), *op cit.*

Harris, R. (1990), 'Social Work Education for the 90s: An Agenda', *Issues in Social Work Education*, Vol. 10, Issues 1 and 2, pp.146-155.

Harris, R. (1996), 'Telling Tales: Probation in the Contemporary Formation', in N. Parton (ed.), *op cit.*

Harris, R., Barker, M., Reading, P., Richards, M. and Youll, P. (eds.) (1985), *Educating Social Workers*, ATSWE, University of Leicester.

Harrison, L. (1990), 'Alcohol and Drugs Education in Social Work Qualification Teaching', *Issues in Social Work Education*, vol. 10, issues 1 and 2, pp.51-68.

Hartman, K.M. (1989), 'Professional Versus Academic Values: Cultural Ambivalence in University Professional Schools in Australia', *Higher Education*, vol. 18, pp.491-509.

Haselgrove, S. (ed.) (1994), *The Student Experience*, SRHE/Open University Press, Buckingham.

HEFCE (1993), *Effective Teaching and Assessment Programme*, Circular 31/93, HEFCE, Bristol.

HEFCE (1995), *Quality Assessment of Applied Social Work, 1994*, QO 5/95, HEFCE, Bristol.

Heidenheimer, A.J. (1989), 'Professional Knowledge and State Policy in Comparative Historical Perspective: Law and Medicine in Britain, Germany and the US', *International Social Science Journal*, vol. 122, pp.529-553.

Henderson, J. (1994), 'Reflecting Oppression: Symmetrical Experiences of Social Work Students and Service Users', *Social Work in Education*, vol. 13, issue 1, pp.16-25.

Henke, D. (1988), 'Will Social Workers be Blamed When Social Policies Backfire?', *Social Work Today*, 26.5.88.

Henkel, M. (1994), 'Social Work: An Incorrigibly Marginal Profession?', in T. Becher (ed.), *op. cit.*

Henkel, M. (1995), 'Conceptions of Knowledge in Social Work Education', in M. Yelloly and M. Henkel (eds.), *op cit.*

Henkel, M. (1997), 'The Impact of HE Reforms on Academic Identities', Paper to HE Studies Group, London, 8/1/97.

Heywood, J.S. (1978), *Children in Care: The Development of the Service for the Deprived Child*, (3rd edn), Routledge, Kegan Paul, London.

Hill, M. and Aldgate, J. (eds.) (1996), *Child Welfare Services: Developments in Law, Policy Practice and Research*, Jessica Kingsley, London.

Hill, M. and Bramley, G. (1990), *Analysing Social Policy*, Blackwell, Oxford.

Hirschman, A.O. (1970), *Exit, Voice and Loyalty: Responses to Decline in Firms, Organisations and States*, Harvard University Press, Cambridge, Massachusetts.

Hixon Cavanagh, S. (1993), 'Connecting Education and Practice', in L. Currey *et al*. (1993).

Hokenstad, M.C., Kinduka, S.K. & Midgley, J. (eds.) (1992), *Profiles in International Social Work*, NASW, Washington, DC.

Holland, R. (1988), 'Visible and Invisible Curricula in Professional Education', *Issues in Social Work Education*, vol. 8, issue 2, pp.83-112.

Hooper, D. and Robb, B. (1986), 'Preparing for Practice: Towards a Future Educational Strategy in Social Work', ATSWE/JUC SWEC/SHOC, Coventry.

Howe, D. (1986), *Social Workers and Their Practice in Welfare Bureaucracies*, Gower, Aldershot.

Howe, D. (1992), 'Child Abuse and the Bureaucratisation of Social Work', *The Sociological Review*, vol. 40, issue 3, pp.491-508.

Humphries, B. (1988), 'Adult Learning in Social Work Education: Towards Liberation of Domestication', *Critical Social Policy*, vol. 23, pp.4-21.

Iredale, R. and Cleverly, A. (1998), 'Research Note: Education and Training in Genetics in Social Work Professional's Across the UK', *British Journal of Social Work*, vol. 28, issue 6, pp.961-968.

Jack, R. (1995), 'Post Qualifying Consortia - An Expensive Waste of Diminishing Resources', *Issues in Social Work Education*, vol. 15, issue 1, pp.78-87.

Jackson, S. and Preston Shoot, M. (1996), *Educating Social Workers in a Changing Policy Context*, Whiting and Birch, London.

Jarrett Report (1985), *Report of the Steering Committee for Efficiency Studies in Universities*, CVCP, London.

JFR Inquiry Group (1995), *Income and Wealth: Report of the JFR Inquiry Group*, Joseph Rowntree Foundation, York.

J.M. Consulting (1998), *Review of the Content of the Diploma in Social Work: Discussion Paper*, J.M. Consulting, London.

Johnson, T.J. (1972), *Professions and Power*, Macmillan, London.

Johnstone, R.J. (1996), 'Managing How Academics Manage' in R. Cuthbert (ed.), *op cit.*

Jones, C. (1978), *An Analysis of the Development of Social Work Education and Social Work 1869-1977: The Making of Citizens and Supercitizens*, Unpublished, PhD Thesis, Durham University.

Jones, C. (1979), 'Social Work Education 1900-1977', in N. Parry, M. Rustin and C. Satyamurti (eds.), *Social Work, Welfare and the State*, Arnold, London.

Jones, C. (1983), *State Social Work and the Working Class*, Macmillan, London.

Jones, C. (1985), *Patterns of Social Policy*, Tavistock, London.

Jones, C. (1992), 'Social Work in Great Britain: Surviving the Challenge of Conservative Ideology', in M. Hokenstad, S.K. Khinduka and J. Midgley (eds.), *Profiles in International Social Work*, NASW, Washington DC.

Jones, C. (1993), 'The Means to a Better End', *Community Care*, 16/9/93, p.11.

Jones, C (1995), 'Demanding Social Work Education', *Issues in Social Work Education*, vol. 15, issue 2, pp.3-17.

Jones, C (1996a), 'Anti-intellectualism and the Peculiarities of British Social Work Education', in N. Parton (ed.), *op cit.*

Jones, C. (1996b), 'Dangerous Times for British Social Work Education', in P. Ford and Hayes (eds.), *op cit.*

Jones, C. (1996c), 'Regulating Social Work: A Review of the Review', in S. Jackson and M. Preston Shoot (eds.), *op cit.*

Jones, S. and Joss, R. (1995), 'Models of Professionalism', in M. Yelloly and M. Henkel (eds.), *op cit.*

Jordan, B. (1991), 'Social Work, Justice and the Common Good', in P. Carter, T. Jeffs and M. Smith (eds.), *op cit.*

Jordan, B., Karban, K., Kazi, M., Masson, H. and O'Byrne, P. (1993), 'Teaching Values: An Experience of the DipSW', *Social Work Education*, vol. 12, issue 1, pp.7-18.

Judge, K. (1978), *Rationing Social Services*, Heinemann, London.

Kelly, A. (1991), 'The "New Managerialism" in the Social Services', in P. Carter, T. Jeffs and M. Smith (eds.), *op cit.*

Kemp, C.H. *et al.* (1962), 'The Battered Child Syndrome', *Journal of the American Medical Association*, vol. 181, pp.17-22.

Kennedy, M. (1987), 'Inexact Sciences: Professional Education and the Development of Expertise', *Review of Research in Education*, vol. 14, pp.133-167.

Knowles, M. (1972), 'Innovations in Teaching Styles and Approaches Based on Adult Learning', *Journal of Education for Social Work*, vol. 8, issue 2, pp.32-39.

Kogan, M. (1975), *Educational Policy-Making: a Study of Interest Groups and Parliament*, George, Allen and Unwin, London.

Kogan, M. (1988), *Education Accountability: an Analytic Overview*, 2nd edn., Hutchinson, London.

Kogan, M. and Henkel, M. (1983), *Government and Research*, Heinemann, London.

Kogan, M. and Kogan, D. (1983), *The Attack on Higher Education*, Kogan Page, London.

Kolb, D.A. (1981), 'Learning Styles and Disciplinary Differences', in A. Chickering (ed.), *The Modern American College*, Jose Bass, San Francisco.

Kuhn, T.S. (1962), *The Structure of Scientific Revolutions*, University of Chicago Press, Chicago.

La Valle, I. and Lyons, K. (1996a), 'The Social Worker Speaks: 1, Perceptions of Recent Changes in British Social Work', *Practice*, vol. 8, issue 2, pp.5-15.

La Valle, I. and Lyons, K. (1996b), 'The Social Worker Speaks: 2, Managing Change in the Personal Social Services', *Practice*, vol. 8, issue 3, pp.63-71.

Langan, M. and Day, L. (eds.), (1992), *Women, Oppression and Social Work*, Routledge, London.

Langan, M. (1993), 'New Directions in Social Work' in J. Clarke (ed.), (1993), *op cit.*

Langan, M. (1993), 'The Rise and Fall of Social Work', in J. Clarke (ed.), (1993), *op cit.*

Letwin, S.R. (1992), *The Anatomy of Thatcherism*, Fortuna, London.

Lindop Report (1985), *Academic Validation in Public Sector Higher Education*, CNAA, London.

Lockwood, G. and Davies, J. (1985), *Universities: the Management Challenge*, NFER-Nelson and SRHE, London.

Lorenz, W. (1991), 'Social Work Practice in Europe', in M. Hill (ed.) *Social Work and the European Community*, Jessica Kingsley, London.

Lorenz, W. (1994), *Social Work in a Changing Europe*, Routledge, London.

Lukes, S. (1974), *Power: A Radical View*, Macmillan, Basingstoke.

Lyons, K. (1996a), 'Education for International Social Work', in IFSW/IASSW Conference Proceedings, *Participating in Change*, IFSW/IASSW, Hong Kong, pp.189-191.

Lyons, K. (1996b), *ERASMUS and the Social Professions in the UK: an Evaluation*, Report for European Union (unpublished).

Lyons, K and Orme, J. (1998), 'The 1996 Research Assessment Exercise and the Response of Social Work Academics', *British Journal of Social Work*, vol. 28, issue 5, pp.783-92.

Lyons, K., La Valle, I. and Grimwood, C. (1995), 'Career Patterns of Qualified Social Workers: Discussion of a Recent Survey', *British Journal of Social Work*, vol. 25, issue 2, pp.173-190.

Macdonald, K. (1995), *'The Sociology of the Professions'*, Sage, London.

Macdonald, K. and Ritzer, G. (1988), 'The Sociology of the Professions, Dead or Alive?', *Work and Occupations*, vol. 15, issue 30, pp.251-272.

Macey, M. and Moxon, E. (1996), 'An Examination of Anti-racist and Anti-oppressive Theory and Practice in Social Work Education', *British Journal of Social Work*, vol. 26, issue 3, pp.297-314.

March, J. and Olsen, M. (1989), *Discovering Institutions*, Free Press, New York.

March, J. and Olsen, M. (1994), 'Institutional Perspectives on Governance', in H.R. Derlien (ed.), *Systemrationalitat und Partialinteresse: Festschrift fur Renate Mayntz Nomos*, Verlagsgesellschaft, Baden Baden.

Marsh, P. and Triselliotis (1996), *Ready to Practice? Social Workers and Probation Officers: Their Training and 1st Year in Work'*, Avebury, Hants.

Matarazzo, I.D. (1977), 'Higher Education, Professional Education and Licensure', *American Psychologist*, vol. 32, pp.856-857.

McDonald, G. and Sheldon, B. (1998), 'Changing One's Mind: the Final Frontier?', *Issues in Social Work Education*, vol. 18, issue 1, pp.3-25.

McNamara, D. (1990), 'Research on Teachers' Thinking: Educating Students to Think Critically', *Journal of Teaching for Education*, vol. 16, issue 2, pp.147-160.

McNay, M. (1992), 'Social Work and Power Relations: Towards a Framework For an Integrated Practice', in M. Langan and L. Day (eds.), *op cit.*

Midgley, J. (1995), *Social Development: The Developmental Perspective in Social Welfare*, Sage, London.

Mishra, R. (1981), *Society and Social Policy*, 2nd edn., Macmillan, London.

Mogissi, H. (1994), 'Racism and Sexism in Academic Practice', in H. Afshar and M. Maynard (eds.), *The Dynamics of Race and Gender*, Taylor and Francis, London.

Nellis, M. (1996), 'What's To Be Done About Probation Training?', in T. Vass and T. May (eds.) (1996) *Working With Offenders*, Sage, London.

NISW (undated), *A Force for the Future: Researching and Planning the Social Services Workforce*, LGMB/NISW, London.

Novak, T. (1995), 'Thinking About a New Social Work Curriculum', *Social Work Education*, vol. 14, issue 4, pp.5-10.

Orme, J. (1994), 'The Case for Research Into Practice', in G. McKenzie and R. Usher (eds.), *Understanding Social Research: Perspectives on Methodology and Practice*, University of Southampton, Southampton.

Otway, O. (1996), 'Social Work With Children and Families: From Child Welfare to Child Protection', in N. Parton (ed.), *op cit.*

Pantin, C.F.A. (1969), *The Relations Between the Sciences*, Cambridge University Press, Cambridge.

Parker, R. (1987), *Planning and Resourcing of Agency Based Placements: Results of a Survey of SSDs in England, Wales and Northern Ireland*, ADSS, Berkshire.

Parker, R. (1991), *Safeguarding Standards: on the Desirability and Feasibility of Establishing a UK Independent Body to Regulate and Promote Good Practice in Social Work and Social Services*, NISW, London.

Parry, N. and Parry, J. (1979), 'Social Work, Professionalism and the State', in N. Parry, M. Rustin and C. Satyamurti, *Social Work, Welfare and the State*, Arnold, London.

Parry, N., Rustin, M. and Satyamurti, C. (eds.) (1979), *Social Work, Welfare and the State*, Arnold, London.

Parsloe, P. (1979), 'Selection for Professional Training: The English and American Experience', *British Journal of Social Work*, vol. 9, issue 3, pp.365-380.

Parsloe, P. (1990), 'The Future of Social Work Education', in P. Carter, T. Jeffs and M. Smith (eds.), *Social Work and Social Welfare Year Book No.2*, Open University Press, Milton Keynes.

Parsloe, P. (1996), 'Managing for Reflective Learning', in N. Gould and I. Taylor (eds.), *op cit.*

Parton, N. (1985), *The Politics of Child Abuse*, Macmillan, London.

Parton, N. (ed.) (1996), *Social Theory, Social Change and Social Work*, Routledge, London.

Payne, M. (1991), *Modern Social Work Theory; a Critical Introduction*, Macmillan, Basingstoke.

Payne, M. (1994), 'Partnership Between Organisations in Social Work Education', *Issues in Social Work Education*, vol. 14, issue 1, pp.53-70.

Phillips, J. (1996), 'The Future of Social Work with Older People in a Changing World' in N. Parton (ed.), *op cit.*

Pierce, R. (1991), *The Funding of Social Work Education and Training*, CCETSW, London.

Pierce, R. (1994), 'PC or not PC: the Facts Behind the Education Debate', *Professional Social Worker*, vol. 4/1994, pp.10-11.

Pietroni, M. (1995), 'The Nature and Aims of Professional Education for Social Workers: A Post Modern Perspective', in M. Yelloly and M. Henkel (eds.), *op cit.*

Pinker, R. (1971), *Social Theory and Social Policy*, Heinemann, London.

Pinker, R. (1993), 'A Lethal Kind of Looniness', *The Times Higher Education Supplement*, 10.9.93.

Polanyi, M. (1962), *Personal Knowledge: Towards a Post-critical Philosophy*, Routledge, Kegan Paul, London.

Polanyi, M, (1967), *The Tacit Dimension*, Routledge, London.

Pollitt, C. (1990), *Managerialism and the Public Services*, Basil Blackwell, Oxford.

Powell, J. (1996), 'The Social Work Practitioner as Researcher: Learning About Research', in P. Ford and P. Hayes (eds.), *op cit.*

Preston-Shoot, M. (ed.) (1993), 'Assessment and Competence in Social Work Law', *Social Work Education*, Special Publication, Bournemouth.

Rafferty, J. (1997), 'Critical Commentary: Shifting Paradigms of Information Technology in Social Work Education and Practice', *British Journal of Social Work*, vol. 27, issue 6, pp.959-969.

Ramon, S. and Sayce, L. (1993), 'Collective User Participation in MH: Implications for Social Work Education and Training', *Issues in Social Work Education*, vol. 13, issue 2, pp.53-70.

Ravn, I. (1991), 'What Should Guide Reality Construction?', in F. Steier (ed.), *Research and Reflexivity*, Sage, London.

Rein, M. (1983), *From Policy to Practice*, Macmillan, Basingstoke.

Reynolds, J. (1994), 'Researching Teaching on Gender in Social Work Education: a Case Study', *Education Action Research*, vol. 2, issue 2, pp.267-280.

Rice, E. and Richlin, J. (1993), 'Broadening the Concept of Research in the Professions', in L. Curry *et al.* (eds.), *op cit.*

Richards, M. (1985), 'In Defence of Social Work Teachers: a Study of Their Development Needs', in R. Harris *et al.*, (eds.), *op cit.*

Riches, P.(1997), *Training for Care*, 97/31, The Learning Agency, London.

Roach Anleu, S. (1992), 'The Professionalisation of Social Work? A Case Study of Three Organisational Settings', *Sociology*, vol. 26, issue 1, pp.23-43.

Robbins Report (1963), *Higher Education*, Cmnd. 2154, HMSO, London.

Robinson, E. (1993), 'Some Psychological Themes in Social Work Education: A Black Perspective', *Social Work Education*, Vol. 12, issue 2, pp.29-34.

Rogers, C. (1961), *On Becoming a Person: a Therapist's View of Psychotherapy*, Constable, London.

Rojek, C., Peacock, G. and Collins, S. (eds.) (1988), *Social Work and Received Ideas*, Routledge, London.

Rowbottom, R., Hey, A. and Billis, D. (1974), *Social Services Departments: Developing Patterns of Work and Organisation*, Heinemann, London.

Rustin, M. and Edwards, J. (1989), *The Costs of Social Work Education*, CCETSW, London.

Schon, D. (1983), *The Reflective Practitioner: How Professionals Think in Action*, Temple Smith, London.

Schon, D. (1987), *Educating the Reflective Practitioner*, Jose Bass, San Francisco.

Schuller, T. (ed.) (1995), *The Changing University?*, SRHE/OUP, Buckingham.

Schuller, T. (ed.) (1991), *The Future of Higher Education*, SRHE/OUP, Buckingham.

Schwieso, J. and Pettit, P. (1995), 'Information Technology Teaching on Diploma in Social Work Programmes in the UK: A Survey and Discussion', *Issues in Social Work Education*, vol. 15, issue 1, pp.33-47.

Scott, P. (1985), *The Crisis in the University*, Croom Helm, Beckenham.

Seebohm Report (1968), *Report of the Committee on Local Authority and Allied Personal Social Services*, Cmnd 3703, HMSO, London.

Shaw, I. (1996), *Evaluating in Practice*, Arena, Aldershot.

Sheldon, B. (1986), 'Social Work Effectiveness Experiments: Review and Implications', *British Journal of Social Work*, vol. 16, issue 2, pp.223-242.

Sheppard, M. (1995), 'Social Work, Social Science and Practice Wisdom', *British Journal of Social Work*, vol. 25, issue 3, pp.265-293.

Sheppard, M. (1997), 'The Preconditions for Social Work as a Distinctive Discipline', *Issues in Social Work Education*, vol. 17, issue 1, pp.82-88.

Sheppard, M. (1998), 'Practice Validity, Reflexivity and Knowledge for Social Work', *British Journal of Social Work*, vol. 28, issue 5, pp.763-778.

Sibeon, R. (1991/2), 'Sociological Reflections on Welfare Politics and Social Work', *Social Work and Social Sciences Review*, vol. 3, issue 3, pp.184-203.

Siegrist, H. (1994), 'The Professions, State and Government in Theory and History', in T. Becher (ed.), (1994) *op cit.*

Silver, H. (1990), *Education Change and the Policy Process*, Falmer, Basingstoke.

Sinclair, I. (1992), 'Social Work Research: Its Relevance to Social Work and Social Work Education', *Issues in Social Work Education*, vol. 11, issue 2, pp.65-80.

Sleeman, S. (1996), 'The Implications of Partnership in Social Work Education', in P. Ford and P. Hayes (eds.), *op cit.*

Smith, D. (1987), 'The Limits of Positivism in Social Work Research', *British Journal of Social Work*, vol. 17, issue 4, pp.573-586.

Smith, D. (1991/2), 'Puritans and Paradigms: a comment', *Social Work and Social Science Review*, vol. 3, issue 2, pp.99-103.

Smith, M. (1965), *Professional Education for Social Work in Britain - an Historical Account*, George, Allen and Unwin/NISW, London.

SSI (1995/96), *Fifth Annual Report of the Chief Inspector of Social Services*, HMSO, London.

Stanford, R. (1992), *A Study of Police and Social Worker Joint Investigations of Cases of Suspected Child Abuse*, M.Phil. Thesis, Brunel University, unpublished.

Statham, D. (1996), *The Future of Social and Personal Care: The Role of Social Service Organisations in the Public, Private and Voluntary Sectors*, NISW, London.

Stephens, M.D. and Roderick, G.W. (1978), *Higher Education Alternatives*, Longman, London.

Stevenson, O. (1988), 'Law and Social Work Education: A Commentary on the Law Report', *Issues in Social Work Education*, vol. 8, issue 1, pp.37-45.

Stevenson, O. (ed.) (1989), *Child Abuse: Public Policy and Professional Practice*, Harvester Wheatsheaf, Hemel Hempstead.

Suin De Boutemard, B. (1990), 'Reflections on the Creation of a Science of Social Work', *International Social Work*, vol. 33, issue 3, pp.255-267.

Sullivan, M. (1994), *Modern Social Policy*, Harvester Wheatsheaf, Hemel Hempstead.

Svenson, L.G. (1994), 'Governmental Control and Professional Education in Sweden', in T. Becher (ed.) (1994) *op cit.*

Tanner, K. and La Riche, P. (1995), 'You See But You do Not Observe: The Art of Observation and its Application to Practice Teaching', *Issues in Social Work Education*, vol. 15, issue 2, pp.66-80.

Tasker, M. and Packard, D. (1993), 'Industry and Higher Education: a Question of Values', *Studies in Higher Education*, vol. 18, issue 2, pp.27-136.

Taylor, I. (1993), 'Evaluating Social Work Education', *British Journal of Social Work*, vol. 23, issue 2, pp.123-138.

Taylor, I. (1996), 'Enquiry and Action Learning', in N. Gould and I. Taylor (eds.), *op cit.*

Taylor, W. (1994), 'Teacher Education: Backstage to Centre Stage', in T. Becher (ed.), *op cit.*

The Times Higher Education Supplement, 'Research Assessments 1996', *The Times Higher Education Supplement*, 20/12/96, p.xii.

Thyer, B. (1993), 'Social Work Theory and Practice Research: The Approach of Logical Positivism', *Social Work and Social Science Review*, vol. 4, issue 1, pp.5-26.

Tight, M. (ed.) (1988), *Academic Freedom and Responsibility*, SRHE/OUP, Buckingham.

Timms, N. (1991), 'A New Diploma for Social Work or Dunkirk as Total Victory', in P. Carter *et al.*, *op cit.*

Torstendahl, R. (1994), 'Engineers and Governments in a Comparative Perspective', in T. Becher (ed.), (1994) *op cit.*

Toulmin, S. (1972), *Human Understanding, Vol. I, General Introduction and Part I*, Clarendon Press, Oxford.

Trist, E. (1972), 'Types of Output Mix of Research Organisations and Their Complementarity', in A.B. Chernz, R. Sinclair and W.I. Jenkins (eds.), *Social Science and Government Policies and Problems*, Tavistock Publications, London.

Turner, J.(1988), 'The Price of Freedom', in M. Tight (ed.), *op cit.*

Utting, W. (1994), 'Almost a Profession', *Professional Social Worker*, January, p.4.

Vang, J. (1994), 'The Case of Medicine', in T. Becher (ed.) (1994), *op cit.*

Vass, A. (1996), 'Competence in Social Work and Probation Practice', in A. Vass (ed.) *Social Work Competences: Core Knowledge, Values and Skills*, Sage, London.

Vass, A. (ed.) (1996), *Social Work Competences, Core Knowledge, Values and Skills*, Sage, London.

Volmer, H. and Mills, D. (eds.) (1966), *Professionalisation*, Prentice Hall, Englewood Cliffs, New Jersey.

Walford, G. (1991), 'Changing Relationship Between Government and Higher Education in Britain', in G. Neave and F.A. Van Vught (eds.), *Prometheus Unbound: the Changing Relationship Between Government and HE in Europe*, Pergamon Press, Oxford.

Walker, J.C. (1992), *Standards and Partnerships in Teaching and Teacher Education: USA and UK Experience*, University of Canberra Centre for Research in Professional Education.

Wallis-Jones, M. and Lyons, K. (1997), *1996 Employment Survey of Newly Qualified Social Workers*, CCETSW, London.

Walton, R. (1975), *Women in Social Work*, Routledge, London.

Ward, D. (1996), 'Probation Training: Celebration or Wake?', in S. Jackson and M. Preston Shoot (eds.), *op cit.*

Warner, D. and Crossthwaite, E. (eds.) (1995). *Human Resource Management in Higher and Further Education*, SRHE/Open University Press, Buckingham.

Warner Report (1992), *Choosing With Care*, HMSO, London.

Watson, D. (1992), 'The Changing Shape of Professional Education', in H. Bines and D. Watson (1992), *op cit.*

Webb, D. (1990), 'Puritans and Paradigms: a Speculation on the New Form of Moralities in Social Work', *Social Work and Social Sciences Review*, vol. 2, issue 2, pp.146-159.

Webb, D. (1991/2), 'A Stranger in the Academy: a Reply to Lena Dominelli', *Social Work and Social Science Review*, vol. 2, issue 3, pp.236-241.

Webb, D. (1992), 'Competencies, Contracts and Cadres: Common Themes in the Social Control of Nurse and Social Work Education', *Journal of Interprofessional Care*, vol. 6, issue 3, pp.223-230.

Webb, D. (1996), 'Regulation for Radicals: the State, CCETSW and the Academy', in N. Parton (ed.), *op cit.*

Williams, B. (1996), 'Probation Training: The Defence of Professionalism', *Social Work Education*, vol. 15, issue 3, pp.5-19.

Williams, B. (ed.) (1995), *Probation Values*, Sage, London.

Wilson, K. and Bradley, G. (1994), 'New Challenges in Social Work Education: Innovation in the Training Programme of Hull University', *Social Work Education*, vol. 13, issue 2, pp.52-73.

Wilson, K. (1992), 'The Place of Observation in Social Work Training', *Journal of Social Work Training*, vol. 5, issue 1, pp.51-60.

Wingard and Williams (1973), 'Grades as Predictors of Physicians Career Performance: An Evaluative Literature Review', *Journal of Medical Education*, vol. 48, pp.311-322.

Winter, R. and Maisch, M. (1992), 'Professionalism and Competence: Towards a Model of Practice-based Post-qualifying Education and Training in Social Work, Anglia/Essex ASSET Programme, Chelmsford.

Wise, S. (1990), 'Becoming a Feminist Social Worker', in L. Stanley (ed.), *Feminist Praxis: Research, Theory and Epistemology*, Routledge, London.

Witz, A. (1991), 'Patriarchy and the Professions: the Gendered Politics of Occupational Closure', *Sociology*, vol. 24, issue 4, pp.675-690.

Wright, P. (1992), 'Learning Through Enterprise: the Enterprise in Higher Education Initiative', in R. Barnett (ed.), *Learning to Effect*, SRHE/OUP, Buckingham.

Yelloly, M. (1995), 'Professional Competence in Higher Education', in M. Yelloly and M. Henkel (eds.) *op cit.*

Yelloly, M. and Henkel, M. (eds.) (1995), *Learning and Teaching in Social Work: Towards Reflective Practice*, Jessica Kingsley, London.

Youll, P. and Walker, C. (1995), 'Great Expectations? Personal, Professional and Institutional Agendas in Advanced Training', in M. Yelloly and M. Henkel (eds.), *op cit.*

Youll, P. (1985), 'Educational Principles and Approaches to Adult Learning in Social Work Education', in R. Harris *et al.* (eds.), *op cit.*

Youll, P. (1996), 'Organisational or Professional Leadership: Managerialism and Social Work Education', in S. Jackson and M. Preston-Shoot (eds.), *op cit.*

Younghusband Report (1959), *Social Work in Britain: a Supplementary Report on the Training and Employment of Social Workers*, Carnegie Trust, Dunfermline.

Younghusband, E. (1951), *Social Work in Britain: A Supplementary Report on the Training and Employment of Social Workers*, Carnegie UK Trust, Dunfermline.

Appendix 1
Research Design and Methodology

Introduction

The research on which this book is based was carried out between 1992 and 1997, and formed the basis for a Ph.D. thesis. The following is an abridged version of the chapter which detailed the research design and process. The research originated from the writer's experience of the day-to-day issues and concerns of social work education, and of its relationships within HEIs and with the external field, as well as a concern about a relative lack of research and writing about social work as a discipline.

The initial literature review suggested several themes about policy development and professional education (outlined in Part 1) which warranted further examination in relation to social work. The research, therefore, was conceived as an exploratory study, using an empirico-inductive approach, and taking the perceptions of social work educators about the subject area and current changes as the database for a case study about the characteristics of one area of professional education. The key question, 'can social work education survive in higher education?' and its elaboration into 'what are the characteristics which make social work education viable or vulnerable as a subject area?' informed the choice and design of the research tools.

Research Design and Methodology

The research therefore set out to identify the characteristics of a subject area perceived as marginal and vulnerable within higher education and to explore why this may be the case. The research design was located within a qualitative frame of reference, considered more appropriate to the exploration of a 'problematic situation' and to the possible development of explanatory theory. The role of the researcher, as an 'insider' or actor in the situation under investigation, was considered to have both potential advantages and disadvantages, and efforts were made to minimise the latter (see later). Similarly, the choice of social work educators as respondents by definition produces only a partial or particular view of the problem, but as Walker suggested, 'what qualitative research can offer the policy maker is a theory of social action grounded on the experience - the world view - of those likely to be affected by a policy decision or thought to be part of the problem' (Walker, 1985, p.19).

The data which formed the empirical basis for this study were collected by three means, postal questionnaires, interviews and documentary sources, in the mid-1990s. This design constituted a form of triangulation which aimed to achieve validity of the data. The incorporation of a survey at an early point in the data collection stage was an important device, both for establishing useful data and for indicating (through a high response rate) the topicality and relevance of the issue to social work educators other than the writer.

The Postal Survey

Self-completion questionnaires were sent to all heads of social work departments or subject areas. The target population was identified as all departments (areas) in HEIs offering a professional course in social work education (at that time a CQSW or DipSW), as listed in the CCETSW publication, *How to Qualify for Social Work 1994-95* (CCETSW, 1993). Issues of access to a population and sampling thus did not arise.

However, identification of respondents was complicated by the fact that a minority of qualifying courses then were delivered outside HEIs (screened out at the mailing stage); and it was conceivable that social work education (research) could exist in institutions which did not offer courses at qualifying level. Some account was taken of the second factor at the interview stage. In the event, 77 departments (subject areas) listed by CCETSW were circulated with a nine-sided questionnaire and covering letter in February 1994, and non-respondents were sent reminder and a second copy in April 1994.

The questionnaire contained a range of closed and open-ended questions aimed at eliciting information about the respondents' circumstances and views on structural and organisational aspects of the subject; the content and pedagogical approaches of the area; its research activities; the characteristics and loyalties of social work educators; and their experience of change. Respondents were also asked an open question about the perceived strengths and weaknesses of the subject and some of the factual questions would illustrate aspects of the resourcing of the area. Questions were not pre-coded since the number to be surveyed was relatively small, and the intention was to interrogate the data manually rather than statistically (see data analysis).

The researcher's knowledge of the target population and area under study enabled formulation of questions in a way which, it was considered, would maximise responses. Additionally, the questionnaire was piloted on a small number of helpful colleagues who would not serve as respondents, but who were able to suggest minor redrafting for clarity, and to indicate how long questionnaire completion might take. Making sense of some of the answers at the data analysis stage was also assisted by the researcher's prior knowledge. It was also likely that some of the information requested might be considered sensitive and that potential respondents would be working under considerable pressure, so the covering letter was carefully worded to explain the purpose of the study, encourage a response, and ensure confidentiality (non-attribution) of the ensuing data. By August 1994, 64 questionnaires had been received (83 per cent).

There followed a temporary interruption to the research process due to external factors, but initial analysis of questionnaires took place. This identified some gaps and areas which would require further exploration or discussion at the interview stage.

The Interviews

The interviews were carried out in the summer of 1996, two years later than the original data collection, with mainly different people from those who had completed postal questionnaires (though this was not a major factor in their selection). Respondents were asked to address both some questions raised in the original questionnaire in more depth, and also other questions omitted from the first stage of data collection and now regarded as important. An initial telephone approach to potential interviewees was followed by a short letter confirming practical arrangements and a note about the research areas to be addressed in the interview.

The interviews were designed as unstructured, non-standardised or focused and were carried out using an interview guide. That is, although topics for exploration were suggested and raised (usually in the order originally notified), interviewees were free to digress and bring in new material or give more emphasis to some areas. Indeed, the selection of twelve respondents had aimed to take account of gender, experience in social work education (including in different types of institution), variations in job definition or emphasis and (known) areas of special interest.

The interviewees were all identified by the researcher as 'leaders in the field', that is people with wide-ranging experience, who have contributed to the literature and debates about social work education in various forums. Only one person, of twelve approached, declined to be interviewed, on the grounds that he no longer held a social work educator post in his institution. Nine interviewees were professors of social work (or similar titles) although this was not an essential requirement. The interviews lasted between 45 and 90 minutes (generally one hour) and with the exception of the first one, were tape-recorded. The researcher also made notes, with the interviewee's agreement.

With regard to 'interviewer effect', the extent to which the researcher knew respondents personally, or knew about them, or was known to them professionally, varied. It has been suggested that sharing a common background and professional language may facilitate the gathering of data via interviews, although the researcher had on occasion to guard against 'assuming meanings', through use of additional questions or probing which required the interviewee to elaborate on their statements. There was, no doubt, a sense in which all respondents 'sought to be helpful' to the researcher, but the range of answers given and ideas expressed did not reflect an agreed assumption about what the researcher wanted to know (other than at the broadest level); and included varying indications of whether particular statements could be attributed to named interviewees (although the researcher had stated that confidentiality would be observed).

Documentary Sources

It was thought that records of an organisation closely involved in developments in relation to social work education would constitute a ready source of documentary evidence from which to supplement other data. JUC SWEC was selected on the grounds that it is a member organisation representing the views and experience of social work educators, and its records were likely to demonstrate the collective concerns and activities of the discipline in recent years. The material analysed (early in 1997) consisted of minutes, annual reports and other papers (for instance, letters or commentaries expressing members' views on particular CCETSW or governmental proposals). By definition, such sources may not address all the questions at issue, but in research concerned in part with policy change, 'records and documents, albeit incomplete accounts, are part of the reality being studied' (Hakim, 1993, p.134).

Ethical Considerations

Insofar as the research was carried out in an open manner, that is, potential respondents were advised of the nature and purpose of the research and could then choose whether or not to participate, this research did not raise ethical questions. None of the questions (in the questionnaire or interview guide) were intended to provoke stress, invade privacy, inappropriate self-disclosure or to have any other adverse effects; and indeed many respondents indicated by additional notes on questionnaires or at the conclusion of interviews that they had found the research intervention stimulating or timely, or otherwise a positive experience.

The researcher did not claim to be value-neutral in this context (Rein, 1981) but an attempt was made to adopt a systematic approach to the research process with the due exercise of objectivity, rationality and rigour throughout. This was assisted by opportunities to relinquish the role of social work educator periodically and to place physical and metaphorical distance from the social work educator role, not least through reference to literature about social work education outside the UK or about other forms of professional education. As mentioned, the normal conventions of confidentiality were stated and observed in relation to data gathering and the writing-up/dissemination stages.

Data Analysis and the Concluding Stage

The data analysis stage is another point at which the 'dual role' of the researcher might be seen as advantageous in understanding the findings, or as introducing (further) bias in how the data are interpreted and communicated. Avoidance of bias at this stage, as earlier, was assisted by efforts to place findings in the context of wider research and literature.

The use of a postal survey might suggest the collection of a large amount of data amenable to statistical analysis. However, the actual number of 'cases' is small in survey terms and for this and other reasons the use of precoding and computer packages to analyse the data was eschewed in favour of a more traditional manual approach. While absolute numbers or proportions are used in some cases in Part II to identify 'facts' about a situation, more often the data reveal trends, opinions or factors which interrelate to build a picture, together with information from other sources, about the characteristics of the subject area in question and the associated issues.

The formulation of themes to be addressed is an important aspect of data analysis and the early identification of themes happened in this instance, since the researcher chose to relate the analysis to the main sections of the questionnaire, 'allocating' material derived from the interviews and records to relevant themes. These themes then constituted the basis for presentation and discussion of the data. The tape recorded interviews were not transcribed, but the use of the researcher's notes, in conjunction with replaying of tapes, enabled the 'extraction' of quotations to illustrate and amplify the material from the survey data at the analysis and writing-up stages. Similarly, the analysis of documentary evidence after the survey and interview stages had been completed enabled easier identification of relevant material from an otherwise unwieldy body of potential data, and sometimes provided illuminating insights into events alluded to in more general terms in the literature.

The extent to which the findings of research *can* be generalised has been seen as an important test of quantitative research but more open to question in relation to qualitative research. However, an aim of this research was to identify whether social work shares any of the characteristics of other forms of professional education, in which case some of the findings might have a wider relevance.

Other sources of 'data' were utilised in the form of reports and items in the general and professional press, which were relevant to an analysis of a 'real life' situation in the process of change, and which provided useful pointers to developments both in the subject and in other forms of professional education not being directly researched. This fell short of a rigorous collection or analysis of secondary data and is more closely related to the use of bibliographic sources to inform research design, execution and conclusions. In this respect, an initial literature search about social work education in 1992 revealed few British texts, and a relatively limited number of articles of the kind the writer was interested in, but the period 1995-1996 was significant for the production of a number of important texts on the subject - a timely reminder that 'stages' in the research process are not discrete nor necessarily sequential, and in this case, exploration of the literature was a concurrent aspect of the research process.

A wide range of literature - pertaining to social work, higher education policy, professional education and research - was utilised to contextualise and guide the researcher. Meanwhile, material more closely related to the empirical findings - frequently derived from articles as well as other material produced by social work educators - has been linked to the data in Part II, to indicate where the researcher's material accords with other findings or concerns, or where a theme has been relatively little explored by other researchers in the discipline.

A further aspect of the research process, concerned with the 'testing' of ideas, also took place, since the researcher took the opportunity to present papers about particular aspects of the findings on two occasions while work was in progress. These presentations were to groups of social work educators, predominantly not departmental managers or academic leaders of the sort included in the data collection stages. Although a form of dissemination, these also provided useful checks on the *credibility* of the data being gathered and indeed were a source of some corroborative data, albeit not included in the initial research design.

Finally, in connection with the later dissemination stage, apart from some presentations of selected aspects to particular audiences, it was not possible to systematically feed back all the findings and conclusions of this study to the people who contributed as respondents or to open them up to wider scrutiny. It was therefore decided to make the study more widely accessible to social work educators and other interested parties through publication.

References

Hakim, C. (1993). 'Research Analysis of Administrative Records', in M. Hammersley (ed.), *Social Research: Philosophy, Politics and Practice*, Sage, London.

Rein, M. (1983). *From Policy to Practice*, Macmillan, Basingstoke.

Walker, A. (1985). *Applied Qualitative Research*, Aldershot, Gower.

Appendix 2
Kolb-Biglan Classification of Academic Knowledge

A Diagrammatic Representation of Beecher's Formulation
(Source: Beecher, 1989, p.12)

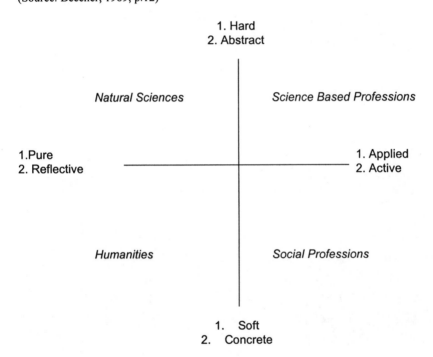

1. Hard
2. Abstract

Natural Sciences   Science Based Professions

1.Pure   1. Applied
2. Reflective   2. Active

Humanities   Social Professions

1. Soft
2. Concrete

Dimensions 1. The Nature of knowledge, after Biglan (1973)
Dimensions 2. Student Learning Styles, after Kolb (1981)

Relevent References: Biglan (1973), Kolb (1981).

239

Appendix 3
JUC Social Work Education
Committee

Joint University Council Social Work Education Committee

The Social Work Education Committee is one of three committees of the Joint University Council. This Council was established by the universities as one body for social studies in 1918, with the object of developing and co-ordinating the new social studies departments.

Various name and constitutional changes followed with the formation of the:

PUBLIC ADMINISTRATION SUB COMMITTEE in 1936
SOCIAL ADMINISTRATION COMMITTEE in 1955
SOCIAL WORK EDUCATION COMMITTEE in 1976

These three Committees now operate in parallel, with separate termly meetings and a combined Annual General Meeting. Each Committee elects its own officers and agrees its own sub-committees, as well as having representation on the JUC Executive Committee.

The organisation is funded by institutional subscriptions, according to the number of Committees to which universities send a representative, and Committees make annual bids for funding, for example for sub-committee activities and conferences.

The Council provides a 'national forum for the discussion of academic issues' related to curricula, resources and standards. Each Committee 'keeps itself closely informed about developments in its subject area' and promotes research, conferences and links with relevant bodies.[1]

---

[1]   Source: Information Sheet issued annually by JUC Secretary.

Membership of the Social Work Education Committee currently covers most institutions which provide qualifying education. Formal minutes of all Committee meetings are circulated to all representatives together with other items which keep members informed of developments or elicit their views.

The Central Council of Education and Training in Social Work normally sends an observer to SWEC meetings and occasionally makes brief presentations about particular developments. Representatives of other bodies are occasionally also invited for specific agenda items.

Appendix 4
Profile of Interviewees

Characteristics of Interviewees

Eleven people (4 women, 7 men, all white) were interviewed in the May-June period, 1996. Interviews lasted between 50 and 90 minutes and were tape-recorded. Selection of interviewees aimed to take account of a number of factors, particularly:

   i. contribution to the area at national level, in various ways;
   ii. range of interests and expertise;
   iii. senior positions in different types of institution and different regions.

Geographical Location

London and south-east - 3   South-west - 2
Wales - 1   North-east - 2   North-west - 2

Distribution by Sector

Old universities -   New universities - 7

Age Distribution

In their forties (4), their fifties (6) or sixty plus (1).

Length of Time in Social Work		Length of Time in Current Post
Less than 3 years		9
Less than 5 years		1
8-10 years	2	1
11-15 years	2	
16-20 years	5	
21 years plus	1	

Posts Held

Head of Section/Director of Studies	2
Professor of Social Work	4
Professor (other)	5
Budget holders	7

Particular Interests

Adult services	3
Child care	5
Probation	2
Organisation of social work (education)	2

(Note: exceeds 11 since some people 'known' for more than one area of work).

Appendix 5
Social Work Education Diagram

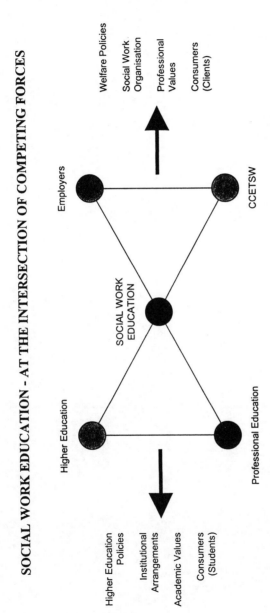

Index of
Authors

Index

Academic (Credentials/Credibility/Status)
10-11, 43, 65, 67, 113, 120, 124,
133, 140, 143, 166, 184, 191, 197,
204
Academic Freedom 19, 48-50, 53
Academic levels 10-11, 14, 19, 21-22, 58,
74-75, 80, 83-84, 86, 109, 116-117,
147, 188-189, 203
Academic Location 22, 66
Academic roles 53, 62, 68, 124, 129, 131
Academic Values 43, 58, 67, 143-144,
180, 210
Access (Recruitment) 10, 43, 104, 156,
161, 168, 189, 194, 203
Accountability 23, 36-37, 45, 47-48, 50,
53, 59, 75, 184
Accreditation 55, 59, 149, 172, 203, 207
Additions 101
Adult Learners 13, 101-102, 104-105,
109, 111
Advanced Award in Social Work
(AASW) 18, 84-85, 89, 99, 103,
117, 147, 157-158
Alliances 79, 90, 125, 144, 177, 180, 196,
211
Anthropology 79, 81
Anti-Discriminatory/Oppressive 14-15,
22, 29, 96, 106, 125, 166-167, 173-
175, 183, 196
Anti-Intellectualism 11, 137-138, 194,
208
Anti-Racism (ART) 14-16, 22, 93
Approval of Prior Experiential Learning
(APEL) 47, 66, 158, 189
Approval of Prior Learning (APL) 47, 66,
103, 158
Approved Social Worker (ASW) 18, 32,
35, 188-189
Areas of Particular Practice (APP) 15, 21,

93, 95, 98
Assessment 30, 32, 65, 66, 68, 97, 103,
105, 107, 149, 154, 166, 169-170,
192, 205, 210
Association of Black Probation Officers
(ABPO) 135
Association of Directors of Social
Services (ADSS) 17, 28-29
Association of Metropolitan Authorities
(AMA) 20
Association of Teachers in Social Work
Education (ATSWE) 15, 22, 89,
124, 130, 136, 163-166, 168, 171
Association of University Professors of
Social Work (AUPSW) 119, 123,
133, 136, 139
Association of University Teachers
(AUT) 45, 125

Banding (see Funding)
Barclay Report 28
Barnett House 6, 20
Basic Unit(s) 48-49, 53, 77-78, 159
Beckford Enquiry 97
Bedford College 6, 14
Binary System/Divide 42-44, 47, 73, 154
Black Perspectives 14-15, 20
Boundaries / Boundary Management (see
also Marginal Position) 77, 80-82,
144, 154, 187, 206, 210
Bristol University 109
British Association of Counsellors (BAC)
135
British Association of Social Workers
(BASW) 10, 26, 37, 85, 123, 135,
177, 188, 191
British Sociological Association (BSA)
125
Brunel University 14

253